ECOLOGY
OF BIOLOGICAL
INVASIONS

ECOLOGY OF BIOLOGICAL INVASIONS

Edited by

R.H. Groves
CSIRO Division of Plant Industry
Canberra, Australia
and
J.J. Burdon
CSIRO Division of Plant Industry
Canberra, Australia

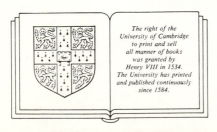

The right of the
University of Cambridge
to print and sell
all manner of books
was granted by
Henry VIII in 1534.
The University has printed
and published continuously
since 1584.

CAMBRIDGE UNIVERSITY PRESS
Cambridge London New York New Rochelle
Melbourne Sydney

Published by the Press Syndicate of the University of Cambridge.
The Pitt Building, Trumpington Street, Cambridge CB2 1RP
32 East 57th Street, New York, NY 10022, USA
PO Box 85, Oakleigh, Victoria 3166, Australia
Saint Martin's Tower, 31 Market Street, Sydney 2000, Australia

First published 1986

Typeset by Jacaranda Publishing, Canberra, ACT.
Printed in Australia by Pirie Printers, Fyshwick, ACT.

British Library Cataloguing in Publication Data
The Ecology of biological invasions
   1. Natural history—Australia
   I. Groves, R.H.   II. Burdon, J.J.
   574.994 QH197

ISBN 0-521-30355-9

PREFACE

The SCOPE project on the 'Ecology of Biological Invasions' is one of a continuing series of projects on key ecological problems which have characterised the SCOPE program since its inception.

The present project was initiated at the SCOPE General Assembly in Ottawa in 1982. It received strong support from the General Assembly as a central problem in the conservation of biological communities and one which was of increasing importance as the mechanism for the transfer of species beyond their natural boundaries increased in number and effectiveness. In fact, the main difficulty encountered by the Assembly was to contain the scope of the project to manageable dimensions. With that in mind, the present focus concentrating on higher plants and animals was adopted.

I would like to congratulate the international steering committee for the project, chaired by Professor Harold Mooney of the United States, and consisting also of Dr F. di Castri (France), Dr R. Groves (Australia), Mr F. Kruger (South Africa), Dr M. Rejmanek (U.S.), Dr J. Sarukhan (Mexico) and Professor M. Williamson (U.K.), for formulating a detailed program from the overall guidance provided by the General Assembly and for the comprehensive series of activities which have made up the project. The present volume, based on the Canberra symposium on 'The Ecology of Biological Invasions in Australia' was an important event in that series.

R.O. Slatyer
SCOPE President

FOREWORD

The project on the 'Ecology of Biological Invasions' was initiated by the Executive Committee of SCOPE (Scientific Committee on Problems of the Environment) in mid 1982, SCOPE being a subsidiary body of the International Council of Scientific Unions. The proposed method of operation of the project followed closely a previous successful SCOPE project on 'The Ecological Effects of Fire'. Many of the same countries which had actively supported the fire project responded enthusiastically to the concept of the new project as did some countries in which fire is not a major ecological factor — for instance, United Kingdom and Czechoslovakia. Australia expressed its support through the National Committee for the Environment of the Australian Academy of Science, who, early in the life of the project, appointed an Organising Committee to begin planning a National Symposium on the subject. The chapters which follow are the final outcome of that initial enthusiastic support and planning.

In editing the chapters which follow we have encountered problems in terminology between the various disciplines of biological science. Even the terminology associated with 'invasions' generally is unsatisfactory with its connotations of a military operation. When botanists refer to plants which have entered a country from outside they may call them variously 'alien', 'introduced', 'exotic' or 'adventive'; when ichthyologists refer to fish species introduced to a country they usually refer to them as 'exotic' (Shafland and Lewis 1984). The latter term of course may be especially appropriate to some introduced fish or even to some herbs because of their bright and varied coloration. As a general term, however, 'exotic' is imprecise. In an effort to be consistent we, as editors, have used the term 'introduced' wherever possible to describe an organism native to a region outside Australia. However, in the chapter by Newsome and Noble we have had to forego even this strong desire for consistency as that chapter refers to three groups of birds — those indigenous to Australia (called 'native'), those indigenous to one region of Australia but introduced deliberately to another Australian region (called 'introduced'), and the third group is those birds introduced from a region outside Australia, for which the term 'foreign' has had to be used. Such are the problems for editors of multidisciplinary volumes in their desire for consistency! When plants become nuisances they are generally termed 'weeds' and when they acquire legal status they are termed 'noxious plants' (which can then lead on to the tautological term 'noxious weeds' that is enshrined in the legislation of some Australian States). Fortunately for us, terminology seems to be simpler with animals — when they become nuisances, animals become 'pests'. Wherever possible and appropriate, we have tried to eliminate emotive terms such as 'weeds' and 'pests', and 'exotic' and 'alien'. 'Adventive' is a relatively neutral term, but with the exception of the chapter by Newsome and Noble, we have chosen to use the even milder term 'introduced' for those organisms which have their origins outside Australia, but which are now an integral and scientifically interesting part of Australia's biota.

Early in the planning of the symposium the decision was taken to encourage authors or pairs of authors to cross their normal disciplinary boundaries and to consider particular aspects of invasions across taxonomic groupings of plants and animals. This decision was taken by the Organising Committee for several reasons. One of the most important reasons was that Australia is a country settled only relatively recently by Europeans and during this 200-year period introduced organisms have played a major role in shaping land-use practices, especially in agricultural and pastoral areas. Accordingly, there has been a considerable research effort on the biology and ecology of the more notable of these introduced organisms; this research has laid a sound basis for their effective control. One has only to think of on-going wheat breeding programs in relation to resistance to wheat stem rust (*Puccinia graminis tritici*), the successful control of prickly pear (*Opuntia* spp.) by the insect *Cactoblastis cactorum* in southern Queensland and northern New South Wales, and the control of rabbits in southern Australia by the release of the myxoma virus. There are other examples of the successful application of research results and some of these have been well described in two previous publications. The Ecological Society of Australia organised a symposium in Adelaide in 1977 on the subject of establishment and success of introduced organisms in Australia. The published account of that symposium (Anderson 1977) presents case histories of a number of introduced species that affect human activities in a major way — from fruit flies and wheat rust to skeleton weed and trout. More recently, a publication on the ecology of introduced organisms (Kitching and Jones 1981) presented detailed case histories of a wide range of organisms with emphasis on insects, but also including one plant, a vertebrate and the crown-of-thorns starfish. In planning a third publication on the subject we thus wished to avoid a 'case history' approach of individual invasive species. It seemed timely to begin to synthesise some generalisations about the ecology of invasive organisms and to test these generalisations, both nationally and internationally.

As well as the two publications mentioned above, some others are relevant to an overall consideration of biological invasions in Australia, and especially to their management using different control methods. A forthcoming volume (Gibbs and Meischke, in press) deals with the invasion of pathogenic organisms, especially those affecting humans directly in a medical sense and also domestic stock. Current methods for chemical control of introduced plants are described by Swarbrick (1984). For a detailed account of research on biological control of insects and plants, Waterhouse (in preparation) is revising Wilson (1960). This will fill a major gap in the present volume, which arose largely because of the co-incidence of the timing of the Canberra symposium with the VI International Symposium on the Biological Control of Weeds in Vancouver (Del Fosse 1985). Thus the present volume does not reflect these often notable aspects of Australian science except peripherally in some chapters.

Introductions and exchanges have always occurred in the Australian biota but at different rates at different times. Williams and Burt (in manuscript) present a history of plant introductions to Australia which excellently characterises the different phases of activity over 200 years. An agricultural and veterinary bias behind the deliberate introductions to Australia has never been stronger than in 1788 when the future of the European settlement at Sydney Cove depended on the success or failure of introduced plants and animals. This utilitarian basis for introductions, including increasingly their use for horticulture or for tropical agriculture, has continued to predominate. The effects of introduced plants and animals on Australian natural ecosystems are important subjects for scientific research. As the SCOPE project on the Ecology of Biological Invasions is concerned primarily with natural ecosystems we hope that the present volume will stimulate further this hitherto neglected aspect of research in Australia. Whilst this stimulating effect is one of our aims, it serves at the same time to explain why there remains considerable emphasis in the present volume on agricultural examples. The two aspects are strongly interconnected in the Australian period of only 200 years of known introduction.

Finally, we wish to thank the many people associated with the preparation of this volume and the mounting of the symposium in August 1984. Members of the National Committee for the Environment strongly supported the idea of an Australian contribution, especially their Chairman Dr M.F. Day, who also chaired the opening session of the symposium. Our fellow members of the Organising Committee — Dr R.D. Hughes, Dr C.R. Krebs, Dr K. Myers, Dr I.R. Noble, and at various times Dr D.T. Briese, Dr J.M. Cullen and Dr A.E. Newsome — were all active in planning the symposium. Mrs R. Green and Ms J. Thomas put those plans into effect, and Mr C.J. Dixon and Mr D. French helped with all aspects of the publication of the proceedings. We thank all the speakers of invited and contributed material presented at the symposium for their contributions. Dr H.A. Mooney (Chairman of the SCOPE Scientific Advisory Committee for the project) enthusiastically agreed to attend and open the symposium and it was a great pleasure to also have two other members of the Scientific Advisory Committee (Dr F. di Castri and Mr F.J. Kruger) actively participate in the symposium as session chairmen. Professor R.O. Slatyer, president of SCOPE, not only played a major role in initiating the project, but since that time has strongly supported Australian participation; Professor Slatyer also chaired the closing session of the symposium. Mrs J. Burdon compiled the index and Ms P. Kaye helped with proof reading. To all these people we express our thanks. The symposium was assisted by a generous grant from the Utah Foundation and support from TAA and the Commonwealth Bank.

R.H. Groves
J.J. Burdon
Canberra, July 1985

References

Anderson, D.J. (ed.) (1977). *Exotic Species in Australia — Their Establishment and Success. Proceedings of the Ecological Society of Australia 10,* 1–186.

Del Fosse, E.S. (ed.) (1985). *Proceedings of the Sixth International Symposium on the Biological Control of Weeds, Vancouver, 1984,* Agriculture Canada, Ottawa.

Gibbs, A.J., and Meischke, H.R.C. (eds) (1985). *Pests and Parasites as Migrants: An Australian Perspective,* Cambridge University Press, Cambridge.

Kitching, R.L., and Jones, R.E. (eds) (1981). *The Ecology of Pests. Some Australian Case Histories,* CSIRO, Melbourne.

Shafland, P.L., and Lewis, W.M. (1984). Terminology associated with introduced organisms. *Fisheries 9,* 17–18.

Swarbrick, J.T. (1984). *The Australian Weed Control Handbook,* 7th edn, Plant Press, Toowoomba.
Williams, W.T., and Burt, R.L. A history of plant introduction in Australia (in manuscript).
Wilson, F. (1960). A review of the biological control of insects and weeds in Australia and Australian New Guinea. *Commonwealth Institute of Biological Control Technical Communication* No. 1.

CONTENTS

INVADING SPECIES

Among species which have been introduced to Australia and become naturalised, there are some which have become especially prominent in an economic or nuisance sense. These plants or animals may not necessarily be a problem in their regions of origin, but often they have become so in several countries to which they have been introduced. Since not all introduced species become invasive, amongst those which have done so is it likely that they have specific features in common? For instance, these species often are commensal with human activities. If looked at widely in a taxonomic sense, are any other attributes identifiable and general? Can we predict which groups of organisms will become invaders? Authors of the three chapters which follow attempt to answer these questions for species and groups of species — both plant and animal, but especially for noxious plants, birds and fish.

ECOLOGICAL AND PHYSIOLOGICAL CHARACTERS OF INVADING SPECIES

A.E. Newsome[1] and I.R. Noble[2]

There is no simple answer to the question of what determines success in colonisation. This is especially true when both plants and animals are considered, as Mayr (1965a) pointed out in comparing the flora with the avian and mammalian faunas in the region between Malaysia and the Solomon Islands. The entire area falls into a single vegetation region whilst the animal communities are divided by Wallace's and Weber's lines.

In this chapter we consider the ecological and physiological characteristics which may distinguish plant and bird invaders of Australia. We have attempted to do this by analysing data sets describing invading species. Neither data set is complete, nor ideal for the task, but they are sufficient to provide a less subjective description of the characters of at least some groups of invasive organisms than the more usual descriptive approach. We are fortunate in having a relatively complete listing of both successful and unsuccessful bird colonisations (and trans-locations) in Australia (Long 1981) and present an analysis of these data. There is no such complete list for plants, so we have restricted our analysis to the noxious plants of Victoria as recognised by Parsons (1973). We have analysed these data sets seeking common physiological and ecological factors which correlate with successful invasion. We then attempt to draw some general conclusions based on these analyses and other descriptions of the colonisation process.

BIRDS

Mayr (1965a) listed six characteristics which he thought diagnostic of successful colonising birds. They should: be social and travel in small flocks; among those commensal with humans, be granivores rather than insectivores; have habitats associated with fresh water; have good powers of dispersal; be able to find unoccupied habitats; and have an ability to shift habitat preferences. The compendium of Long (1981) has allowed us to compare some behavioural, ecological and physiological attributes of the invaders for success and failure among 65 foreign and 34 native birds. Those numbers were brought up to date by adding 13 more known examples (I. Mason, pers. comm.). A full species list, their scientific and common names, the approximate numbers introduced and their fates, are given in Appendix 1. Species evaluated are those recorded for mainland Australia, Tasmania, the off-shore islands and Territories (e.g. Macquarie and Norfolk Islands). A full bibliography (133 papers) of the history of introductions is not included here; nor is a listing of papers mentioning species. They have been deposited in the library of the CSIRO Division of Wildlife and Rangelands Research, Canberra, Australia. General texts followed here are: for common names, Long (1981) and Schodde et al. (1978); for nomenclature and taxonomy, Condon (1975), Morony, Bock and Farrand (1975) and Schodde (1975); and for current distributions of all successful species, Anonymous (1948), Fullagar and Disney (1975), Schodde, Fullagar and Hermes (1983) and Blakers, Davies and Reilly (1984).

Analyses

The data are analysed below for success rates under ten ecophysiological attributes. Chi-square analyses presented in Tables 1 to 10 are based on the G-statistic (Sokal and Rohlf 1969).

Origin. Of the 112 invading species, five (which were eradicated by humans) and the woodlark (see footnote 7, Appendix 1) have been excluded from analyses. Thus, 59 out of 107 (55%) were successful (Table 1). One third of the foreign species were imported from England to southeastern Australia by acclimatisation societies, mostly in the late 1800s or early 1900s (see later). Significantly more native than foreign species were

[1] CSIRO, Division of Wildlife and Rangelands Research, Canberra, A.C.T. 2602
[2] Research School of Biological Sciences, Australian National University, Canberra, A.C.T. 2601

successful invaders (X_1^2 5.15; $P < 0.05$). Twelve of the 32 successful native species were Psittaciformes (cockatoos, lorikeets and parrots), renowned for their success as invaders. Only on three occasions did they fail to establish themselves when translocated. The crimson rosella failed only on Lord Howe Island (31°32′S, 159°06′E), and the eastern rosella and sulphur-crested cockatoo failed on Maria Island (42°44′S, 148°01′E) having flown to nearby Tasmania (Rounsevell, Blackhall and Thomas 1977).

TABLE 1. *Origin and fate of foreign (n = 65) and native (n = 47) bird species introduced to Australia.*

Origin	Successful	Survived many years before failing	Other failures	Eradicated by humans
England	12	1	10	0
Europe	0	0	1	1
Eurasia	0	0	5	0
Canary Is.	0	0	1	0
N. America	3	0	3	0
S.E. Asia/Japan	8	3	3	2
Africa	3	4	2	0
New Zealand	1	1	0	0
Australia	32	3	12	2
Totals	59	12	37	5

Success of native vs. foreign: $X_1^2 = 5.15$; $P < 0.05$ (excluding eradicated).

Number of propagules. For this analysis totals for all documented introductions of each species whether in one place at one time or in many, are used. Escapees are assumed to have been in small numbers. Doubtless there were other escapees and introductions (especially self-introductions and the more usual foreign imports) which were in such low numbers as to have gone unrecorded (Balmford 1978). As it is, numbers for three species (weka, sulphur-crested cockatoo and laughing kookaburra) are unknown and so they were excluded from

TABLE 2. *Success and failure of foreign and native bird species and the number of propagules.*

Propagule number	Foreign birds				Native birds			
	Succeed		Fail		Succeed		Fail	
Unknown and escapees*	4		10		14		1	
< 10	1	} 5	10	} 25	8	} 25	8	} 12
11-20	0		5		3		3	
21-50	2		2		2		3	
51-100	4	} 6	4	} 6	3	} 5	0	} 3
101-500	11		3					
> 500	4	} 15	0	} 3				
	$X_2^2 = 22.22$; $P < 0.001$				$X_1^2 = 0.06$; N.S.			

Comparison: $X_1^2 = 9.82$; N.S.
Success $\times$ Numbers: $X_2^2 = 9.20$; $P < 0.02$

* Assumed to be few; see footnote 3, Appendix 1.

analyses. Numbers did not influence success significantly among native birds but did so for foreign species which were released in greater numbers on average than Australian species (Table 2). No native bird was released in numbers exceeding 100, compared with 18 introduced species which exceeded this number. Four foreign species (ostrich, ring-necked pheasant, skylark and the ubiquitous house sparrow) were released in large numbers (> 500) and were all successful. Native species were very successful (68%) despite low numbers of propagules.

The history of the Java sparrow shows that success or failure was not always immediate. Large numbers (200-235) were released in Melbourne and the species persisted for about 25 years before dying out for unknown reasons. The large number of propagules may have aided survival in the short run. In all, six species persisted for some time before dying out.

Primary nesting sites. Where birds nested made no significant difference to success or failure within foreign or native species (Table 3); but the pooled data indicated significant differences (P < 0.05) because of the success of so many native hollow-nesters (16), and the failure of so many foreign ground-nesters (19). Twelve of the former were again the Psittaciformes. Of the 12 successful foreign ground-nesting species, seven were introduced to islands, and of 19 species which failed, thirteen were released on the mainland only. Twelve had less than 20 propagules and 3 more were escapees presumably in low numbers also, a characteristic which was not propitious. Thirteen were game species (Anatidae, Phasianidae, Pteroclididae). Their failure may have been aided by other factors such as incorrect climate and habitat (e.g. pintailed sandgrouse) and human hunting pressures (Balmford 1978) which was also the case in New Zealand for a number of geese (Long 1981).

TABLE 3. *Success and failure of foreign and native bird species and their primary nesting sites.*

Nesting sites		Foreign birds		Native birds	
		Succeed	Fail	Succeed	Fail
Forks, shrubs and trees	Dome nests	1 ⎫ 10	5 ⎫ 12	3 ⎫ 9	1 ⎫ 6
	Cup nests	9 ⎭	7 ⎭	6 ⎭	5 ⎭
Ground	Grassland/low shrubs	10 ⎫	15 ⎫	3 ⎫	1 ⎫
	Islands/swamps	2 ⎬ 12	4 ⎬ 19	3 ⎬ 7	2 ⎬ 5
	Mound builders	0 ⎭	0 ⎭	1 ⎭	2 ⎭
Hollows	Landbirds	2 ⎫	2 ⎫	14 ⎫	2 ⎫
	Waterbirds	0 ⎬ 5	0 ⎬ 3	1 ⎬ 16	2 ⎬ 4
Human dwellings		3 ⎭	1 ⎭	1 ⎭	0 ⎭
		$X_2^2 = 1.48$; N S.		$X_2^2 = 2.36$; N.S.	

Success × Nest Site Overall: $X_2^2 = 7.01$; P < 0.05.

Basic diets. Success was not related significantly overall to basic diets (P > 0.05), but there was a large anomaly in the two groups of seed-eaters (P > 0.05) (Table 4). Only 34% of the foreign species succeeded compared with 61% of the native species (P < 0.05). Of the 25 foreign failures, 11 were gamebirds (see earlier), and at least 14 were either escapees or released in low numbers (also see earlier). However, five failures were not small releases, e.g. 110 European partridges in Tasmania, and 52 common sandgrouse on Phillip Island. The cockatoos and parrots were well represented in the successful native contingent, plus the finches. Five of the 10 unsuccessful native species were pigeons and doves introduced to Kangaroo Island (see later).

Primary habitats in homeland. There was no significant difference in success rates for donor habitats for either foreign or native birds or overall (P > 0.05) (Table 5). However, within the forest and woodland habitats, native species succeeded more often than their foreign counterparts (P < 0.05), but 12 of those successful native species were, once again, the Psittaciformes. At least five other of those Australian successes are generalist feeders (laughing kookaburra, superb lyrebird, silvereye, Australian magpie-lark and Australian magpie). All 15 native failures were introduced to islands. Three of them were water-birds (Australian shelduck, grey teal and Australian shoveler) which flew from Maria Island to nearby Tasmania (Rounsevell,

Blackhall and Thomas 1977) (cf. above). Two others were owls (southern boobook and barn owl) taken to Lord Howe Island in the forlorn hope that they would eradicate the introduced black rat (*Rattus rattus*) which was endangering endemic species of birds (Hindwood 1940).

The most successful foreign groups were from suburbia, orchards and vineyards (12/16) (see next section). Twenty of the 34 foreign species which failed were in low numbers; thirteen were introduced deliberately (< 10), six were escapees (see before) and one was self-introduced. The red jungle fowl was originally from Southeast Asian jungles. They live in similar habitats on two tropical and one subtropical island [viz. Northwest, Heron and Norfolk].

Suitability of receptor habitats. Although details were not as good as for donor habitats, the results are unequivocal (Table 6). All 27 species introduced into highly suitable habitat succeeded, but only one of 27 introduced to unsuitable habitat may have done so. That one species was the king quail which inhabits grasslands in Australia and Southeast Asia. Its origins are uncertain; whether the stock surviving today around Melbourne are from early overseas introductions, native escapees, or original Australian stock is unknown (see footnote 4, Appendix 1).

The large difference between success rates of native and foreign birds lay not with prime or unsuitable habitats, but with those of intermediate status where the native species (75%) fared better than the foreign (45%). Another clear distinction is between foreign birds succeeding in artificial and altered habitats, and native birds succeeding in original habitats. Green's (1984) study is most telling. In Melbourne suburbs she found that although 52 native species occurred compared to 12 introduced species, the former were outnumbered by the latter by about 2:1. Moreover, the proportion of foreign birds in exotic habitats was far greater than in native ones.

The successful foreign species in grasslands, a habitat being created continually by clearing of forests for agriculture, were the Phasianidae (gamebirds), which includes the turkey. Turkeys survive only on Flinders

TABLE 4. *Success and failure of foreign and native bird species and their basic diets.*

Basic diet	Foreign birds		Native birds	
	Succeed	Fail	Succeed	Fail
Insects — generalists	—	—	2 } 2	0 } 0
Insects, grain, fruit, invertebrates (land)	9 } 9	7 } 7	2 } 2	1 } 1
Insects, bulbs, invertebrates (water)	0	0	0	0
Insects, invertebrates (land)	0 } 3	1 } 2	2 } 4	1 } 2
Insects, invertebrates, aquatic vegetation (water)	3	1	2	1
Carnivore/omnivore-invertebrates, vertebrates, scavenger (land)	2 } 2	0 } 0	4 } 5	1 } 1
Carnivore/omnivore-invertebrates, vertebrates (water)	0	0	1	0
Seeds, fruit, bulbs, vegetation, invertebrates (land)	13 } 13	21 } 25	14 } 16	7 } 10
Seeds, bulbs, aquatic vegetation, invertebrates (water)	0	4	2	3
Fruit	—	—	0 } 3	1 } 1
Nectar	—	—	3	0
	$X_3^2 = 6.27$; N.S.		$X_6^2 = 2.86$; N.S.	

Success × Diet Overall: $X_5^2 = 9.82$; N S.
Success × Seed-Eaters: $X_1^2 = 4.68$; P < 0.05

Island on grazing land held in common to the Islanders who protect the species but reserve the right of harvest.

Size of flocks and clutches. There was no evidence that these qualities provided any advantage to foreign or native species, or overall (Tables 7 and 8).

TABLE 5. *Success and failure of foreign and native bird species and their primary habitats in homelands.*

Primary donor habitat	Foreign birds		Native birds	
	Succeed	Fail	Succeed	Fail
Tropical forests	1 } 4	1 } 7	1 } 13	1 } 4
Other forests	3	6	12	3
Savanna woodland	0 } 1	2 } 6	8 } 9	4 } 7
Semi-arid shrubland	1	4	1	3
Rivers and swamps	3 } 3	5 } 5	5 } 5	4 } 4
Grasslands	2 } 6	3 } 10	5 } 5	0 } 0
Cultivated pastures	4	7	—	—
Pine plantations	1	2	—	—
Orchards and vineyards	2 } 13	0 } 6	—	—
Suburban	10	4	—	—

$$X_4^2 = 8.14;\ \text{N.S.} \qquad X_3^2 = 6.02;\ \text{N.S.}$$

Success $\times$ Habitat Overall: $X_4^2 = 3.51$; N.S.
Success $\times$ Forest and Woodland: $X_1^2 = 6.48$; $P < 0.05$

TABLE 6. *Success and failure of foreign and native bird species and the suitability of receptor habitats.*

Receptor habitat	Foreign birds		Native birds	
	Succeed	Fail	Succeed	Fail
Prime	13	0	14	0
Intermediate	13	16	18	6
Unsuitable	1*	18	0	9

$$X_2^2 = 36.03;\ P < 0.001 \qquad X_2^2 = 31.87;\ P < 0.001$$

Success $\times$ Suitability Overall: $X_2^2 = 68.23$; $P < 0.001$

* See comments on king quail in text and footnote 4, Appendix 1.

Historical timing of introductions. From about 1840 to 1899, the success rate of both foreign and native birds was 50%, but it rose to 89% between 1950 to 1984 (Table 9). Some species failed early but succeeded later, e.g. the self-introduced cattle egret from Asia, and the emu, a human introduction to Kangaroo Island. The greatest numbers of introductions were in the latter half of the 1800s (Figure 1) when acclimatisation societies were active, especially in Victoria. The two main factors involved were the continual expansion of ranges of established species (e.g. blackbird, common starling, laughing kookaburra and Australian magpie-lark) and some aviary escapees (e.g. nutmeg mannikin and red-browed firetail) as the landscapes of the mainland and islands were continually altered by humans.

Comparison of islands and mainland. Table 10 compares success rates of various groups of birds on the mainland and Tasmania and islands. The numbers of species in the Table are greater than in Appendix 1 because some species were introduced to both the mainland and islands. Overall, there was no significant difference in success in either locale. However, when results for Kangaroo Island are removed, the success rate on islands increased to significance ($P < 0.05$). Kangaroo Island is the largest (4350 sq km) used in the analysis, is close to the mainland (13 km) and had the greatest number of introductions (27) of which ten failed (37%) (see next section).

In general, ground-nesting species succeeded least among foreign birds (Table 3), but the results in Table 10 show that islands were exceptions for game-birds (80% cf. 16% success on the mainland; $X_1^2 = 9.50$; $P < 0.01$). The reasons may be the general difficulty of dispersing from distant islands, the greater degree of protection from predation there (including human), and the grossly altered habitats of islands as a result of human pressures. The presence of humans can work both ways, however. For example, the Californian quail

TABLE 7. *Success and failure of foreign and native bird species and the size of flocks.*

Size of flocks	Foreign birds		Native birds	
	Succeed	Fail	Succeed	Fail
Solitary/pairs	6	4	6	5
< 10-20	13	18	16	5
> 20	8	12	10	5
	$X_2^2 = 1.21$; N.S.		$X_2^2 = 1.56$; N.S.	

Success × Flocking: $X_2^2 = 0.25$; N.S.
Total $X_7^2 = 9.82$; N.S.

TABLE 8. *Success and failure of foreign and native bird species and their clutch sizes.*

Clutch size	Foreign birds		Native birds	
	Succeed	Fail	Succeed	Fail
1	0	0	1	0
2–3	4	6	10	7
4–5	15	19	14	2
7–8	4	4	2	2
10–12	4	4	4	2
>15	0	1	1	2
	$X_4^2 = 1.46$; N.S.		$X_5^2 = 6.77$; N.S.	

Success × Clutch Size: $X_5^2 = 3.11$; N.S.
Total $X_{16}^2 = 25.12$; $P > 0.05$

TABLE 9. *Success and failure of foreign and native bird species and the historical timing of introductions.*

Period of introduction	Foreign birds		Native birds	
	Succeed	Fail	Succeed	Fail
c. 1840-1899	99	100	2	1
1900-1949	60	23	27	21
1950-1984	34	3	43	6
	$X_2^2 = 32.63; P < 0.001$		$X_2^2 = 11.98; P < 0.001$	

Success $\times$ Timing: $X_2^2 = 139.62; P < 0.001$

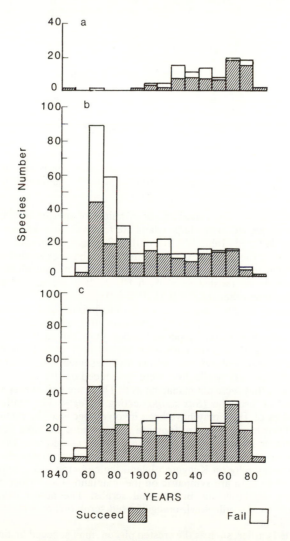

Fig. 1. Total numbers of introductions of species which succeeded (hatched) or failed (unhatched) per decade: (a) native birds; (b) foreign birds; and (c) both groups together.

TABLE 10. *Success and failure of groups of birds introduced to islands and the mainland of Australia (including Tasmania).*

Groups of birds	Islands		Mainland	
	Succeed	Fail	Succeed	Fail
Rattites	1	0	1	0
Megapodes	1	2	—	—
Waterbirds and rails	9	7	3	4
Gamebirds	8	2	2	10
Pigeons and doves	4	7	3	4
Raptors	1	0	—	—
Cockatoos and parrots	3	2	10	1
Owls	1	2	—	—
Kookaburra	1	0	1	0
Finches and associated groups	4	2	7	14
Insectivores	6	0	6	5
Generalist feeders	2	0	1	0
Totals	41	24	34	38

$$X_1^2 = 2.52; \text{N.S.}$$

Totals excluding Kangaroo Is .	38	14	34	38

$$X_1^2 = 6.45; P < 0.05$$

was once abundant on Lord Howe Island but became extinct after the black rat arrived from a ship-wreck (Fullagar and Disney 1975). The rats were also credited with the demise of five endemic species on the island.

Introductions to Kangaroo Island. The actual causes of failure of species are rarely known but the detailed histories of the 27 species introduced to this large island are relatively well known so that the possible reasons for success or failure can be deduced (Table 11). Ten of the 17 successful species were self-introduced from the mainland 13 km away. Most utilise urban or agrarian sites which have expanded with time. All native species were introduced to the Island in low numbers (2–27) which was not a problem for them overall (Table 2). However, on numbers introduced (scaled at < 5, 6–10, > 10), native species with higher numbers of propagules failed more often than others ($X_1^2 = 9.71; P < 0.01$).

The failure of nine species is attributed to incompatible habitat and climate. Kangaroo Island has a mediterranean to cool temperate climate, yet four species came from arid and semi-arid regions, three from the tropics, and two from sub-tropical to warm temperate regions. Only two each of the spinifex pigeon and magpie goose were introduced, however, so that the odds were against them even if the habitats were suitable. With plenty of mallee eucalypts present, only the malleefowl was presented with suitable habitat, and perhaps also the crested pigeon and wonga pigeon. Malleefowl were introduced on five occasions between 1911 and 1936 (Abbott 1974), indicating that they were not managing well. There are earlier records (Sutton 1926) of mounds being destroyed by fire and of feral pigs (*Sus scrofa*) eating the eggs. The malleefowl's survival today is in doubt (Ford 1979). The fires of 1958 may have been involved because the malleefowl and another mound-builder, the orange-footed scrubfowl (see also footnote 3, Appendix 1), have not been seen since (Wheeler 1960). Why a related mound-builder, the Australian brush-turkey, should have survived is not known although it is a most versatile species living in a variety of mainland habitats from rainforests to fire-prone sclerophyllous woodlands. Nor can we explain why on Kangaroo Island the common bronzewing should survive whilst the wonga pigeon should fail when both are sympatric on the mainland. The former does utilise a wider range of mainland habitats whereas the latter inhabits coastal scrubs. The above examples suggest that habitat specificity of certain species (e.g. malleefowl, orange-footed scrubfowl and wonga pigeon) may restrict their ability to colonise other habitats.

Some species which failed earlier, such as the crested pigeon, may succeed unaided eventually (Ford 1979), because the crested pigeon, like the galah, has been extending its range from inland Australia to the coast (Blakers, Davies and Reilly 1984). The latter became established on Kangaroo Island in the 1920s (Cooper

1947; Abbott 1974). Recent expansion of range in native species is associated with habitat alteration by humans (Blakers, Davies and Reilly 1984). The success of the mainland emu is not surprising because a dwarf species of emu *Dromaius minor* was exterminated on Kangaroo Island early in the history of European settlement, probably because of bushfires and hunting (Ford 1979). However, there were several introductions of the mainland species before success was attained, and it was even reduced to one individual at one time (Condon 1968).

Other eco-physiological qualities. Other qualities were examined, e.g. breeding seasons and patterns, the number of clutches per season, foraging patterns, and territoriality. As the analyses of these data contributed little to further understanding, results are not presented.

Discussion

No single eco-physiological quality among those examined nor any simple selection of them typified a successful coloniser among the foreign and native birds examined, which confirms Mayr's conclusions (1965a). Also confirmatory was that the chief factor contributing to success among foreign birds was being a

TABLE 11. *History and numbers of introductions of bird species to Kangaroo Island and reasons for success and failure.*

Succeed			Fail	
Into human-made habitats	Lack of competition and predation	Unknown	Wrong habitat	Predation, fire
INTRODUCED BY HUMANS 6 Cape Barren goose (1923) Common peafowl?* (semi-domesticated) SELF-INTRODUCED NATIVE Aust. magpie (1900s) Galah (1920s) Aust. magpie-lark (1950s) FOREIGN House sparrow (1890s) Comm. starling (1900s) Europ. goldfinch (c.1917) Blackbird (c. 1947) Spotted turtle dove (c. 1953) Skylark (c. 1960) Feral pigeon (c. 1967)	9 Emu (1926-57) 2 Australian brush-turkey (1936) 4 Laughing kookaburra (1926) 8 Gang-gang cockatoo? (1940)	4 Common bronzewing (1937)	4 Wonga pigeon (1946) 4 Diamond dove (1937) 22 Peaceful dove (1937-1940) 2 Magpie goose (1940) 2 Spinifex pigeon (1940) 4 Bar-shouldered dove (1940) 12 Zebra finch (1940) 4 Wonga pigeon (1946)	27 Malleefowl (1911-1936) Orange-footed scrubfowl (?)
Total number of species 12	4	1	8	1

* Foreign species.

human commensal (see Green 1984), as has been shown previously for New Zealand (Wodzicki 1965). Some conclusions, however, appear contrary to Mayr. There was no special advantage for water-birds, not even on islands, and no indication that birds shifted habitats in order to succeed. Indeed, there was 100% success for birds moved or moving to concordant habitats, and high failure rates otherwise. Also, insectivores and omnivores succeeded overall more often than granivores ($X_i^2 = 103.6$; $P < 0.001$) although Mayr was restricting his comparison to birds commensal with humans. Native granivores were more successful than foreign ones (62% vs 34%; $X_i^2 = 5.08$; $P < 0.05$).

Flock size was not a significant factor in our analyses. Mayr contended that birds which travel in small flocks would be favoured, as in Polynesia, because once they had arrived, reproduction could succeed. He was referring only to self-introduced birds colonising a series of oceanic islands, whereas we have spread a wider net. If we restrict our data to species (both native and foreign) which naturally colonise islands, Mayr's point is favoured: 11 species commonly form flocks greater than 20, eight form smaller flocks (2-20), and one is solitary or travels in pairs. But two species which form large flocks and two which function as pairs or small family parties failed. Analysing our data as a set, the influence of flocking size on success was not quite significant ($X_i^2 = 3.45$; $P < 0.1$).

Mayr's point, however, dealt with the number of propagules as much as anything and that was an important factor for success in foreign birds. It was not important in native species, but characteristics of the cockatoos, lorikeets and parrots continually dominated analyses. Such birds possess a quality which Mayr (1965b) termed "toughness" (p.555); they range widely in search of resources (food, nesting holes in trees), have generally unspecialised diets (seeds, fruits) and also travel in flocks. Although we have no analyses for two others of Mayr's points, viz. the powers of dispersal and the ability to find unoccupied habitat, clearly data from the parrot group support them.

The parrots are the main reason also why the most successful native species were hole-nesters. There were seven other hole-nesters from the Anatidae (ducks), Strigiformes (nocturnal raptors) and Coraciiformes (kingfishers and allies). Taken together, native hole-nesters had a success rate of 74% compared with 81% for the parrot group. Only one foreign parrot has been an invader, the peach-faced lovebird, an aviary escapee which failed to establish itself. Three other hole-nesters were introduced, the tree sparrow which survived locally and commensally with humans, the common starling which is a successful commensal, and the European robin which died out.

Species introduced to islands had a better chance of surviving than on the mainland (excepting Kangaroo Island — see earlier topic). Traditionally, islands are far less resistant to colonisation (Mayr 1965a). Lack of complex faunas probably reduces competitive and predatory interactions. Wherever exotic mammalian predators have arrived, as on Lord Howe (e.g. black rat) and Kangaroo Islands (e.g. feral pig), they were implicated in extinctions (Hindwood 1940; Sutton 1926, respectively). This was also found for New Zealand (Wodzicki 1965) and in Fiji (Mayr 1965a). We have also argued for the difficulty to disperse from islands (although Maria Island, which is very close to Tasmania, was an exception), and the extreme habitat alteration by humans in changing forests to grasslands on islands cannot be overlooked.

Although some Australian birds have extended their ranges into the artificial grasslands of cereal crops and cultivated pastures and do utilise introduced plants in suburbia, by and large, the latter is the preserve of foreign birds even though the species diversity of introduced plants is lower than for that of natives (Green 1984). There is little evidence of secondary invasion away from primary habitats by either native or foreign birds.

Time in which to succeed and perhaps the timing of invasion were other factors. The cattle egret was first introduced to northwestern Australia in 1933 (Hewitt 1960) but was not observed again until 1948 in Arnhem land, northern Australia (Deignan 1964). The species has since spread to much of eastern, southern and southwestern Australia (Blakers, Davies and Reilly 1984), helped almost certainly by environments increasingly altered for agriculture and livestock grazing.

Timing is also related to the higher success rate recently than a century or more ago. Changes caused by humans would again be involved. As well, recent successes have been mostly self-introduced or escapees from aviaries. The introduction of foreign species is no longer in vogue, and many earlier failures were improbable species, e.g. the impejan pheasant from Himalayan rainforests.

Time in which to die out also played a part. A number of foreign species survived sparsely for some years before disappearing, often with no apparent reason (see also Mayr 1965a), e.g. the escaped red-vented bulbul in Melbourne after 25 years. And humans were involved directly in some failures (e.g. the ostrich; see also Table 1). After being successfully farmed for their plumes in South Australia, ostriches were released when the industry collapsed in the 1920s and 1930s and became a pest. Large numbers were shot during the 1950s (Parker *et al.* 1976), and have since declined almost to the point of extinction, possibly because of predation and drought. Unpredictable events may have intervened, like wildfire on Kangaroo Island, and the advent of the black rat on Lord Howe Island.

PLANTS

The ideal weed

Baker (1965) listed the characteristics of an ideal weed (Table 12). In summary, an ideal weed is a plastic perennial which will germinate in a wide range of conditions, grow quickly, flower early, is self-compatible, produces many seeds which disperse widely, reproduces vegetatively and is a good competitor (i.e. occupier of space).

TABLE 12. *The characteristics of an ideal(?) weed (from Baker 1965).*

1. Has no special environmental requirements for germination.

2. Has discontinuous germination (self-controlled) and great longevity of seed.

3. Shows rapid seedling growth.

4. Spends only a short period of time in the vegetative condition before beginning to flower.

5. Maintains a continuous seed production for as long as growing conditions permit.

6. Is self-compatible, but not obligatorily self-pollinated or apomictic.

7. When cross-pollinated, this can be achieved by a nonspecialised flower visitor or by wind.

8. Has very high seed output in favorable environmental circumstances.

9. Can produce some seed in a very wide range of environmental circumstances. Has high tolerance of (and often plasticity in face of) climatic and edaphic variation.

10. Has special adaptations for both long-distance and short-distance dispersal.

11. If a perennial, has vigorous vegetative reproduction.

12. If a perennial, has brittleness at the lower nodes or of the rhizomes or rootstocks.

13. If a perennial, shows an ability to regenerate from severed portions of the root-stock.

14. Has ability to compete by special means: rosette formation, choking growth, exocrine production (but no fouling of soil for itself), etc.

Table 12 provides a useful checklist of points to be considered when assessing whether a plant may become a successful invader. However, it is a 'wish list'. As Baker points out, no one plant will possess all the characters on the list and nor does it need to in order to be successful. Conversely, the possession of any single, or several, characteristics from the list does not necessarily mean that the species will be a successful invader. In fact, it is easy to demonstrate that one must be cautious in adding an attribute to the list simply because it would seem to be useful. An example of this is the assumption that the C_4 photosynthetic pathway is competitively superior to the C_3 pathway and therefore advantageous to invading plants (Black 1971). This belief is given support by a listing of the world's worst weeds (Holm *et al.* 1977) in which 14/18 of the top ranked weeds are C_4 species in contrast to only 3/15 of the world's crop plants (Harlan 1975). Elmore and Paul (1983) claim that C_4 species appear in weed lists 17 times more often than expected by chance. But do these observations reflect a true superiority of the C_4 mechanism or a predilection of compilers of weed lists to recognise a weed if it competes with crop plants and especially with crops growing in the hotter areas of the world where agricultural practices tend to be less rigorous? In Parsons' (1973) description of the noxious plants of Victoria, only 5/83 species for which the photosynthetic pathway was known are C_4 species. Why does this discrepancy occur in the representation of C_4 species in weed lists?

The C_4 pathway tends to be most advantageous in environments characterised by high temperatures and low light and, although the photosynthetic rates of C_4 plants tend to be higher than C_3 plants, the realised capacities are similar when the physical environment, seasonal displacement of activity and leaf arrangement are taken into account (Pearcy and Ehrlinger 1984). At low leaf temperatures ($< 20°C$) there is little, if any, advantage in the C_4 pathway and it has often been noted that in arid regions there tends to be a winter ephemeral flora dominated by C_3 species and a summer ephemeral flora dominated by C_4. When we look at the list of Victorian noxious plants we find that groups of species with similar characteristics can be found. For example, 26/85 species belong to the Asteraceae, most of which show a particular suite of ecological characteristics. All are C_3 species and 17/26 germinate in autumn. Other suites of ecological characteristics can also be recognised. Among them is a group of spring-germinating (often with an autumn seed dormancy), fast-growing and fast-maturing C_4 plants which accounts for 4/5 of the C_4 species.

Suites of eco-physiological characters

It is not possible to carry out a complete analysis of successful versus unsuccessful invaders as was done for birds. Parsons' compendium is not a complete list of successful invaders (i.e. species which have become naturalised) but only of those which for some reason have been proclaimed as 'noxious' in a legal sense, and we have no information about failures. However, the list does contain information about a group of species which have successfully invaded particular habitats of Victoria and thus may provide some insights into those eco-physiological characteristics which are associated with that success.

We have drawn up a list of properties of Victorian noxious plants (Table 13) and have used a clustering technique (CLUSTAN package using Ward's method and Euclidian distance based on normalised scores) to group the species. At the 10-group stage (Figure 2) the following groups were recognised.

TABLE 13. *Species characters used in analysis of Parsons' (1973) data on noxious plants in Victoria.*

Longevity — annual, biennial, perennial
Size — height in cm
Origin — Europe, Europe/W. Asia/N. Africa/Asia-minor, Americas, Africa (S.), Australia, Asia
Root — shallow, deep, parasitic
Rhizome — rhizomes or corms present or absent
Mat — mat or clump forming — yes or no
Germination — autumn, autumn/spring, spring, any season, summer
Rosette — yes or no
Layering — yes or no
Vegetative dispersal — ability of plant to establish from plant material broken away and transported elsewhere
Habit — prostrate, erect, sprawling/tangled
Stem — no stems, single stemmed, multi-stemmed
Leaf size — measured along longest axis < 2.5 cm, 2.5-5.0, 5.0-10.0, 10.0-20.0, 20.0-30.0, 30.0-60.0, > 60.0, grasses
Seed size — < 2 mm, 2-3, 3-5, 5-7, 7-10, 10-12
Habitat — crops, pasture, disturbed land, fallow, native communities
Dispersal mechanism — no specialised mechanism, spined, pappus/bristles
C_3/C_4 — photosynthetic pathway

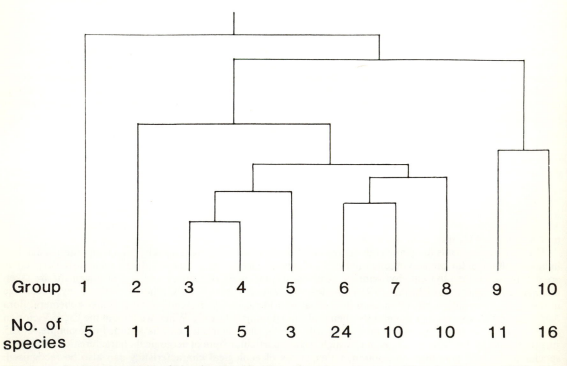

Fig. 2. A dendrogram arising from the classification of noxious plants in Victoria (Parsons 1973). The analysis is based on the characters listed in Table 13.

Group 1. The C_4 species which tend to be spring-germinating, rhizomatous (or similar), mat-forming species with spiny or bristled fruits or seeds (4/5 species spiny compared with 16/86 for the list as a whole) (e.g. khaki weed, *Alternanthera repens*).

Group 4. Sprawling or layering perennials (e.g. blackberry, *Rubus fruticosus*).

Group 5. The cactus (*Opuntia*) species.

Group 6. Erect, single-stemmed plants with 'large' leaves and mostly perennial. These are essentially the remaining species ('the rest'), as is commonly found in cluster analyses. It includes species ranging from the Cape tulips (*Homeria* spp.) to thorn apple (*Datura ferox*).

Group 7. Mat-forming, multistemmed perennials with non-rhizomatous shallow root systems, 'large' leaves and ability to germinate all year round (e.g. fennel, *Foeniculum vulgare*).

Group 8. Mat-forming, multistemmed perennials with rhizomatous, deep root systems, smaller leaves than Group 7 and germinating in autumn or spring (e.g. *Hypericum* spp.).

Group 9. Mainly annual composites which germinate in autumn. This group tends to have spiny or bristled fruit or flower heads, shallow roots and large leaves; most species originate from the cooler areas of Europe and America (e.g. slender thistle, *Carduus tenuiflorus*, but also spiny emex, *Emex australis*).

Group 10. Again, mainly annual composites which germinate in autumn, but this group tends to have seeds with a pappus, forms rosettes, has a deep root system and small leaves and most species are of Mediterranean origin (e.g. spear thistle, *Cirsium vulgare*, but also Paterson's curse, *Echium* sp.).

There were two single species groups. The only tree in the list, tree of heaven (*Ailanthus altissima*), formed one and dodder (*Cuscuta* sp.), the other. Dodder was unusual in being a twining parasitic species.

There are strong taxonomic links between the species of some of the groups, but this is not always the case. For example, group 10 contains 13 species of the Asteraceae and a small group of three species — Paterson's curse, musk weed (*Myagrum perfoliatum*) and wild teasel (*Dipsacus follonum*). They appear to occur with the composites as a result of their establishment behaviour of autumn germination and the formation of an overwintering rosette — characteristics otherwise not found in this list of noxious plants outside of the composites. By contrast 7/26 species of composites do not occur in Groups 9 or 10. Four fall in the variable Group 6, but 3 rhizomatous, mat-forming composites fall in Group 8. Hence, it appears that these groups do largely represent eco-physiological groups rather than simple taxonomic groupings.

Discussion

The above groups represent suites of eco-physiological characters which are associated with success in invasion of Victorian ecosystems. They probably represent only a small portion of the suites of characteristics which may be associated with successful invaders since the list is biased towards species which are a problem in agricultural habitats. Nor are we able to demonstrate that these suites are associated preferentially with successful invaders. However, suites of eco-physiological characters can be recognised. Based on this list and other descriptions of invasive plants, we propose the following eco-physiological types of successful invaders and qualities of habitats which favour success. Although these categories are based largely on plant invaders, some are also applicable to birds (see later).

Gap grabbers. Early germinators with fast initial growth or rosette formation can occupy the available space before the later germinators. Examples are the species germinating in autumn which overwinter as a rosette before making rapid growth in early spring, such as the thistles of Groups 9 and 10 above. Fox (1984) has shown that bridal creeper (*Asparagus asparagoides*) has an advantage in establishment over native *Clematis* species because of its ability to germinate a few days earlier in the season.

The use of false breaks is a variant of the gap-grabbing suite of properties. Seedlings of these species must mature rapidly or be drought tolerant in order to take advantage of short growth periods. The species must also possess a seed pool since many germination pulses will fail, as with *Echium* (Piggin 1982). Both suites of properties are examples of specialisation in the establishment niche (Grubb 1977).

Competitors. Species in this group usually out-extend their competitors either by holding their leaves higher in light-limited environments or pushing their roots deeper or further in water- or nutrient-limited environments. Groups 1 and 6 above contain many of these species. *Tribulus* is an example with its very rapid early growth which leads to the quick development of a deep root system (Squires 1979). Another is the competitive interaction between *Chrysanthemoides* and *Acacia* in dune communities. Weiss and Noble (1984b) found that *Acacia* has a greater photosynthetic rate per unit leaf area under ideal conditions but in the field, *Chrysanthemoides* reached a higher biomass by a more effective arrangement of its leaves to achieve greater effective leaf area. *Chrysanthemoides* also appeared to develop a deeper rooting system, thereby tapping a greater water supply.

It is possible that the success of the parrots, lorikeets and cockatoos may also be ascribed to competitive superiority for both food resources and nesting sites. However, it would appear that direct competition is a less important factor in birds than it is in plants, a view supported by Mayr (1965a).

Survivors. This group includes long-lived individuals which are resistant to most causes of mortality. Few of these species occur in the list of Victorian noxious plants, but such species tend to be weeds of grazed areas (e.g. *Eremophila*, Hodgkinson and Beeston 1982; and *Nassella*, Campbell 1982). Another variant is the mat- or thicket-forming species which spread vegetatively and have an indefinite life span (e.g. blackberry, Amor and Richardson 1980; and groups 4, 7 and 8 above). The success of ostriches and emus may be partly because of their longevity.

Swampers. Some species show a mass germination of seedlings (without necessarily having an early start). This tactic is only useful where mortality is not dependent on density but there were insufficient data available for the Victorian noxious plants to determine how common this suite of properties might be.

Obviously many invading species fall into more than one of these groups, but the possession of any one of these sets of characters will usually be sufficient to allow a species to be an invader in appropriate physical environments.

The question remains — why do some species act as invaders (i.e. species which spread and achieve a degree of dominance of the community) in some communities and not in others (including their native environment). We suggest that there are four processes which may be involved.

Habitat changes. The impact of human settlement has greatly increased the availability of some habitats. Species which specialise in these habitats have the opportunity to become invaders. Examples include the noxious plants of fallow land such as skeleton weed (*Chondrilla juncea*) in Australia, or the birds of human settlements.

Gap filling. It has been suggested that many invaders succeed by occupying niches which had remained vacant (or ineffectively used) until their arrival. Just why a niche should be vacant is an interesting area for evolutionary speculation (Walker and Valentine 1984) but we can give no examples of where this occurs (also see Fox and Fox, this volume). It had been suggested that *Chrysanthemoides* is in fact filling gaps on the dunes of the east coast of Australia. Weiss and Noble (1984a) checked this, however, and found evidence that it is displacing *Acacia longifolia* (i.e. its 'structural analogue') but having no detectable effect on the other species of the community. The filling of vacant niches is often assumed to be a factor in the increased success of birds in invading islands, but other factors such as reduced predation and habitat modification by humans cannot be overlooked.

Risk taking. It is possible that some invaders have ecological characteristics which allow them to survive at their new locality for some years but which will not allow them to survive extreme events. Thus the invader may appear to be successful for some years. This strategy will be effective in the longer term only if the species is able to regularly recolonise a site or if it has a long-lived propagule pool. *Pinus radiata*, which is invading dry sclerophyll eucalypt forest, probably falls into this category. The patchiness of prescribed fires and the suppression of wildfire allow pines to become established and grow to maturity; however, it is unlikely that they will be able to survive the inevitable wildfire. The extinction of malleefowl on Kangaroo Island on several occasions because of fire may be an example of this.

Competitive superiority. In any situation where organisms are transported around the world and are subject to competition for resources at their new localities, there will be winners and losers. We must expect a progressive simplification of the world's biota as superior species arrive in suitable habitats and displace the local species. (Note that we may not see a complete extinction of the local species and therefore species richness may increase.)

Predator release. There is another process which may often be involved in the 'risk taking' or 'competitively superior' categories. This is what we will term 'compensation'. In their native habitats many species are subject to heavy predation levels and only survive by undergoing selection which enables them to cope with these losses. When these species are introduced to areas lacking their predators, the compensatory mechanism confers a great advantage and often allows them to outcompete the local species. The massive seedling inputs by *Acacia* species in South Africa or by *Chrysanthemoides* in Australia is an example of this (Weiss 1983). In Australia, Weiss and Milton (1984) found that the seed pool of *Acacia* is *c.* $6/m^2$, whereas in South Africa, where it is largely free of pre- and post-dispersal predation, it achieves seed pools of $> 7000/m^2$. The reverse is true for *Chrysanthemoides* where seed pools in South Africa are *c.* $50/m^2$, whereas in Australia it suffers much less loss of viability and achieves seed pools of *c.* $2000/m^2$. Whether *Acacia* and *Chrysanthemoides* fall into the risk taking or competitively superior groups is not known yet.

CONCLUSIONS

Three questions remain to be answered. Are there any eco-physiological characters which indicate whether a species is likely to be a successful invader? If there are, are these characteristics similar or analogous in birds and plants? And, what is the relative importance of intrinsic versus extrinsic factors in determining the likelihood of success of an invading species.

Baker (1965) and Mayr (1965a) listed the characteristics likely to be associated with colonising species of plants and birds respectively. Although our data sets are not ideally suited to testing these propositions, we can find only limited support for them. In the plants, we found that suites of eco-physiological characteristics tend to be found in the introduced species of a temperate rural region. These suites allow the species to exploit particular opportunities for invasion and imply that most introduced plants tend to be 'specialists' with particular requirements for germination, sometimes with extended vegetative stages and relatively poor plasticity, rather than the super generalists described by Baker (Table 12).

In the bird data as a whole we found no support for the contention (Mayr 1965a) that social birds travelling in small flocks or that seed-eaters and freshwater birds would be most successful, although when our analysis was based on invaders of islands only (as was most of Mayr's data) we find that flocking birds were more successful. Native seed-eaters were successful in translocating and this perhaps may have reduced the success of introduced seed-eaters. Although there are no data on that point, it demonstrates the difficulty of testing specific hypotheses with limited data sets. Mayr also referred to ecological flexibility, and the ability to discover unoccupied habitats, but these properties are too vague to be tested directly. Mayr's final characteristic of a colonising species was the ability to shift habitat preference. Our data show that most successful invasions were into habitats similar to the original prime habitat.

Some similarities in the intrinsic characteristics of successful plant and bird species can be found. These include commensalism and occupation of disturbed habitats by foreign invaders mainly, longevity of individuals, risk taking and escape from predators. However, our analyses for both birds and plants show that there is no one suite of eco-physiological characteristics which may allow successful invasion. Although our analyses show certain analogies between birds and plants, what is more important is that in both groups successful invaders tend to be relative specialists often having few of the characters specified in lists of characteristics of 'ideal' invaders.

The history of invasion by both plants and birds in Australia shows that environmental circumstances extrinsic to the invader are often the most important factor in determining its success. Most of the successful invasions by introduced birds were to habitats very similar to the primary habitat of their homeland and in the majority of cases these were habitats associated with human activity. It seems highly likely that suburban areas lacking native trees and shrubs are essentially 'biological deserts' for native birds. There has been very little dispersal of introduced birds from areas of human occupation to native bushland and *vice versa* for Australian birds. This is true numerically for plants — although we recognise that the data set analysed was biased to emphasise plants of agricultural or otherwise modified land. A more interesting difference between birds and plants are the examples of truly successful invasions of native bushland by introduced plants; examples include prickly pear (*Opuntia* sp.), *Chrysanthemoides* sp., *Lantana* and many successfully naturalised forage species. On the face of it, this difference appears to reflect an oddity in the invasion by birds, since other vertebrate species have been able to invade native habitats successfully; examples include rabbits, goats, pigs, buffaloes, camels, horses, mice, trout, cats and dogs (Fox and Adamson 1979). However, all but two of these species are domestic, which accords with the relative success of commensal birds.

The mobility of modern society has probably changed the characteristics of the ideal invader. The ability to disperse great distances is no longer as important as it was even a millennium ago, since many species will be translocated from one habitat to another at regular intervals intentionally or unintentionally by humans. This will allow an increase in the 'risk-taking' category of invaders, since multiple introductions may allow some invaders to persist which, otherwise, would be eradicated in the long term by extreme environmental events or hazards. The modification of large regions of the globe as a result of occupation by European cultures has also provided an enormous expansion of habitat for the commensal species of that culture.

Thus, we conclude that there is not a single collection of eco-physiological characters possessed by successful invaders, but rather a number of suites of characters depending on the specialisation of the invader. However, factors extrinsic to the invader are likely to be the most important determinant of its success in a new habitat.

ACKNOWLEDGMENTS

The section on birds could not have been written without the knowledge, skill and energies of Mr I. Mason. He added to the original list of invading birds, extracted all biological information on species, consulted with other ornithological experts on details, and provided time and again the examples required. The statistical analyses were conducted by Mr D. Allen with biological inputs from Mr I. Mason. We are extremely pleased to acknowledge them both with the utmost gratitude for their invaluable assistance. Mrs H.B. Gill and Mr D.E. Rounsevell provided additional information on the status of species on islands, and Mr F. Knight drew Figure 1.

REFERENCES

Abbott, I. (1974). The avifauna of Kangaroo Island and causes of its impoverishment. *Emu 74*, 124–134.

Amor, R.L., and Richardson, R.G. (1980). The biology of Australian weeds. 2. *Rubus fruticosus* L. agg. *Journal of the Australian Institute of Agricultural Science 46*, 87–97.

Anonymous (1948). Flinders Chase, Kangaroo Island. *South Australian Ornithologist 18*, 76–77.

Baker, H.G. (1965). Characteristics and modes of origin of weeds. In *The Genetics of Colonizing Species* (eds H.G. Baker and G.L. Stebbins) pp. 147–169, Academic Press, New York.

Balmford, R. (1978). Early introductions of birds to Victoria. *Australian Bird Watcher 7*, 237–248; 262–265.

Black, C.C. (1971). Ecological implications of dividing plants into groups with distinct photosynthetic production capacities. *Advances in Ecological Research 7*, 87–114.

Blakers, M., Davies, S., and Reilly, P. (1984). *The Atlas of Australian Birds*, Melbourne University Press, Melbourne.

Campbell, M.H. (1982). The biology of Australian weeds. 9. *Nassella trichotoma* (Nees) Arech. *Journal of the Australian Institute of Agricultural Science 48*, 76–84.

Condon, H.T. (1968). *A Handlist of the Birds of South Australia, 2nd edn*, South Australian Ornithologists Association, Adelaide.

Condon, H.T. (1975). *Checklist of the Birds of Australia, Part 1, Non-Passerines*, Royal Australasian Ornithologists Union, Melbourne.

Cooper, H.M. (1947). Some notes on Kangaroo Island birds. *South Australian Ornithologist 18*, 48.

Deignan, H.G. (1964). Birds of the Arnhemland Expedition. In *Records of the American-Australian Scientific Expedition of Arnhemland, Zoology, Vol.4* (ed. R.L. Specht) pp. 345–425, Melbourne University Press, Melbourne.

Elmore, C.D.and Paul, R.N. (1983). Composite list of C_4 weeds. *Weed Science 31*, 686–692.

Ford, H.A. (1979). Birds. In *Natural History of Kangaroo Island* (eds M.J. Tyler, C.R. Twidale and J.K. Ling) pp. 103–114, Royal Society of South Australia, Adelaide.

Fox, J. (1984). A comparison of two climbing plant species (one native and one exotic) at Woodman Point, Western Australia. *Western Australian Naturalist 16*, 11–15.

Fox, M.D., and Adamson, D. (1979). The ecology of invasions. In *A Natural Legacy* (eds H.F. Recher, D. Lunney and I. Dunn) pp. 135–151, Pergamon Press, Sydney.

Fullagar, P.J., and Disney, H.J. de S. (1975). The birds of Lord Howe Island: A report on the rare and endangered species. In *XII Bulletin of the International Council for Bird Preservation* (eds P. Barclay-Smith and R.D. Chancellor) pp. 187–202, International Council for Bird Preservation, London.

Green, R.J. (1984). Native and exotic birds in a suburban habitat. *Australian Wildlife Research 11*, 181–190.

Grubb, P.J. (1977). The maintenance of species richness in plant communities: the importance of the regeneration niche. *Biological Reviews 52*, 107–145.

Harlan, J. (1975). *Crops and Man*, American Society of Agronomy, Madison, Wisconsin.

Hewitt, J.M. (1960). The Cattle Egret in Australia. *Emu 60*, 99–102.

Hindwood, K.A. (1940). The birds of Lord Howe Island. *Emu 40*, 1–86.

Hodgkinson, K.C., and Beeston, G.R. (1982). The biology of Australian weeds. 10. *Eremophila mitchellii* Benth. *Journal of the Australian Institute of Agricultural Science 48*, 200–208.

Holm, L.G., Plucknett, D.L., Pancho, J.V., and Herberger, J.P. (1977). *The World's Worst Weeds, Distribution and Biology*, University Press, Hawaii.

Jenkins, C.F.H. (1977). *The Noah's Ark Syndrome*, General Printing, Perth.

Long, J.L. (1981). *Introduced Birds of the World*, Reed, Sydney.

Mayr, E. (1965a). The nature of colonising birds. In *The Genetics of Colonizing Species* (eds H.G. Baker and G.L. Stebbins) pp. 29–43, Academic Press, New York.

Mayr, E. (1965b). Summary. In *The Genetics of Colonizing Species* (eds H.G. Baker and G.L. Stebbins) pp. 553–563, Academic Press, New York.

McCance, N. (1962). Reckless acclimatisation. *Australian Aviculture*, pp. 105–106.

Morony, J.J., Bock, W.J., and Farrand, J. (1975). *Reference List of the Birds of the World*, American Museum of Natural History, New York.

Parker, S.A., Eckert, H.J., Ragless, G.B., Cox, J.B., and Reid, N.C.H. (1976). *An Annotated Checklist of the Birds of South Australia, Part 1, Emus to Spoonbills*, South Australian Ornithologists Association, Adelaide.

Parsons, W.T. (1973). *Noxious Weeds of Victoria*, Inkata Press, Melbourne and Sydney.

Pearcy, R.W., and Ehrlinger, J. (1984). Comparative eco-physiology of C_3 and C_4 plants. *Plant, Cell and Environment 7*, 1–13.

Piggin, C.M. (1982). The biology of Australian weeds. 8. *Echium plantagineum* L. *Journal of the Australian Institute of Agricultural Science 48*, 3–16.

Rounsevell, D.E., Blackhall, S.A., and Thomas, D.G. (1977). *Birds of Maria Island*, Tasmanian National Parks and Wildlife Service, Wildlife Division, Technical Report No. 77/3.

Schodde, R. (1975). *Interim List of Australian Songbirds, Passerines*, Royal Australasian Ornithologists Union, Melbourne.

Schodde, R., Fullagar, P., and Hermes, N. (1983). *A Review of Norfolk Island Birds: Past and Present*, Australian National Parks and Wildlife Service Special Publication, Australian Government Publishing Service, Canberra.

Schodde, R., Glover, B., Kinsky, F.C., Marchant, S., McGill, A.R., and Parker, S.A. (1978). Recommended English names for Australian birds. *Emu 77*, 245–307.

Sokal, R.R., and Rohlf, F.J. (1969). *Biometry*, 1st edn, H.H. Freeman and Company, San Francisco.

Squires, V.R. (1979). The biology of Australian weeds. 1. *Tribulus terrestris* L. *Journal of the Australian Institute of Agricultural Science 45*, 75–82.

Sutton, J. (1926). Malleefowl (*Leipoa occellata*) on Kangaroo Island. *South Australian Ornithology 13*, 92–103.

Walker, T.D., and Valentine, J.W. (1984). Equilibrium models of evolutionary species diversity and the number of empty niches. *American Naturalist 124*, 887–899.

Weiss, P.W. (1983). Invasion of coastal *Acacia* communities by *Chrysanthemoides*. Ph.D. thesis, Australian National University, Canberra.

Weiss, P.W., and Milton, S. (1984). *Chrysanthemoides monilifera* and *Acacia longifolia* in Australia and South Africa. In *Proceedings of the 4th International Conference on Mediterranean Ecosystems* (ed. B. Dell) pp. 159–160, Botany Department, University of Western Australia.

Weiss, P.W., and Noble, I.R. (1984a). Status of coastal dune communities invaded by *Chrysanthemoides monilifera*. *Australian Journal of Ecology 9*, 93–98.

Weiss, P.W., and Noble, I.R. (1984b). Interactions between seedlings of *Chrysanthemoides* and *Acacia longifolia*. *Australian Journal of Ecology 9*, 107–115.

Wheeler, J.R. (1960). The RAOU camp-out at Kangaroo Island, South Australia, 1959. *Emu 60*, 265–280.

Wheeler, W.R. (1979). *The Birds of Victoria and Where to Find Them*, Nelson, Melbourne.

Wodzicki, K. (1965). The status of some exotic vertebrates in the ecology of New Zealand. In *The Genetics of Colonizing Species* (eds H.G. Baker and G.L. Stebbins) pp. 425–460, Academic Press, New York.

APPENDIX 1.

*List of all foreign and native species of birds introduced anywhere into Australia.**
Successful introductions are in capitals, and approximate numbers introduced overall are in parenthesis.

FAMILY	FOREIGN	NATIVE
STRUTHIANIDAE	OSTRICH *Struthio camelus*[1] (? > 500)	
DROMAIIDAE		EMU *Dromaius novaehollandiae* (18)
ARDEIDAE	CATTLE EGRET *Ardeola ibis* (self introduced)	WHITE-FACED HERON *Ardea novaehollandiae* (self introduced)
		Rufous night heron *Nycticorax caledonicus* (7; eradicated)
ANATIDAE	MUTE SWAN *Cygnus olor* (? > 20)	Magpie goose *Anseranas semipalmata*[2] (2)
	Canada goose *Branta canadensis* (? > 6)	Black swan *Cygnus atratus* (11; eradicated)
	Egyptian goose *Alopchen aegyptiacus* (? > 4)	CAPE BARREN GOOSE *Cereopsis novaehollandiae* (89 +)
		Australian shelduck *Tadorna tadornoides* (10)
	Paradise shelduck *Tadorna variegata* (self introduced)	PACIFIC BLACK DUCK *Anas superciliosa* (4)
	Spur-winged goose *Plectropterus gambensis* (? > 4)	Grey teal *Anas gibberifrons* (3)
	Mandarin duck *Aix galericulata* (2)	CHESTNUT TEAL *Anas castanea* (8)
	MALLARD *Anas platyrhynchos* (? 136)	Australasian shoveller *Anas rhynchotis* (2)
FALCONIDAE		AUSTRALIAN KESTREL *Falco cenchroides* (self introduced)

APPENDIX 1. (continued)

FAMILY	FOREIGN	NATIVE
MEGAPODIIDAE		Orange-footed scrubfowl *Megapodius reinwardt*[3] (?) Malleefowl *Leipoa ocellata* (< 30) AUSTRALIAN BRUSH-TURKEY *Alectura lathami* (2)
PHASIANIDAE	TURKEY *Meleagris gallopavo*[3] (?) CALIFORNIA QUAIL *Lophortyx californica* (? > 2-300) Chukar partridge *Alectoris graeca* (< 50) Red-legged partridge *Alectoris rufa* (< 20) European partridge *Perdix perdix* (< 200) Common quail *Coturnix coturnix*[3] (?) KING QUAIL *Coturnix chinensis*[4] (< 250) Impejan pheasant *Lophophorus impejanus* (< 10) RED JUNGLE FOWL *Gallus gallus* (? 20-30 +) Silver pheasant *Lophura nycthemera* (escapee; eradicated) Crested fireback *Lophura ignita*[3] (?) RING-NECKED PHEASANT *Phasianus colchicus* (< 1-2000) COMMON PEAFOWL *Pavo cristatus* (? < 100) HELMETED GUINEAFOWL *Numida meleagris* (< 400)	BROWN QUAIL *Coturnix ypsilophora* (< 80)
RALLIDAE	WEKA *Gallirallus australis* (?)	TASMANIAN NATIVE-HEN *Gallinula mortierii* (3) PURPLE SWAMPHEN *Porphyrio porphyrio* (2)
PTEROCLIDIDAE	Pintailed sandgrouse *Pterocles alchata* (10) Common sandgrouse *Pterocles exustus* (< 80)	
COLUMBIDAE	FERAL PIGEON *Columba livia* (? 100's) Common turtle-dove *Streptopelia tutor* (8) Collared turtle-dove *Streptopelia decaocto*[5] (escapee; eradicated) SPOTTED TURLE-DOVE *Streptopelia chinensis* (? > 100) LAUGHING TURTLE-DOVE *Streptopelia senegalensis* (? >> 50) Namaqua dove *Oena capensis* (escapee)	Peaceful dove *Geopelia placida* (22) Diamond dove *Geopelia cuneata* (4) Bar-shouldered dove *Geopelia humeralis* (4) COMMON BRONZEWING *Phaps chalcoptera* (4) Crested pigeon *Ocyphaps lophotes*[6] (12) Spinifex pigeon *Petrophassa plumifera* (2) Wonga pigeon *Leucosarcia melanoleuca* (4)
CACATUIDAE		GANG-GANG COCKATOO *Callocephalon fimbriatum* (8 +) GALAH *Cacatua roseicapilla* (self introduced)

APPENDIX 1. (continued)

FAMILY	FOREIGN	NATIVE
		LONG-BILLED CORELLA *Cacatua tenuirostris* (30 +)
		SULPHUR-CRESTED COCKATOO *Cacatua galerita* (?)
LORIIDAE		RAINBOW LORIKEET *Trichoglossus haematodus* (? 2; escapee)
		SCALY-BREASTED LORIKEET *Trichoglossus chlorolepidotus* (? 2; escapee)
		MUSK LORIKEET *Glossopsitta concinna* (? 2; escapee)
PSITTACIDAE	Peach-faced lovebird *Agapornis roseicollis* (escapee)	CRIMSON ROSELLA *Platycercus elegans* (escapee; human introduced)
		EASTERN ROSELLA *Platycercus eximius* (12 +; escapee; human introduced)
		PALE-HEADED ROSELLA *Platycercus adscitus* (escapee)
		PORT LINCOLN PARROT *Barnardius zonarius* (escapee)
		RED-RUMPED PARROT *Psephotus haematonotus* (escapee)
STRIGIDAE		Southern boobook *Ninox novaeseelandia* (? < 10)
		Barn owl *Tyto alba* (? < 20)
TYTONIDAE		MASKED OWL *Tyto novaehollandiae* (? < 100)
ALCEDINIDAE		LAUGHING KOOKABURRA *Dacelo novaeguineae* (?; human and self introduced)
MENURIDAE		SUPERB LYREBIRD *Menura novaehollandiae* (21)
ALAUDIDAE	Woodlark *Lullula arborea*[7] (?)	
	SKYLARK *Alauda arvensis* (> 700)	
HIRUNDINIDAE		WELCOME SWALLOW *Hirundo neoxena* (self introduced)
PYCNONOTIDAE	RED-WHISKERED BULBUL *Pycnonotus jocosus* (escapee)	
	Red-vented bulbul *Pycnonotus cafer* (escapee)	
MUSCICAPIDAE	European robin *Erithacus rubecula* (47)	
	Nightingale *Erithacus megarhynchos* (2)	
	Hermit thrush *Hylocichla guttata*[3] (3)	
	BLACKBIRD *Turdus merula* (> 150)	
	SONG THRUSH *Turdus philomelos* (> 70)	
ZOSTEROPIDAE		SILVEREYE *Zosterops lateralis*[3] (?; human and self introduced)
EMBERIZIDAE	Yellowhammer *Emberiza citrinella* (> 15)	
	Ortolan bunting *Emberiza hortulana* (16)	
	Common cardinal *Cardinalis cardinalis*[3] (?)	

APPENDIX 1. (continued)

FAMILY	FOREIGN	NATIVE
FRINGILLIDAE	Chaffinch *Fringilla coelebes* (< 200) Bramble finch *Fringilla montifringilla* (< 80) Canary *Serinus canaria* (18) EUROPEAN GREENFINCH *Carduelis chloris* (< 150) Siskin *Carduelis spinus* (80) EUROPEAN GOLDFINCH *Carduelis carduelis* (< 500) COMMON REDPOLL *Acanthis flammea* (self introduced) Linnet *Acanthis cannabina* (? < 50) Bullfinch *Pyrrhula pyrrhula* (14) Hawfinch *Coccothraustes coccothraustes*[3] (?)	
PLOCEIDAE	HOUSE SPARROW *Passer domesticus* (? >> 100) TREE SPARROW *Passer montanus* (? < 70) Red bishop *Euplectes orix* (escapee) White-winged wydah *Euplectes albonotatus* (escapee)	
ESTRILDIDAE	NUTMEG MANNIKIN *Lonchura punctulata* (escapee) Black-headed mannikin *Lonchura malacca* (escapee) Java sparrow *Padda oryzivora* (>> 100)	RED-BROWED FIRETAIL *Emblema temporalis* (escapee) Zebra finch *Poephila guttata* (12) CHESTNUT-BREASTED MANNIKIN *Lonchura castaneothorax* (escapee)
STURNIDAE	COMMON STARLING *Sturnus vulgaris* (> 450) COMMON MYNAH *Acridotheres tristis* (> 350)	
GRALLINIDAE		AUSTRALIAN MAGPIE-LARK *Grallina cyanoleuca* (10)
CRACTICIDAE		AUSTRALIAN MAGPIE *Gymnorhina tibicen*[3] (?; human and self introduced)
CORVIDAE	House Crow *Corvus splendens* (self introduced; eradicated)	

* The five species eradicated by humans and the woodlark (see footnote 7) are not used in any analyses.

1 Ostrich. Almost extinct (Parker *et al.* 1976); remaining populations in semi-domesticated conditions (I. Mason, pers. comm.).
2 Some 300 magpie geese have been introduced to Victoria since 1973 but few remain (Blakers, Davies and Reilly 1984).
3 No details of release exist (e.g. McCance 1962; Jenkins 1977; Long 1981) but low numbers (< 10) are assumed here.
4 King quail still exist in Victoria (Wheeler 1979) but whether they are of Australian or foreign stock will not be known until specimens are collected (I. Mason, pers. comm.).
5 Collared turtle-doves (escapees) are still occasionally observed around the Melbourne district (Wheeler 1979).
6 Crested pigeons did not survive on Kangaroo Island from the original introduction of 12 birds in 1937 but the occasional vagrant arrives from the mainland (Abbott 1974; Ford 1979).
7 The woodlark was brought to Australia but it is not certain that any were released (Long 1981).

GENETIC ATTRIBUTES OF INVADING SPECIES

S.C.H. Barrett[1] and B.J. Richardson[2]

A consideration of the genetic attributes of invading species, and the genetic consequences of colonisation, depends on the concept of colonisation that is used. Clearly the process of colonisation is an integral component of the population biology of all plants and animals. In this volume, however, we are concerned with biological invasions and hence colonisation on a grand scale. We therefore define an invasion as the successful founding of a colony in a region where none previously existed followed by rapid expansion of the range of the invading species. Biological invasions may occur on various geographical scales from simple extension of range to intercontinental migration. The effects of such movement may involve the entry into a new physical or biological environment, sharp reductions in population size, restricted gene flow, and difficulty in finding mates. These influences can have major effects on colonisation; the ability of a species to cope with them may determine the likelihood of a successful biological invasion. In this chapter we examine the importance of these influences and whether successful invading species as a group share similar genetic characteristics.

Several detailed works on the genetics of colonising species are available (e.g. Baker and Stebbins 1965; Parsons 1983) and therefore there is no need for an exhaustive treatment of the subject. Instead we organise this chapter by posing a number of inter-related questions regarding the genetic aspects of biological invasions:
1) What is the effect of the invasion process on the amount of genetic variation in populations?
2) What levels of genetic variation are found in species that are successful invaders?
3) What genetic systems are associated with colonising success?
4) What are the relative contributions of inherited and environmentally controlled variation in life history traits of colonising species?
5) What evidence exists for local genetic differentiation following invasions?
Where possible we answer the above questions using examples of plant and animal invasions of Australia.

WHAT IS THE EFFECT OF THE INVASION PROCESS ON THE AMOUNT OF GENETIC VARIATION IN POPULATIONS?

A new colony is usually, but not always, established by a small number of immigrants. In theory this could lead to a loss of genetic variation through sampling effects during the population bottleneck as a small random sample of individuals may not contain all the variation present in the parent population. Nei, Maruyama and Chakraborty (1975) studied the theoretical consequences of this process and concluded that the level of variability does in fact decline but that this depends not only on the size of the founder population, but also on the speed of recovery of large population size (i.e. for how many generations the population remains small). The theoretical effect of founder population size and speed of recovery are shown in Table 1. Nei, Maruyama and Chakraborty (1975) also point out that the effect of a bottleneck in population size on average heterozygosity (i.e. proportion of loci in an individual present in the heterozygous state) is smaller than on the average number of alleles at each locus. Most additional alleles are at very low frequency and contribute little to heterozygosity. These alleles are most easily lost by sampling effects.

An example of the effect of the colonisation process on the level of genetic variation was reported by Richardson, Rogers and Hewitt (1980) for the rabbit (*Oryctolagus cuniculus*) which occurs naturally in Spain.

[1] CSIRO, Division of Plant Industry, G.P.O. Box 1600, Canberra, A.C.T. 2601. Permanent address: Department of Botany, University of Toronto, Toronto, Ontario, Canada M5S 1A1

[2] Bureau of Flora and Fauna, G.P.O. Box 1383, Canberra, A.C.T. 2601

After domestication it was taken to England by the Normans and later to Australia in the mid 19th century. From the twenty or so animals released in Victoria the species increased rapidly in number and range until it reached Western Australia. During this latter phase of range expansion the 'rabbit front' apparently moved at a rate of 100 km/year (Myers 1971). The colonisation process in Australia therefore consisted of several stages. As well as the original colonisation event there was a sequence of founder events of local populations as the rabbit spread westward continuously over a period of 60 years and 3000 km. From the changes in allele frequencies of electrophoretic loci that accompanied this series of events (Table 2) it can be seen that domestication apparently led to significant changes in allele frequencies, the move to Australia little change, and the spread to Western Australia no change in frequency of common alleles but the apparent loss of a rare carbonic anhydrase allele. These results are in accord with the theoretical expectations and show that long-distance migration involving relatively few immigrants may have little effect on the amount of genetic variation if rapid population increase follows the initial establishment.

Marked reductions in genetic variation accompanying continental migration can occur in selfing species if propagules originate from a limited sampling of populations in the native range. Surveys of isozyme variation in native North American populations of barnyard grass (*Echinochloa microstachya*) reveal considerable variation among populations but little variation within populations (S.C.H. Barrett and A.H.D. Brown, unpublished data). Most populations surveyed were composed of a single homozygous genotype. The species was introduced this century to rice fields in New South Wales, probably as a contaminant of imported rice stocks from California (McIntyre and Barrett 1985). Since introduction, *E. microstachya* has spread throughout the rice-growing area as a weed of rice. The amount of genetic variation in Australian rice field populations is very restricted compared with the native range, although individual populations in the two regions are equally depauperate in variation. Brown and Marshall (1981) reviewed other comparisons of genetic variation in the native and introduced range of weeds. Where the reproductive system of weeds involves predominant selfing or apomixis (see below) we may expect marked reduction of genetic variation in the introduced range. In contrast, in outbreeding species relatively small differences may be evident if large population sizes are maintained following introduction.

WHAT LEVELS OF GENETIC VARIATION ARE FOUND IN SPECIES THAT ARE SUCCESSFUL INVADERS?

The level of genetic variation within a population largely determines its capacity to respond, in an evolutionary sense, to changes in environment. Skibinski and Ward (1982) showed, for example, using

TABLE 1. *The effect of size of the founder population and the speed of recovery of large population size on the loss of heterozygosity (H).*
Calculated from Nei *et al.* (1975).

Size of founder population	After one generation	Proportion of H remaining When large population size recovered*				
		200%	100%	50%	20%	10%
1	0.50	0.41	0.31	0.18	0.03	0.02
2	0.75	0.66	0.58	0.45	0.20	0.05
5	0.90	0.86	0.81	0.73	0.54	0.32
10	0.95	0.93	0.90	0.86	0.74	0.57
100	0.99	0.99	0.99	0.99	0.97	0.95
1000	1.00	1.00	1.00	1.00	1.00	0.99

* (% population increase/generation).

TABLE 2. *Allele frequencies in rabbit populations from Europe and Australia.*
After Richardson *et al.* (1980).

Location	Ada^1	Ada^2	Pgd^1	Est^1	Ca^1	Dia^1
s. France	0.75	0.01	0.01	0.69	0.66	1.00
Britain	0.42	0.20	0	0.64	0.16	—
Victoria	0.56	0.02	0	0.77	—	—
w. N.S.W.	0.54	0.03	0.07	0.55	0.11	0.76
s. W.A.	0.52	0.09	0.03	0.64	0	0.71

Ada, adenosine deaminase; *Pgd*, phosphoglucosedehydrogenase; *Est*, esterase; *Ca*, carbonic anhydrase; *Dia*, diaphorase.

electrophoretic and amino acid sequence data drawn from vertebrates, that the rate of evolutionary change in amino acid sequence is correlated with the average heterozygosity of the protein. Of prime importance is variation underlying characters of ecological significance. The genetic basis of these traits is often difficult to establish, however, and population geneticists have resorted to other measurements that are presumed to reflect the overall level of variation in populations. The simplest of these is 'H', the proportion of loci that are carried in the heterozygous condition in an average individual. An estimate of 'H' can be obtained from measurements of the amount of genetic polymorphism in enzymes and other proteins detected using electrophoresis. These estimates assume that the electrophoretically detectable proteins coded by structural genes vary in populations in a fashion similar to other classes of genes, such as those involved with gene regulation. Zouros, Singh and Miles (1980) studied the effect of average heterozygosity of seven enzyme loci on growth rates of individual oysters in a natural population. They found growth rate to be related linearly to average heterozygosity, thereby supporting the contention that 'H' is a biologically meaningful measurement.

Information from electrophoretic studies of isozyme variation in natural populations of 228 animal species has been summarised by Nevo (1978). He found significant differences in the amount of genetic variation for subsets of the data subdivided using different biological criteria. Cosmopolitan species exhibited higher levels of genetic variation than temperate species, but were not necessarily more variable than tropical species. This indicates that cosmopolitan species, which are frequently successful invaders, do have, on average, high levels of variation, but a wide range of heterozygosity values was found and successful animal invaders with little variation are known.

Successful colonists are frequently considered to be generalists and Nevo's analysis showed that generalists on average carry significantly more variation than specialists. However, some specialists harbour high levels of variation, e.g., the curculionid beetle *Otiorrhynchus scaber* has an 'H' value of 0.31 (Suomalainen and Saura 1973), which is 25% more than the next highest species reported by Nevo (1978), whilst some generalists carry little or no variation.

Nevo's analysis involves comparison of a large number of unrelated species and it would be useful to test his proposals in a closely related group of species where phylogenetic variation is restricted. Lewis (1981) examined the relationship between heterozygosity and a number of biological variables using data for tuna and other scombrid fishes. He found that the level of heterozygosity was correlated with size, vagility and geographical range of the species in the group. Species with high vagility, wide distribution and large size could be considered equivalent to the generalists or cosmopolitan species groups examined by Nevo (1978) and a similar result was obtained. Again, however, the range of heterozygosities observed by Lewis was very large in each class and it is clear that there is no necessary relationship between level of inherited variation and success as a coloniser in the animals surveyed to date.

A similar analysis involving exclusively plant data from 113 taxa revealed somewhat different patterns (Hamrick, Linhart and Mitton 1979). Mean levels of genetic variation were lowest in species with restricted distributions (endemics), increased for the regional category but declined in species with widespread distributions. The decrease was attributed to the large number of weedy, predominantly selfing species whose population variability was relatively low (see below). In a separate analysis of genetic variation in species of contrasting stages of succession, Hamrick, Linhart and Mitton (1979) found that weed species, which predominate in early successional stages, were significantly less variable than species of middle and late successional stages.

The amount of genetic variation in weed populations may also be associated with the life history strategy and ecological characteristics of the species. Some weeds have broad ecological tolerances and colonise a wide range of environments whereas others are highly specialised in their habitat requirements (Baker 1974). Among the world's most successful colonising species are members of the barnyard grass genus *Echinochloa* (Holm *et al.* 1977). *Echinochloa crus-galli* and *E. oryzoides* are both annual, self-fertilising hexaploid weeds of world-wide distribution. *Echinochloa crus-galli* invades a broad spectrum of disturbed habitats and agricultural crops whereas *E. oryzoides* is a satellite weed of cultivated rice restricted to flooded rice fields (Barrett 1983). A study of genetic variation at enzyme loci and quantitative characters in Californian and Australian populations of the two taxa (S.C.H. Barrett and A.H.D. Brown, unpublished data) found that the generalist *E. crus-galli* was more variable both within and between populations than *E. oryzoides* (Table 3).

Of particular interest was the contrast in patterns of variation exhibited by loci controlling the enzyme alcohol dehydrogenase (*Adh*). In *E. crus-galli* a total of 12 homozygous *Adh* multilocus genotypes were evident among populations as a result of polymorphism at 2 or 3 loci. Virtually all populations which were surveyed in both regions contained several *Adh* genotypes. In contrast all *E. oryzoides* populations, except one in California, were composed of individuals with the same multilocus genotype. The exceptional population was monomorphic for a variant *Adh* genotype. Although populations of *E. oryzoides* were monomorphic for *Adh* loci, polymorphism for other enzyme loci (e.g. aconitase, diaphorase, phosphoglucomutase) was apparent but the level of polymorphism was reduced in comparison with *E. crus-galli*.

Whilst historical factors associated with plant introduction obviously influence the variation exhibited by the two *Echinochloa* species it is also possible that the absence of *Adh* variation in populations of the obligate rice

TABLE 3. *Genetic variation in Californian populations of* Echinochloa crus-galli *and* E. oryzoides.

Species	X̄ Coefficient of variation (%) of between family variation within populations		Percentage loci polymorphic	Total *Adh* genotypes
	Time to flowering	Fecundity	(n = loci surveyed)	
E. crus-galli	13.84	29.74	51.6 (31)	12
E. oryzoides	6.85	23.46	15.6 (32)	2

Quantitative traits based on 15 families from each of 10 populations grown under uniform glasshouse conditions .Electrophoretic analysis on 15 families from 12 populations (S C H .Barrett and A H.D. Brown, unpublished data).

weed may reflect selection of an 'optimum' *Adh* genotype adapted to the relatively uniform and predictable conditions of flooded rice fields. In contrast, the polymorphism at *Adh* genes in *E. crus-galli* may be maintained by the heterogeneous nature of the disturbed habitats it occupies. Elsewhere it has been demonstrated that *Adh* enzymes may function to enable plants to tolerate the anaerobic conditions associated with flooded environments (Crawford 1967; Marshall, Broué and Pryor 1973).

A significant number of surveys of isozyme variation in weed species document depauperate amounts of genetic diversity both within and between populations, particularly following continental migration. Weed groups for which recent surveys have revealed highly homozygous populations or populations composed of a few genotypes include the examples reviewed in Brown and Marshall (1981) and Barrett (1982) and, in addition, *Amaranthus* spp. (Hauptli and Jain 1978), *Polygonum pensylvanicum* (Kubetin and Schaal 1979), *Capsella bursa-pastoris* (Bosbach and Hurka 1981), *Senecio viscosus* (Koniuszek and Verkeij 1982), *Lolium temulentum* (Hayward and Zaruk 1982), *Hordeum murinum* (Giles 1983) and *Echinochloa* spp. (S.C.H. Barrett and A.H.D. Brown, unpublished data). All these findings clearly indicate that high levels of genetic diversity are not a prerequisite for a successful invading species.

It is important to note, however, that populations of weeds that are genetically uniform for isozyme variation at single loci may in fact carry more genetic variation than may be appreciated if they are polyploid, through the presence of fixed heterozygosity (different alleles at homoeologous loci). Many cosmopolitan weeds are, in fact, inbreeding, polyploid annuals and the genetic systems of these plants may maintain high biochemical versatility contributing towards individual buffering in the varying environments they encounter (Roose and Gottlieb 1976; Babbel and Wain 1977; Allard, Miller and Kahler 1978). The role of polyploidy *per se* in colonising success is considered below.

Another reason for not assuming that weeds exhibiting uniformity for enzyme loci are entirely devoid of genetic variation comes from parallel studies involving both quantitative characters and isozymes. Where these have been undertaken it has often been shown that populations apparently monomorphic for enzyme loci contain significant genetically-based variation for important life history traits. An example of the disparity between the two classes of loci involves one of the most widespread and successful weeds, the inbreeding annual *Xanthium strumarium* noogoora burr). Moran and Marshall (1978) surveyed 12 populations of this species complex in Australia, comprising four taxonomic races, for isozyme variation at 13 loci. They found that within three of the four races, all populations were composed of the same homozygous multilocus isozyme genotype. However, a study of 15 quantitative characters revealed significant genetic variation within and between populations (Moran, Marshall and Muller 1981). Since the patterns of genetic variation were uncorrelated with differences in the distribution of the four races in Australia, it appears that the amount of genetic variation *per se* may be unimportant in explaining racial differences in colonising success within the group. Moran, Marshall and Muller (1981) suggest that differences in reproductive output and photoperiodic requirements for flowering may be more important attributes in accounting for the contrasting distributional patterns of the four races in Australia.

Normally, genetic variation at different loci within populations is distributed independently and all possible combinations of alleles at different loci may be found. However, self-fertilisation and population bottlenecks during the early stages of colonisation can produce linkage disequilibrium between loci. Such effects can generate a limited number of multilocus associations within populations; they have been documented in Californian populations of slender wild oat, *Avena barbata* (Allard *et al.* 1972) and Israeli populations of wild barley, *Hordeum spontaneum* (Brown, Feldman and Nevo 1980). Both of these weed species are highly self-pollinating. In Australia only three distinct multilocus genotypes are evident in introduced populations of skeleton weed, *Chondrilla juncea* (Burdon, Marshall and Groves 1980). Here triploidy in association with the apomictic mode of reproduction prevents recombination and the three genotypes presumably result from separate introductions from Europe.

At the other extreme, in terms of multilocus structure, is the annual outbreeding weed *Echium plantagineum* (Paterson's curse), one of the most successful invaders of temperate Australia. In a survey of the genetic structure of a population at Gundagai, New South Wales, Brown and Burdon (1983) revealed remarkably high levels of genetic diversity. A vast array of multilocus genotypes was present, with no detectable non-random association among the 11 polymorphic enzyme loci which were assayed. The organisation of genetic variation within the population suggests that the outcrossed mating system of *E. plantagineum* encourages sufficient recombination to overcome the effects of bottlenecks on multilocus structure.

To date, the population of *E. plantagineum* at Gundagai not only represents the most isozymically variable weed population which has been assayed but is also among the most diverse of any plant population which has been studied electrophoretically (Hamrick, Linhart and Mitton 1979). Brown and Burdon's findings raise several interesting questions concerning the invasive properties of the species in Australia. Are other *E. plantagineum* populations in Australia as diverse as the one they studied? How variable are populations in the native European range and to what extent has the dramatic spread of *E. plantagineum* been aided by high levels of genetic variation? Further comparative ecogenetic studies of the species in Australia and Europe would seem warranted. If high genetic diversity is a general feature of Australian populations of *E. plantagineum*, the rapid evolution of races locally adapted to Australian conditions would be anticipated.

Together these surveys suggest that the patterns of genetic variation in colonising plants and animals of widespread distribution may often differ. Where differences are evident they are most likely associated with the contrasting genetic systems found in the two groups.

WHAT GENETIC SYSTEMS ARE ASSOCIATED WITH COLONISING SUCCESS?

Mating systems

Colonisation of unoccupied territory is often associated with periods of low population density. The difficulties of mating under these circumstances may be expected to impose severe restrictions on the colonising potential of non-motile, outbreeding organisms. In plants an association between unsaturated habitats and self-fertilisation was first noted by Henslow (1879) who reported that most weeds in Britain were selfers. More recently the search for correlations between colonising ability and uniparental modes of reproduction, either by selfing or apomixis, has been a repeated theme in studies of weed groups (Stebbins 1957, 1965; Allard 1965; Baker 1965; Mulligan and Findlay 1970). Two main advantages have been proposed to explain why plants capable of uniparental reproduction should be more effective colonisers. The first, originally proposed by Baker (1955, 1967), concerns the ability of selfing or apomictic colonists to start reproducing colonies following long-distance dispersal of a single individual. In addition, Stebbins (1957) and Allard (1965), among others, have argued that following successful establishment selfing allows the rapid fixation and multiplication of adapted genotypes. Two recent surveys of colonising plants support the general association first observed by Henslow. Price and Jain (1981) surveyed 400 species from 43 plant families from the flora of the British Isles in an attempt to see whether plants capable of uniparental reproduction were better colonists than outcrossers. They found that predominant selfing or apomixis was significantly more common among plants they classified as colonisers than was outbreeding. However, as Price and Jain (1981) note, many cases occur, particularly among perennial weeds, where both obligate outbreeding, through self-incompatibility or dioecism, and clonal propagation are associated. Among the plants judged to be the world's most successful invaders (see Holm *et al.* 1977) Brown and Marshall (1981) found that about half reproduced predominantly by selfing and most of the remainder multiplied primarily by asexual means.

With their diversity of reproductive systems, it is not unexpected that both inbreeding and outbreeding weeds should occur. What is required, however, are experimental ecological studies of successful, outbreeding invaders to examine how they overcome the constraints imposed by the requirement for mates during colonisation. Temporary reversals to self-compatibility in multilocus incompatibility systems (Pandey 1980), 'leaky' dioecism (Baker and Cox 1984), multiseeded diaspores, individual longevity and extended reproductive periods can all reduce in different ways the likelihood of reproductive failure during the establishment phase in outbreeding colonising plants.

Although the majority of animal invaders reproduce exclusively by outbreeding, a growing number of examples involving parthenogenesis or self-fertilisation in hermaphrodite species are coming to light. For example, the parthenogenetic gecko, *Lepidodactylus lugubris*, is an extremely successful coloniser of new islands and is now found in Australia and widely throughout the Indo-Pacific region from India to Tahiti (Cuellar and Kluge 1972). Recent work by Selander and his colleagues (McCracken and Selander 1980; Foltz *et al.* 1982; Selander 1983) on the breeding systems of two families of terrestrial slugs (Arionidae and Limacidae) demonstrates that selfing is a major mode of reproduction in this group. Most of the selfing species consist entirely of homozygous genotypes throughout much of their range. In *Arion circumscriptus* and *A. silvaticus* both native (Europe) and introduced (North America) populations are composed of a single monogenic strain. Among the European species which have invaded North America self-fertilising forms are disproportionately represented. Of the 10 such species so far identified in Europe only two have failed to invade North America. In contrast nine of the 13 outcrossing species have not become established. Among the introduced species in North America the selfers apparently occupy a wider range of habitats than the outcrossers. It appears that, in common with many weeds, colonising success in these slugs may be relatively independent of the amount of genetic variation carried by populations and be more strongly influenced by the problem of finding mates in new areas.

Whilst many successful plant invaders reproduce primarily by selfing or asexual means there is some evidence that increased outcrossing in selfing species can follow continental migration (Brown and Marshall 1981). In the Mediterranean grasses *Avena barbata* (wild oat) and *Bromus mollis* (soft brome) estimates of outcrossing, based on isozyme markers, in populations from the native and alien range indicate significantly higher outcrossing in the latter (Kahler *et al*. 1980; Brown and Marshall 1981). In both studies increased outcrossing was also associated with greater heterozygosity in the introduced region. Since colonisation of new territory may be associated with altered selection pressures it seems plausible that such modifications in mating systems are adaptive. Where novel environments are encountered there may be selection for genetical innovation through increased recombination. In contrast, where pre-adapted gene combinations are favoured, high selfing may be maintained to restrict the disruptive effects of outcrossing.

Modifications of the mating system of wind-pollinated plant species, such as the grasses mentioned above, usually involve small alterations in floral structure and reproductive timing. However, in animal-pollinated species the mating system will be strongly influenced by the abundance and type of pollen vectors in the introduced region. Where colonisation of new territory is associated with a loss of specialised pollinators, modifications favouring autogamy may be selected (Baker 1967; Barrett 1979; Lloyd 1980). In such cases ensuring the production of offspring (by selfing) may outweigh any requirement for developing new gene combinations. It is notable that among the most successful insect-pollinated invaders most have unspecialised floral structures and are fed upon by generalist flower visitors (e.g. the combination of *Echium plantagineum* and *Apis mellifera* in Australia).

Although selfing variants of normally outcrossing plant species are often found at the margins of their range (Lloyd 1980), in some cases the presence of suitable pollinator guilds and the advantages of increased recombination may result in the development of new floral traits favouring outcrossing in selfing colonists. The geographical patterns of breeding system distribution in the neotropical weed complex *Turnera ulmifolia* suggest that this process has taken place (S.C.H. Barrett and J.S. Shore, unpublished data). Populations from continental South and Central America are primarily distylous and self-incompatible (Barrett 1978). However, on many of the Caribbean Islands autogamous homostyles replace the outcrossers probably because the selfing habit was favoured during colonisation of these islands. On some of the larger islands which are more complex ecologically, such as Jamaica, selection for herkogamy (separation of anthers and stigmas) has resulted in the re-establishment of outcrossing in the homostylous colonists. These changes emphasise the lability of plant mating systems and cast doubt on the commonly held view (reviewed by Jain 1976) that the evolution of selfing from outcrossing is a 'one way street'.

Asexual reproduction

Among plant invaders with perennial growth most possess some means of vegetative multiplication. This can be by stolons, runners, rhizomes etc. or by the production of viable seeds without fertilisation (apomixis). In plants, asexual reproduction, particularly clonal propagation, is often associated with long generation times and large size, whereas among animal groups it is more frequently found in small organisms with short generation times (e.g. parthenogenesis in *Daphnia* and *Aphis*). The adaptive features of parthenogenesis in invading species are numerous and include high reproductive rates, the ability of single isolated females to establish colonies, and the fixation of adaptive heterotic gene combinations (White 1973; Williams 1975). In some animal groups a mixed strategy, consisting of an alternation of sexual and asexual generations is found (e.g. in coelenterates and in protozoan and platyhelminth parasites).

The evolution of parthenogenetic races among insect groups is often associated with the invasion of areas unoccupied by the ancestral bisexual forms (Vandel 1928; Suomalainen 1962; White 1973; Lokki and Saura 1980). An example involves the parthenogenetic cockroach *Pycnoscelus surinamensis* which has a pan-tropical distribution. Examination of enzyme polymorphisms at five loci in diploid and triploid races of this widespread species indicate multiple origins from the restricted bisexual diploid *P. indicus* (Parker *et al*. 1977). Similar patterns are evident among the numerous apomictic plant taxa where interspecific hybridisation and polyploidy are often also involved.

Several of the classic cases of plant invasion on the Australian continent involve apomictic groups, including *Opuntia* spp., *Rubus* spp., *Chondrilla juncea* and *Hypericum perforatum*. Several of these taxa have been successful targets in biological control schemes. Burdon and Marshall (1981) have argued that this largely results from the restricted recombination and low levels of genetic diversity which characterise populations in the introduced range. Unfortunately in comparison with sexually-reproducing weeds there have been relatively few electrophoretic analyses of populations of apomictic species (Solbrig and Simpson 1974; Usberti and Jain 1978; Burdon, Marshall and Groves 1980) and despite the development of theoretical models for estimating the degree of sexuality in facultative apomicts (Marshall and Brown 1974) relatively little is known of their reproductive behaviour in natural populations.

Of particular interest for studies of genetic systems in invading species are closely related groups, with diverse reproductive systems, where a single species has become a successful weed whilst close relatives are relatively innocuous (Baker 1965). An outstanding example is the aquatic plant genus *Eichhornia* comprised of seven species, one of which, *E. crassipes* (water hyacinth), is perhaps the world's most successful weed of natural and artificial water bodies (Sculthorpe 1967; Holm *et al*. 1977). The remaining species of *Eichhornia* all have widespread distributions in their native regions and colonise, to varying degrees, a range of wetland habitats including lakeshores, rivers, seasonal pools, drainage canals and rice fields. However, none has shown the dramatic world-wide spread exhibited by *E. crassipes* during the past century.

Examination of the breeding systems of *Eichhornia* species provides few clues to account for this difference in behaviour (Table 4). Although selfing has evolved on a number of occasions in the genus in association with the breakdown of trimorphic incompatibility (Barrett 1979, 1985), the selfers have shown no tendency to become aggressive weeds, despite the increased colonising potential selfing may give. Selfing variants of the normally outbreeding *E. paniculata* have colonised Jamaica and the successful establishment of *E. natans* on the African continent was no doubt aided by its selfing habit (Table 4).

TABLE 4. *Genetic systems and colonising ability in* Eichhornia *species*. Data of S.C.H. Barrett.

Taxon	Ploidy level	Breeding system	Asexual reproduction	Distribution	Weed status
E. paniculata	2x	tristylous	none	N. Brazil & Caribbean	occasional in rice fields
E. paradoxa	2x	S. homostylous	none	neotropics rare disjunct	no reports
E. azurea	4x	tristylous	moderate	neotropics widespread	local problem
E. crassipes	4x	tristylous	highly developed	worldwide	noxious aquatic weed
E. heterosperma	4x	S. homostylous	moderate	neotropics local	no reports
E. diversifolia	4x	S. homostylous	moderate	neotropics widespread	occasional in rice fields
E. natans	—	S. homostylous	moderate	Africa widespread	occasional in rice fields

Water hyacinth's aggressive behaviour is principally the result of its prolific powers of asexual reproduction by stolons and possession of the free-floating life form. Under favourable conditions it has been estimated that 10 plants of *E. crassipes* can produce 0.4 ha of plants in 8 months by clonal propagation (Penfound and Earle 1948). No other member of the genus possesses the clonal architecture and free-floating habit which are adaptations to the periodic water-level fluctuations and temporary aquatic habitats that *E. crassipes* inhabits in its native Amazon Basin (Barrett 1977). In many parts of its adventive range water hyacinth is represented by relatively few asexually-reproducing clones and the development of genetic diversity is restricted because of the failure of seeds to germinate and establish (Barrett 1980). However, limited sexual reproduction in these areas has little effect on its invasive power which results from its rapid powers of clonal multiplication and water dispersal of vegetative fragments.

Polyploidy

Polyploidy is a widespread and common condition among eukaryotes, particularly flowering plants and ferns. Today it is recognised that 70–80% of the Angiosperms are of polyploid origin (Goldblatt 1980; Lewis 1980). Accordingly, attempts to demonstrate a general relationship between polyploidy and colonising success are fraught with difficulty. This theme has been examined in numerous biosystematic studies (reviewed by Ehrendorfer 1980) with the distinction usually being made between the differences in ecological behaviour of autopolyploids and allopolyploids (Stebbins 1942; Love and Love 1943; Lewis 1980; Levin 1983). In particular it has often been stressed that neopolyploids of hybrid origin will usually surpass their ancestors in genetic variation, heterosis, adaptability and potential to invade novel environments. Among diploid-polyploid complexes there is often a greater likelihood of the polyploids exhibiting weediness and in some cases this tendency increases with ploidy level. It is noteworthy in this connection that of the 18 most widespread and successful weeds all are believed to be of polyploid origin (Brown and Marshall 1981; Clegg and Brown 1983). Despite these patterns many successful colonisers are diploid and polyploids of restricted distribution are also known.

The wide adaptability of many polyploid species is believed to stem from extensive gene duplication and subsequent diversification, fixed heterozygosity, and the reduced effects of inbreeding depression. Whilst it would appear that heterosis is involved in the success of many polyploids of hybrid origin, clear experimental verification of their superior fitness under field conditions is still lacking. Detailed comparative measures of fitness components from natural populations of progenitor and derivative species are often complicated in polyploid groups owing to the rapid divergence in ecological preferences of polyploids following their origin. These ecological effects may not be limited solely to polyploids of hybrid origin, but may also arise from chromosome doubling alone (Levin 1983).

In plants with well developed powers of clonal propagation sterile polyploids arising from wide hybridisation can possess remarkable invasive powers as a result of the effects of heterosis on vegetative vigour. For example, the neotropical aquatic fern *Salvinia molesta* has become one of the world's most noxious aquatic weeds during the past century (Mitchell 1972). The plant is a sterile pentaploid in which spore production is largely abortive and spore germination does not occur (Loyal and Grewal 1966). In common with water hyacinth the multiplicative pattern of growth and free-floating habit of *S. molesta* results in rapid regeneration and wide dispersal of vegetative fragments by water. Clones in the two species, both of which occur in Australia, occupy large areas and may be near immortal. Another successful weed in Australia, which like *S. molesta* is also sterile, is the pentaploid *Oxalis pes-caprae* which reproduces vegetatively by means of underground bulbils (Baker 1965). Clearly the absence of genetical recombination in these plants has not been an impediment to colonising success, although the genetic uniformity of populations may make them more prone to natural or managed pest attack (Levin 1975; Burdon and Marshall 1981; Room *et al.* 1981).

Among insects polyploidy is rare and is reported from less than one hundred species. Of these, several have been examined in detail providing an opportunity to compare the colonising ability of diploid and polyploid forms (Suomalainen, Saura and Lokki 1976). All documented cases of polyploidy in the insects are associated with parthenogenesis and in several groups the polyploids have become highly successful at invading vast land areas (cases reviewed in Lokki and Saura 1980). Part of this success doubtless lies in the acquisition of uniparental reproduction (see above); however, it appears that in many cases parthenogenetic species are often only successful as invaders when they are polyploid, apparently indicating a direct advantage to chromosome increase. The benefits may arise from the greater genetic versatility engendered by gene duplication and heterozygosity. In a survey of the degree of heterozygosity per locus in various diploid and polyploid insect populations, Lokki and Saura (1980) found that a general increase in heterozygosity was associated with polyploidy. However, as yet there is only limited evidence available to test whether polyploid populations are more polymorphic intragenomically than related diploids, or whether intergenomic diversity is the basis of their success (Brown and Marshall 1981).

WHAT ARE THE RELATIVE CONTRIBUTIONS OF INHERITED AND ENVIRONMENTALLY CONTROLLED VARIATION IN LIFE HISTORY TRAITS OF COLONISING SPECIES?

Many invading species establish in a wide range of environments, some of which can be highly heterogeneous in space and time. Two contrasting modes of adaptation to variable environments have been proposed for colonising species. These involve either genetic polymorphism (population buffering) on the one hand or phenotypic plasticity (individual buffering) on the other (Thoday 1953; Lewontin 1957; Bradshaw 1965; Lande 1982). Whilst colonising plant species frequently exhibit marked inter-population genetic differentiation (Baker 1974; Brown and Marshall 1981) in many instances, as we have seen, populations may contain relatively low levels of genetic polymorphism. In such cases, and these frequently involve selfing annual weeds, it is probable that phenotypic plasticity plays a significant role in enabling populations to survive and reproduce in unpredictable environments. Nevertheless, how phenotypic plasticity is directly related to the fitness of individuals in natural populations has rarely been investigated.

An unresolved issue concerns the relationship between the degree of phenotypic plasticity exhibited by a species or population and its genetic variation and heterozygosity. Both positive (Wilken 1977) and negative associations have been demonstrated (Marshall and Jain 1968). One difficulty in investigating this relationship involves the choice of characters which are measured in experimental manipulations. Schlichting and Levin (1984) demonstrated markedly different patterns of response among 18 characters, measured over six environments, in three annual species of *Phlox*, with contrasting heterozygosities. The results provided few clear relationships and the authors concluded that whilst heterozygosity may influence the degree of plasticity exhibited by some characters, other features of the biology of organisms, such as their ecology and phylogeny, are likely to shape the response of others.

Another difficulty in studies of the relationship between plasticity and heterozygosity concerns the distinction between the adaptive and maladaptive features of phenotypic and developmental variation. Intra-organismal variation can take the form of developmental instability brought about by inbreeding and homozygosity (Lerner 1954). Here such variation is usually maladaptive, thereby reducing the fitness of individuals (Soulé 1973). However, under certain circumstances developmental instabilities may give rise to novel phenotypic expressions which are at a selective advantage (Levin 1970; Barrett 1985). Invading species may be particularly prone to these effects since colonisation is frequently associated with strong directional selection, inbreeding, and genetic drift. These influences can result in the disruption of balanced gene complexes and developmental instability. Whether such variation, much of which can be modified by environmental stimuli, should be regarded as plasticity will depend on its effects on fitness.

Whilst many weeds display marked phenotypic plasticity this does not preclude populations from containing significant amounts of genetic variation for important life history traits such as development rate and reproductive output (Hamrick and Allard 1975; Law, Bradshaw and Putwain 1977). Earlier, Lewontin (1965) predicted that, based on theoretical studies of selection in colonising species, populations of colonisers should contain low amounts of additive genetic variance for development time but relatively high amounts for fecundity. Among animal groups Istock (1981) showed that in the mosquito *Wyeonyia smithii* there was considerable genetic variation for development rate. This led to adaptive local variation in development associated with seasonality and density-dependent effects. Dawson (1977) also reviewed evidence contradictory to Lewontin's prediction. At present it is clear that more studies of the quantitative genetics of life history traits in colonising species are required before we can confidently predict the responses to selection imposed by repeated colonising episodes.

WHAT EVIDENCE EXISTS FOR LOCAL GENETIC DIFFERENTIATION FOLLOWING INVASION?

Whether local adaptation following invasion occurs will depend on the kinds of environments a colonist encounters, the range and distribution of genetic variation available to populations, and the inheritance patterns of traits conferring increased fitness. Where there is correlated variation among individual traits, selection for 'improvement' in one trait may result in deterioration of another (Lande 1982). For example, selection for more rapid development may result in reduced fecundity (Lewontin 1965). These effects, which have been demonstrated in numerous artificial selection experiments, have usually involved polygenic characters (Falconer 1960).

Where the genetic basis of traits important to colonising success are relatively simple then rapid changes in behaviour or ecology may occur. Carson and Ohta (1981) reported that an ecological shift from a specialist monophagous habit to a generalist polyphagous habit in the *Drosophila grimshawi* species complex of Hawaii is apparently under control of one gene and two alleles with the generalist behaviour dominant. In plants, Gottlieb (1984) recently detailed many cases of control, by one or two genes, of morphological traits many of which are of ecological significance. Notwithstanding such examples, although shifts in ecology may be initiated by mutation at major genes, it seems likely that selection operating on many genes with small effects is required to achieve a well integrated phenotype.

Several studies have examined adaptive changes following colonisation events. Myers and Sabath (1980) found that larval dispersal and the temperature threshold for adult emergence, in North American populations of the European cinnabar moth (*Tyria jacobaea*) had changed value significantly following colonisation. These changes appear to be in response to different food plant spacing and early spring temperatures in their new environment. Similarly, Cocks and Phillips (1979) were able to document strains of the introduced subterranean clover (*Trifolium subterraneum*) in Australia with divergent flowering times. The strains appear to have resulted from hybridisation between different introductions followed by local selection. Other cases of intraspecific and interspecific hybridisation among weeds giving rise to locally adapted as well as aggressive variants are reviewed in Barrett (1982).

Unfortunately few workers have artificially founded colonies with known genotypes and followed their survival. One attempt involved establishing colonies of rose clover (*Trifolium hirtum*) outside of the range of the species in California with low versus high levels of genetic variation (Martins and Jain 1978). Surveys of establishment over 2 years provided evidence that the more variable populations had the highest levels of colonising success. More studies of this sort are required before we can fully evaluate whether genetic variation plays an important role in successful colonising events. Similarly, to evaluate whether local genetic differentiation following invasion has occurred, detailed comparisons of populations from the native and introduced range are needed. Where the species in question has a widespread distribution in its native area problems of sampling will inevitably be involved unless historical information on the source of immigrants is available.

CONCLUSION

One of the major difficulties in the study of the biology of invasions is the lack of information on the early stages of colonisation. For most successful invaders no genetic data are available from the founding populations. In the case of biological control programs, many of which are being carried out in Australia, this information could be readily obtained. However, for most introductions, retrospective analyses of contemporary populations are all we have. A particular deficiency is our ignorance of why some colonists fail to establish. Is this because of the absence of suitable genetic variation, lack of broad ecophysiological adaptation to the new environment, or merely chance?

The range of genetic attributes found in successful invaders suggests that there is no single optimal solution to the challenges facing the colonist. There is rather a series of ways to improve the chances of success. It is clearly an advantage for a colonising population to contain much genetic variation, to be able to produce offspring even though mates are hard to find, and to be able to rapidly develop adaptive phenotypes in the face of new challenges. Whilst some invaders do indeed contain significant stores of genetic variation others are genetically uniform. Whilst many successful invaders are capable of uniparental reproduction some are obligate outbreeders. Colonising success may be achieved by relatively simple genetic changes in some species whereas in others more complex adaptations are involved. These contrasting patterns highlight the importance of comparative experimental studies of related groups containing both successful invaders and taxa of restricted distribution.

ACKNOWLEDGMENTS

We thank Tony Brown, Jeremy Burdon and Richard Groves for advice and CSIRO and NSERC (Canada) for travel and research funds to S.C.H.B.

REFERENCES

Allard, R.W. (1965). Genetic systems associated with colonizing ability in predominantly self-pollinated species. In *The Genetics of Colonizing Species* (eds. H.G. Baker and G.L. Stebbins) pp. 49–75, Academic Press, London.

Allard, R.W., Babbel, G.R., Clegg, M.T., and Kahler, A.L. (1972). Evidence for coadaptation in *Avena barbata*. *Proceedings of the National Academy of Science USA 69*, 3043–3048.

Allard, R.W., Miller, R.D., and Kahler, A.L. (1978). The relationship between degree of environmental heterogeneity and genetic polymorphism. In *Structure and Functioning of Plant Populations*, Verhandelingen der Koninklijke Nederlandse Akademie van Wetenschappen, Afdeling Natuurkunde, Tweede Reeks.

Babbel, G.R., and Wain, R.P. (1977). Genetic structure of *Hordeum jubatum*. I. Outcrossing rates and heterozygosity levels. *Canadian Journal of Genetics and Cytology 19*, 143–152.

Baker, H.G. (1955). Self-compatibility and establishment after 'long-distance' dispersal. *Evolution 9*, 347–349.

Baker, H.G. (1965). Characteristics and modes of origins of weeds. In *The Genetics of Colonizing Species* (eds. H.G. Baker and G.L. Stebbins) pp. 141–172, Academic Press, London.

Baker, H.G. (1967). Support for Baker's law — as a rule. *Evolution 21*, 853–856.

Baker, H.G. (1974). The evolution of weeds. *Annual Review of Ecology and Systematics 5*, 1–24.

Baker, H.G., and Cox, P.A. (1984). Further thoughts on dioecism and islands. *Annals of Missouri Botanical Gardens 71*, 230–239.

Baker, H.G., and Stebbins, G.L. (1965). *The Genetics of Colonizing Species*, Academic Press, London.

Barrett, S.C.H. (1977). Tristyly in *Eichhornia crassipes* (Mart.) Solms (Water Hyacinth). *Biotropica 9*, 230–238.

Barrett, S.C.H. (1978). Heterostyly in a tropical weed: the reproductive biology of the *Turnera ulmifolia* complex (Turneraceae). *Canadian Journal of Botany 56*, 1713–1725.

Barrett, S.C.H. (1979). The evolutionary breakdown of tristyly in *Eichhornia crassipes* (Mart.) Solms. *Evolution 33*, 499–510.

Barrett, S.C.H. (1980). Sexual reproduction in *Eichhornia crassipes* (Water Hyacinth). II. Seed production in natural populations. *Journal of Applied Ecology 17*, 113–124.

Barrett, S.C.H. (1982). Genetic variation in weeds. In *Biological Control of Weeds with Plant Pathogens* (eds. R. Charudattan and H. Walker) pp. 73–98, John Wiley, New York.

Barrett, S.C.H. (1983). Crop mimicry in weeds. *Economic Botany 37*, 255–282

Barrett, S.C.H. (1985). Floral trimorphism and monomorphism in continental and island populations of *Eichhornia paniculata* (Pontederiaceae). *Biological Journal of the Linnean Society*, in press.

Bosbach, K., and Hurka, H. (1981). Biosystematic studies on *Capsella bursa-pastoris* (Brassicaceae) : enzyme polymorphism in natural populations. *Plant Systematics and Evolution 137*, 73–94.

Bradshaw, A.D. (1965). Evolutionary significance of phenotypic plasticity in plants. *Advances in Genetics 13*, 115–155.

Brown, A.H.D., Feldman, M.W., and Nevo, E. (1980). Multilocus structure of natural populations of *Hordeum spontaneum*. *Genetics 96*, 523–536.

Brown, A.H.D., and Marshall, D.R. (1981). Evolutionary changes accompanying colonisation in plants. In *Evolution Today*, Proceedings of the Second International Congress of Systematic and Evolutionary Biology (eds. G.E.C. Scudder and J.L. Reveal) pp. 351–363, Hunt Institute for Botanical Documentation, Carnegie-Mellon University, Pittsburgh.

Brown, A.H.D., and Burdon, J.J. (1983). Multilocus diversity in an outbreeding weed, *Echium plantagineum* L. *Australian Journal of Biological Sciences 36*, 503–509.

Burdon, J.J., and Marshall, D.R. (1981). Biological control and the reproductive mode of weeds. *Journal of Applied Ecology 18*, 649–658.

Burdon, J.J., Marshall, D.R., and Groves, R.H. (1980). Isozyme variation in *Chondrilla juncea* L. in Australia. *Australian Journal of Botany 28*, 193–198.

Carson, H.L., and Ohta, A.T. (1981). Origin of the genetic basis of colonising ability. In *Evolution Today*, Proceedings of the Second International Congress of Systematic and Evolutionary Biology (eds. G.E.C. Scudder and J.L. Reveal) pp. 365–370, Hunt Institute for Botanical Documentation, Carnegie-Mellon University, Pittsburgh.

Clegg, M.T., and Brown, A.H.D. (1983). The founding of plant populations. In *Genetics and Conservation* (eds. C.M. Schonewald-Cox, S.M. Chambers, B. MacBryde and W.L. Thomas) pp. 216–228, Benjamin/Cummings, California.

Cocks, P.S., and Phillips, J.R. (1979). Evolution of subterranean clover in South Australia. I. The strains and their distribution. *Australian Journal of Agricultural Research 30*, 1035–1052.

Crawford, R.M.M. (1967). Alcohol dehydrogenase activity in relation to flooding tolerance in roots. *Journal of Experimental Botany 18*, 458–464.

Cuellar, O., and Kluge, A.G. (1972). Natural parthenogenesis in the gekkonid lizard *Lepidodactylus lugubris*. *Journal of Genetics 61*, 14–26.

Dawson, P.S. (1977). Life history strategy and evolutionary history of *Tribolium* flour beetles. *Evolution 31*, 226–229.

Ehrendorfer, F. (1980). Polyploidy and distribution. In *Polyploidy Biological Relevance* (ed. W.H. Lewis) pp. 45–60, Plenum Press, New York.

Falconer, D.S. (1960). *Introduction to Quantitative Genetics*, Longman, London.

Foltz, D.W., Ochman, H., Jones, J.S., Evangelisti, S.M., and Selander, R.H. (1982). Genetic population structure and breeding systems in Arionid slugs (Mollusca, Pulmonarta). *Biological Journal of the Linnean Society 17*, 225–241.

Giles, B.E. (1983). A comparison between quantitative and biochemical variation in the wild barley *Hordeum murinum. Evolution 38*, 34–41.

Goldblatt, P. (1980). Polyploidy in Angiosperms: Monocotyledons. In *Polyploidy Biological Relevance* (ed. W.H. Lewis) pp. 219–240, Plenum Press, New York.

Gottlieb, L. (1984). Genetics and morphological evolution in plants. *American Naturalist 123*, 681–709.

Hamrick, J.L., and Allard, R.W. (1975). Correlations between quantitative characters and enzyme genotypes in *Avena barbata. Evolution 29*, 438–442.

Hamrick, J.L., Linhart, Y.B., and Mitton, J.B. (1979). Relationships between life history characteristics and electrophoretically detectable genetic variation in plants. *Annual Review of Ecology and Systematics 10*, 173–200.

Hauptli, H., and Jain, S.K. (1978). Biosystematic and agronomic potential of some weedy and cultivated amaranths. *Theoretical and Applied Genetics 52*, 177–185.

Hayward, M.D., and Zaruk, M.T.M. (1982). Allozyme variation in the inbreeding species *Lolium temulentum* L. *Heredity 49*, 255–257.

Henslow, (1879). On the self-fertilisation of plants. *Transactions of the Linnean Society Series II. Botany 1*, 317–398.

Holm, L.G., Plucknett, D.L., Pancho, J.V., and Herberger, H.P. (1977). *The World's Worst Weeds: Distribution and Biology*, The University Press of Hawaii, Honolulu.

Istock, C.A. (1980). Natural selection and life history variation: theory plus lessons from a mosquito. In *Insect Life History Patterns* (eds. R.F. Denno and H. Dingle) pp. 113–127, Springer-Verlag, New York.

Jain, S.K. (1976). The evolution of inbreeding in plants. *Annual Review of Ecology and Systematics 7*, 469–495.

Kahler, A.L., Allard, R.W., Krzakowa, M., Wehrhahn, C.F., and Nevo, E. (1980). Associations between isozyme phenotypes and environment in the slender wild oat (*Avena barbata*) in Israel. *Theoretical and Applied Genetics 56*, 31–47.

Koniuszek, J.W.J., and Verkeij, J.A.C. (1982). Genetical variation in two related annual *Senecio* species occurring in the same habitat. *Genetica 59*, 133–137.

Kubetin, W.R., and Schaal, B.A. (1979). Apportionment of isozyme variability in *Polygonum pensylvanicum* (Polygonaceae). *Systematic Botany 4*, 148–156.

Lande, R. (1982). A quantitative genetic theory of life history evolution. *Ecology 63*, 607–615.

Law, R., Bradshaw, A.D., and Putwain, P.D. (1977). Life history variation in *Poa annua. Evolution 31*, 233–246.

Lerner, I.M. (1954). *Genetic Homeostasis*, Oliver and Boyd, London.

Levin, D.A. (1970). Developmental instability and evolution in peripheral isolates. *American Naturalist 104*, 343–353.

Levin, D.A. (1975). Pest pressure and recombination systems in plants. *American Naturalist 109*, 437–451.

Levin, D.A. (1983). Polyploidy and novelty in flowering plants. *American Naturalist 122*, 1–25.

Lewis, A.D. (1981). Population genetics, ecology and systematics of Indo-Australian scombrid fishes, with particular reference to skipjack tuna (*Katsuwonus pelamis*). Ph. D. thesis, Australian National University.

Lewis, W.H. (1980). Polyploidy in Angiosperms: Dicotyledons. In *Polyploidy Biological Relevance* (ed. W.H. Lewis) pp. 241–268, Plenum Press, New York.

Lewontin, R.C. (1957). The adaptations of populations to varying environments. *Cold Spring Harbour Symposium in Quantitative Biology 22*, 395–408.

Lewontin, R.C. (1965). Selection for colonising ability. In *The Genetics of Colonizing Species* (eds. H.G. Baker and G.L. Stebbins) pp. 79–92, Academic Press, London.

Lloyd, D.G. (1980). Demographic factors and mating patterns in Angiosperms. In *Demography and Evolution in Plant Populations* (ed. O.T. Solbrig) pp. 67–88, Blackwell, Oxford.

Lokki, J., and Saura, A. (1980). Polyploidy in insect evolution. In *Polyploidy Biological Relevance* (ed. W.H. Lewis) pp. 277–312, Plenum Press, New York.

Love, A., and Love, D. (1943). The significance of differences in the distribution of diploids and polyploids. *Hereditas 29*, 145–163.

Loyal, D.S., and Grewal, R.K. (1966). Cytological study on sterility in *Salvinia auriculata* Aublet with a bearing on its reproductive mechanism. *Cytologia 31*, 330–338.

Marshall, D.R., Broué, P., and Pryor, A.J. (1973). Adaptive significance of alcohol dehydrogenase isozymes in maize. *Nature 244*, 17–18.

Marshall, D.R., and Brown, A.H.D. (1974). Estimation of the level of apomixis in plant populations. *Heredity 32*, 321–333.

Marshall, D.R., and Jain, S.K. (1968). Phenotypic plasticity of *Avena fatua* and *A. barbata*. *American Naturalist 102*, 457–467.

Martins, P.S., and Jain, S.K. (1979). The role of genetic variation in the colonising ability of rose clover (*Trifolium hirtum* All.). *American Naturalist 114*, 591–595.

McCracken, G.F., and Selander, R.K. (1980). Self-fertilisation and monogenic strains in natural populations of terrestrial slugs. *Proceedings of the National Academy of Science USA 77*, 684–688.

McIntyre, S., and Barrett, S.C.H. (1985). A comparison of weed communities of rice in Australia and California. In *Are Australian Ecosystems Different?* (ed. M. Westoby) pp. 237–250, Ecological Society of Australia.

Mitchell, D.S. (1972). The Kariba weed: *Salvinia molesta*. *British Fern Gazette 10*, 251–252.

Moran, G.F., and Marshall, D.R. (1978). Allozyme uniformity within and variation between races of the colonising species *Xanthium strumarium* L. (Noogoora Burr). *Australian Journal of Biological Sciences 31*, 282–291.

Moran, G.F., Marshall, D.R., and Muller, W.J. (1981). Phenotypic variation and plasticity in the colonising species *Xanthium strumarium* L. (Noogoora Burr). *Australian Journal of Biological Sciences 34*, 639–648.

Mulligan, G.A., and Findlay, J.D. (1970). Reproductive systems and colonisation in Canadian weeds. *Canadian Journal of Botany 48*, 859–860.

Myers, K. (1971). The rabbit in Australia. In *Dynamics of Populations* (eds. P.S. den Boer and G.R. Gradwell) pp. 478–503, Centre for Agricultural Publishing and Documentation, Wageningen, The Netherlands.

Myers, J.H., and Sabath, M.D. (1980). Genetic and phenotypic variability, genetic variance, and the success of establishment of insect introductions for the biological control of weeds. *Proceedings Fifth International Symposium on the Biological Control of Weeds, Brisbane, Australia*, pp. 91–102, CSIRO, Melbourne.

Nei, M., Maruyama, T., and Chakraborty, R. (1975). The bottleneck effect and genetic variability in populations. *Evolution 29*, 1–10.

Nevo, E. (1978). Genetic variation in natural populations: patterns and theory. *Theoretical Population Biology 13*, 121–177.

Pandey, K.K. (1980). Evolution of incompatibility systems in plants: origin of 'independent' and 'complementary' control of incompatibility in Angiosperms. *New Phytologist 84*, 381–400.

Parker, E.D., Selander, R.K., Hudson, R.O., and Lester, L.J. (1977). Genetic diversity in colonising parthenogenetic cockroaches. *Evolution 31*, 836–842.

Parsons, P.A. (1983). *The Evolutionary Biology of Colonizing Species*, Cambridge University Press, Cambridge.

Penfound, W.T., and Earle, T.T. (1984). The biology of the water hyacinth. *Ecological Monographs 18*, 447–472.

Price, S.C., and Jain, S.K. (1981). Are inbreeders better colonisers? *Oecologia 49*, 283–286.

Richardson, B.J., Rogers, P.M., and Hewitt, G.M. (1980). Ecological genetics of the wild rabbit in Australia. II. Protein variation in British, French and Australian rabbits and the geographical distribution of the variation in Australia. *Australian Journal of Biological Sciences 33*, 371–383.

Room, P.M., Hartley, K.L.S., Forno, I.W., and Sands, D.P.A. (1981). Successful biological control of the floating weed salvinia. *Nature 294*, 78–80.

Roose, M.L., and Gottlieb, L.D. (1976). Genetic and biochemical consequences of polyploidy in *Tragopogon*. *Evolution 30*, 818–830.

Schlichting, C.D., and Levin, D.A. (1984). Phenotypic plasticity of annual *Phlox*: tests of some hypotheses. *American Journal of Botany 71*, 252–260.

Sculthorpe, C.D. (1967). *The Biology of Aquatic Vascular Plants*, Edward Arnold, London.

Selander, R.K., (1983). Evolutionary consequences of inbreeding. In *Genetics and Conservation* (eds. C.M. Schonewald-Cox, S.M. Chambers, B. MacBryde and W.L. Thomas) pp. 201–215, Benjamin/Cummings, California.

Selander, R.K., and Kaufman, D.W. (1973). Self-fertilisation and genic population structure in a colonising land snail. *Proceedings of the National Academy of Science USA 70*, 1186–1190.

Skibinski, D.O.F., and Ward, R.D. (1982). Correlations between heterozygosity and evolutionary rate of proteins. *Nature 298*, 490–492.

Solbrig, O.T., and Simpson, B.B. (1974). Components of regulation of a population of dandelions in Michigan. *Journal of Ecology 62*, 473–486.

Soulé M. (1979). Heterozygosity and developmental stability: another look. *Evolution 33*, 396–401.

Stebbins, G.L. (1942). Polyploid complexes in relation to ecology and the history of floras. *American Naturalist 76*, 36–45.

Stebbins, G.L. (1957). Self-fertilisation and population variability in the higher plants. *American Naturalist 91*, 337–354.

Stebbins, G.L. (1965). Colonising species of the native California flora. In *The Genetics of Colonizing Species* (eds. H.G. Baker and G.L. Stebbins) pp. 173–192, Academic Press, London.

Suomalainen, E. (1962). Significance of parthenogenesis in the evolution of insects. *Annual Review of Entomology 7*, 349–366.

Suomalainen, E., and Saura, A. (1973). Genetic polymorphism and evolution in parthenogenetic animals. I. Polyploid Curculionidae. *Genetics 74*, 489–508.

Suomalainen, E., Saura, A., and Lokki, J. (1976). Evolution of parthenogenetic insects. In *Evolutionary Biology* Vol. 9 (eds. M. Hecht, W. Steer and B. Wallace) pp. 209–257, Plenum Press, New York.

Thoday, J.M. (1953). Components of fitness. *Symposium of the Society of Experimental Biology VIII*, 96–113, Academic Press, New York.

Usberti, J.A. jr., and Jain, S.K. (1978). Variation in *Panicum maximum*: A comparison of sexual and asexual populations. *Botanical Gazette 139*, 112–116.

Vandel, A. (1928). Le rôle de la polyploidie dans le rêne animal. *Archives Julius Klaus-Stift 21*, 397–410.

White, M.J.D. (1973). *Animal Cytology and Evolution,* Cambridge University Press, Cambridge.

Wilken, D.H. (1977). Local differentiation for phenotypic plasticity in the wild annual *Collomia linearis* (Polemoniaceae). *Systematic Botany 2,* 99–108.

Williams, G.C. (1975). *Sex and Evolution*, Princeton University Press, Princeton.

Zouros, E., Singh, S.M., and Miles, H.E. (1980). Growth-rate in oysters: an overdominant phenotype and its possible explanations. *Evolution 34*, 856–867.

AQUATIC INVADING SPECIES

Angela H. Arthington[1] and David S. Mitchell[2]

Australian aquatic ecosystems have been invaded successfully by both plants and animals that are introduced to the continent. Some of these invasions have been spectacular and have occasioned considerable concern. Despite suspicion that Australian aquatic ecosystems are more susceptible to invasion than those of other continents, there is no evidence to test rigorously this hypothesis. In this chapter we give an account of the progress of selected aquatic plant and animal invasions, mainly but not exclusively in Australia. Our purposes are to identify a common framework for the biological invasions of aquatic ecosystems and common features of aquatic invading species in order to direct attention to the measures needed to guard against unwanted invasions, predict the likely occurrence and nature of invasions from particular introduced species, and improve the management of invasions when they occur.

AQUATIC PLANTS

Several aquatic plant species have provided spectacular examples of extensive population growth following invasion of ecosystems to which they have been introduced. In some cases population growths have been so rapid that the phenomena have been described as biological explosions. Yet, in spite of the remarkable nature of such events, we have few data quantifying the factors which cause them to occur. Elton (1958) and Salisbury (1961) have laid a basis for understanding these processes. Relatively little reference was made to aquatic systems in these accounts, however. Nevertheless, there are a number of descriptions in the literature of the adventive spread of aquatic plants (e.g. Sculthorpe 1967), though because available resources are usually diverted to short-term investigations of suitable control methods, little is known about their cause.

In Australia, Aston (1973, 1977) included 26 and Sainty and Jacobs (1981) 46 introduced species in their treatments of aquatic plants of Australia and New South Wales respectively (Table 1). The difference in numbers largely reflects differences in definition of what constitutes an aquatic species. Mitchell (1978) listed 126 aquatic vascular species which cause weed problems or have the potential to do so. Of these, 24 were introduced to Australia. Thirty-two species were considered to cause serious problems and 11 of these were introduced. It is clear from these lists that a number of introduced plants have become naturalised successfully in Australian aquatic ecosystems. A high proportion of these have caused problems as weeds. These plants are usually species which have spread adventively in other parts of the world and generally constitute the best documented cases of invasion. Thus the phenomenon can be described by reference to representative examples of such species in each of the main growth forms of aquatic plants: floating, submerged and emergent.

THE ADVENTIVE SPREAD OF FLOATING AQUATIC SPECIES

Eichhornia crassipes

Water hyacinth (*Eichhornia crassipes*) is probably the most widely known tropical weed. Its beautiful spikes of blue flowers, floating habit, bulbous petioles and capacity for rapid vegetative reproduction attract attention. A weed of the tropics and subtropics, it started to spread through the world from its native habitat in South and Central America during the last decade of the last century. It now occurs in most tropical countries (Robson 1976; Holm *et al.* 1977; Gopal and Sharma 1981).

Eichhornia crassipes first invaded Australia in 1894. By the turn of the century it was established successfully in coastal areas of Queensland and New South Wales (Aston 1973). By 1976 infestations of the

[1]   School of Australian Environmental Studies, Griffith University, Nathan, Qld 4111
[2]   CSIRO, Centre for Irrigation Research, Private Mail Bag, Griffith, N.S.W. 2680

TABLE 1. *Introduced aquatic vascular plants in Australia.*

Family and species	Common name	Significance/comments
Alismataceae		
Alisma lanceolatum (1)		One locality in Victoria
Sagittaria engelmanniana (1)		Found once in Victoria in 1910
Sagittaria graminea (1,2,3)	Sagittaria	Rice and channel plant
Sagittaria montevidensis (1,2,3)	Arrowhead	Rice and channel plant
Amaranthaceae		
Alternanthera philoxeroides (2,3,4)	Alligator weed	Noxious emergent plant
Apiaceae		
Hydrocotyle bonariensis (2)		Sandy soils near the coast
Sium latifolium (2)	Broadleaf water parsnip	Water margins, occasionally in drains.
Aponogetonaceae		
Aponogeton distachyos (1,2,3)	Cape pond lily	Ornamental
Araceae		
Zantedeschia aethiopica (2)	Arum lily	Ornamental
Brassicaceae		
Rorippa nasturtium-aquaticum (1,2,3)	Watercress	Food plant
Rorippa microphylla (1)	One-row watercress	Food plant
Callitrichaceae		
Callitriche hamulata (1)	Starwort	Well established in Victoria
Callitriche stagnalis (1,2,3)	Common starwort	In drains
Compositae		
Aster subulatus (2)	Bushy starwort	Ruderal in damp places
Cyperaceae		
Cyperus involucratus (2)		Ornamental
Cyperus papyrus (2)	Papyrus	Ornamental
Eleocharis sp. (2)		Rice weed
Schoenoplectus prolifer (2)		Potential plant of irrigation systems
Gramineae		
Arundo donax (1)	Giant reed	Ornamental
Brachiaria mutica (2,3)	Para grass	Tropical and subtropical plant of channels and drains
Echinochloa oryzoides (2,3)	Hairy millet	Rice weed
Glyceria declinata (2)	Glaucous sweetgrass	In drains
Glyceria maxima (2,3)	Reed sweetgrass	In temperate waters
Leersia oryzoides (2)		In slow-flowing waters and rice paddies
Panicum repens (2,3)	Torpedo grass	In crops and pastures
Paspalum dilatatum (2,3)		Important pasture species but weedy in irrigation areas
Phalaris arundinaceae (2)	Reed canary grass	Pasture species, occasionally in irrigation systems
Polypogon monspeliensis (2,3)	Beard grass	In irrigation drains
Haloragaceae		
Myriophyllum aquaticum (*M. brasiliense*) (1,2,3,4)	Parrot's feather	Aquarium plant
Hydrocharitaceae		
Egeria densa (1,2,3)	Leafy elodea	Aquarium plant; submerged
Elodea canadensis (1,2,3)	Canadian pond weed	Aquarium plant; noxious submerged plant

TABLE 1. *Introduced aquatic vascular plants in Australia* **(continued).**

Family and species	Common name	Significance/comments
Lagarosiphon major (1,2,3,4)	Lagarosiphon	Aquarium plant; noxious submerged plant
Juncaceae		
Juncus acutus (2,3)	Spiny rush	In channels and drains
Juncus articulatus (2,3)	Jointed rush	In channels and drains
Lilaeaceae		
Lilaea scilloides (1)	Lilaea	Water margins submerged/ emergent
Marantaceae		
Thalia dealbata (2)		Ornamental
Nymphaceae		
Nuphar lutea (2)		Ornamental
Nymphaea capensis (1,2,3)	Water lily	Ornamental
Nymphaea flava (1)	Water lily	Ornamental
Nymphaea mexicana (2)	Water lily	Ornamental
nymphaea alba hybrids (2)	Water lily	Ornamental
Nymphaea tuberosa hybrids (2)	Water lily	Ornamental
(all these species have the potential to obstruct water flow)		
Onagraceae		
Ludwigia palustris (1)	Marsh water primrose	Naturalised in Victoria, occasionally in damp places
Ludwigia peruviana (2)		Naturalised in Sydney region, in slow water courses
Polygonaceae		
Polygonum orientale (2)	Prince's feather	
Rumex crispus (2,3)	Curled dock	In wetlands and water edges
Pontederiaceae		
Eichhornia crassipes (1,2,3)	Water hyacinth	Ornamental; noxious floating plant
Pontederia cordata (1,2,3)	Pickerel weed	Ornamental
Ranunculaceae		
Ranunculus muricatus (2)	Sharp buttercup	Minor in damp areas
Ranunculus repens (2)	Creeping buttercup	Minor in damp areas
Ranunculus sceleratus (2,3)	Celery buttercup	Minor in drains and water margins, can be poisonous to stock
Salviniaceae		
Salvinia molesta (*S. auriculata*) (1,2,3,4)	Salvinia	Ornamental; aquarium plant; noxious floating plant
Scrophulariaceae		
Veronica anagallis-aquatica (1,2)	Blue water speedwell	Minor in drains
Veronica catenata (1)	Pink water speedwell	Naturalised in Victoria and South Australia
Typhaceae		
Typha latifolia (1,3)	Bulrush, cattail	Major weed of N. America, naturalised in Tasmania

(1) Cited by Aston (1973).
(2) Cited by Sainty and Jacobs (1981).
(3) Cited by Mitchell (1978).
(4) Cited by Aston (1977).

plant had been reported from every State or Territory in Australia except Tasmania and the Australian Capital Territory (Mitchell 1978) although infestations reported from Victoria and South Australia have been eliminated as a matter of policy.

Eichhornia crassipes reproduces vegetatively by means of offsets which break free from parent plants. It is capable of doubling the number of plants in a population every 6.2 days in good conditions (Bagnall *et al*. 1974). It is also capable of sexual reproduction, though many populations fail to produce viable seeds. When produced, seeds germinate most readily on exposed moist substrates (Pettet 1964).

Eichhornia crassipes has been spread by humans as a horticultural plant. Within a river or lake system, it is spread by currents, wind or it may be transported accidentally by boats. There is no evidence of it being dispersed between water systems by other than human agencies.

Salvinia molesta

The aquatic fern *Salvinia molesta* is another notorious floating weed. This plant has spread into the tropics and subtropics of the world from its native locality in southern Brazil (Forno and Harley 1979) since the 1930s. The plant was first reported as a weed from Sri Lanka in 1943 (Seneratna 1943). Subsequently it has spread and become a major problem in many countries.

Salvinia molesta was first reported in Australia in 1952 (Harley and Mitchell 1981) and has now been reported from every State or Territory except Tasmania and the Australian Capital Territory (Finlayson and Mitchell 1983). In this respect it parallels *Eichhornia crassipes*, though it has spread through Australia more rapidly.

Salvinia molesta is a pentaploid that is apparently incapable of producing viable spores. Consequently, it is dependent on vegetative reproduction. Under good growth conditions it is capable of doubling every 2.2 days (Cary and Weerts 1983).

Like *Eichhornia crassipes*, *Salvinia molesta* is dispersed by wind and current within water bodies and between water bodies by humans. At first, it was cultivated as a botanical curiosity, but more recently it has been spread as an aquarium plant.

THE ADVENTIVE SPREAD OF SUBMERGED AQUATIC PLANTS

Elodea canadensis

The first example of the spectacular spread of an aquatic plant in an alien environment was furnished by Canadian pondweed, *Elodea canadensis*. During the latter half of the last century, the plant which is native to North America progressively invaded the waters of western Europe. The canal systems that formed an important network for the transport of goods provided a ready means for its spread and were especially severely affected. The plant was also introduced to Victoria, Tasmania and New Zealand during the last century (about 1860) probably at the same time as the introduction of trout from Europe. It soon formed troublesome populations in parts of New Zealand but was apparently less aggressive there than in Europe (Mason 1960; Chapman *et al*. 1974). By contrast it did not spread vigorously in Australia until recently. Thus, from about 1968, the plant rapidly colonised the irrigation systems of Victoria and southern New South Wales, occasioning considerable alarm (Mitchell 1978). However, by the late 1970s, populations were apparently declining in their extent and density. In this regard it behaved as it did in western Europe where populations seemed to increase markedly for about seven years and then enter into a decline until only small numbers of plants were present (Sculthorpe 1967). In all these cases, there has been no record of sexual reproduction. Spread has been due to vegetative growth following fragmentation and the production of overwintering dormant apices (Bowmer, Mitchell and Short 1984). Again, humans have been the main, and probably the only, agent for dispersing the plant between water bodies and between continents.

Hydrilla verticillata

The vigorous growth of submerged aquatic plants in Florida that superficially resembled *Elodea* was first noticed in 1959. Eventually identified as *Hydrilla verticillata*, introduced from Africa, Asia and Australasia, the plant provided an interesting example of a reciprocal biological invasion as it had invaded marginal areas of the native distribution of *Elodea canadensis*.

In Florida, *Hydrilla* rapidly replaced the native submerged species and formed dense stands which rendered waterbodies next to useless for boating and other forms of recreational use. The aesthetic appeal of waters was downgraded and the value of adjacent land was adversely affected. Lakes and other suitable waters were first colonised by vegetative spread but the plant is also able to multiply through two types of perennating organs: subterranean tubers and leafy turions.

Hydrilla is continuing to spread in the United States and was recently reported from California. It also often forms troublesome growths in eutrophic waters in its native environments (Swarbrick, Finlayson and Cauldwell 1981).

Lagarosiphon major

The genus *Lagarosiphon* is endemic to Africa and contains several species capable of vigorous growth to form large populations (e.g. *L. verticillifolius* on Lake Kariba). One species *L. major*, which has a temperate to subtropical distribution in South Africa, has become a major weed following its invasion of New Zealand in about 1950. It is especially troublesome in the Waikato River system of the North Island where it forms dense stands in deep, shaded or swiftly flowing waters (Mason 1960). Little is known of the relative contribution of vegetative reproduction to its spread. In the absence of other evidence, it can be assumed that the plant has been dispersed by humans as an aquarium plant. It was certainly brought into Australia in this guise, though, so far, no naturalised populations have been reported.

THE ADVENTIVE SPREAD OF EMERGENT AQUATIC PLANTS

Alternanthera philoxeroides

Alligator weed (*Alternanthera philoxeroides*) is a native of tropical South America that has caused weed problems in situations to which it has been introduced, especially in the southeastern United States, where it was first recorded in 1894 (Maddox *et al.* 1971). It now occurs in India, Southeast Asia and Australia. It was probably introduced into Australia in the mid 1940s (Hockley 1974).

The plant typically grows in shallow marginal waters where it becomes firmly rooted in the substratum. It spreads along shores by rooting readily at nodes on decumbent stems, and grows out over the water forming thick tangled mats of vegetation. However, it does not seem to be capable of sustaining a totally floating habit indefinitely. It is also able to grow in moist wetland soils, although it grows less vigorously (but more persistently) in such situations.

Throughout its adventive distribution the plant appears to be incapable of setting viable seed and depends on vegetative reproduction for spread. Since rooting from nodes readily occurs following fragmentation, each node is a potential and effective propagule.

Alternanthera philoxeroides is thought to have spread between continents as packing material or as a contaminant of the ballast of ships. The plant has no obvious attraction for humans and its spread can only have been opportunistic. Certainly, spread following invasion has always been slow and in this regard it differs from the more attractive introduced plants such as water hyacinth and *Salvinia*.

Myriophyllum aquaticum

Parrotfeather (*Myriophyllum aquaticum,* syn. *M. brasiliense*) is a widely grown aquarium plant that has escaped and become naturalised in a number of places. The plant is native to South America but now occurs in North America, Europe, Africa and Australasia. The plant occupies a similar habitat to *A. philoxeroides*, rooting in shallow water and forming tangled floating masses of stems half in and half out of the water. In flowing water portions of the floating masses break free and are swept downstream to establish new colonies. Outside South America the plant produces only female flowers and vegetative reproduction alone is responsible for its spread and persistence. It is a popular aquarium plant and is also grown widely in garden ponds. Again humans are the main dispersal agent.

Other emergent aquatic plants

Serious weed problems are caused by the invasion of newly formed waters of shallow depth by emergent swamp plants such as *Phragmites* spp. and *Typha* spp. For the most part these weed problems occur within the native distribution range of these plants and are the result of seed dispersal. Indeed it is remarkable that some of the most vigorously growing and troublesome emergent aquatic weeds have not been successful adventive species. For example, *Typha latifolia*, which is a economic problem in the United States where it is native, became naturalised in a few localities in New South Wales but gave no evidence of aggressive spread beyond these sites (Aston 1973). It is not listed as present in that State by Sainty and Jacobs (1981) and has presumably died out. *Cyperus papyrus*, a native of Africa and western Asia, has similarly become naturalised at isolated sites in a number of countries, including Australia, as a garden escape. In spite of its capacity for vigorous growth and relatively wide latitudinal spread (35°N to 25°S) in its native environment, it has also shown no evidence of aggressive invasive behaviour. Superficial examination indicates that the naturalised populations do not set seeds and this may be the reason for the plant's inability to spread.

FACTORS THAT FAVOUR THE ADVENTIVE SPREAD OF AQUATIC PLANTS

Several common features can be distinguished amongst aquatic plants which have demonstrated a capacity for adventive spread in alien environments:
1. Vegetative reproduction is common and often the only method of reproduction.
2. Humans are the main agents for dispersing freshwater plants both between and within continents.
3. Invading plants that are capable of very rapid rates of reproduction often become serious weeds.
4. Invading plants which exhibit sexual sterility only become locally naturalised, unless they are capable of wide dispersal through small vegetative propagules or are purposely spread by humans.

It is significant that all these factors deal with dispersal and reproduction. On this basis, the same three main stages in successful invasion that occur in terrestrial plants (see previous chapters) can also be recognised in aquatic plants; namely, invasion; establishment of the population through reproduction; and dispersal.

Each of these stages involves interaction between environmental factors and characteristics of the invading plants which promote, delay, or prevent successful completion of the stage. The successful dispersal of a propagule to a new locality starts the whole process again. It is also obvious that the rate at which the process takes place depends, in the first instance, on the number of population units in the initial inoculum and in the dispersal stage. An exponential increase in these will ensure an exponential acceleration in the apparent rate at which the invasion occurs until environmental factors becoming limiting.

These features can be illustrated further by reference to the invasions by *Salvinia molesta* of Lake Kariba, central Africa, and of the Sepik River, Papua New Guinea.

Salvinia molesta (then identified as *S. auriculata*) was first recorded for the Zambezi River system in 1949. However, there were no reports of it forming large troublesome populations in the river until 1959 when Lake Kariba formed behind a dam constructed in the Middle Zambezi. There, the plant was able to take advantage of calm nutrient-enriched waters. The dam was closed in December 1958 and, by April 1960, *S. molesta* was estimated to occupy 285 km² (11.5%) of the lake's surface. The area covered by the plant rose to a peak in May 1962 when it occupied 1003 km² (21.5%) of the lake's surface. Subsequently, the area fell and from 1964 to 1972 it fluctuated between about 400 and 800 km². There was then a dramatic drop in area to about 100 km² approximately 2 years after liberation of an aquatic Acridid grasshopper (*Paulinia acuminata*) as a biological control agent. The introduction of *Paulinia* together with a decline in nutrient content of the lake water, a decrease in sheltered habitat as the lake matured and increasing competition from native aquatic plants were considered to be the main factors responsible for the eventual marked decline in the area of the plant (Mitchell and Rose 1979; Marshall and Junor 1981). *Salvinia molesta* is still present in relatively small quantities in Lake Kariba, with the area of weed fluctuating in response to seasonal changes in lake level and influent river floods.

Salvinia molesta was probably introduced into the Sepik River system in 1971 (Mitchell 1979). However, it was not reported to the authorities until 1977 by which time it was already beginning to interfere with water transport and fisheries. By August 1977, *Salvinia* was estimated to occupy 32 km². In September the plant invaded Chambri Lake and rapidly spread. By May 1979 it was estimated to occupy 47 km² of the lake and 32 km² in the rest of the system, while by 1981 it was estimated to occupy a total of 200 km². The appointment of a Salvinia Control Coordinator in December 1980 and the subsequent release of a biological control agent *Cyrtobagous salvinae* (a weevil), have decreased the rate of spread and recent indications are that the area occupied by the plant has decreased (P.A. Thomas, personal communication).

There are several features of the invasion and explosive growth of *Salvinia* in the Zambezi and Sepik River systems which warrant comment.

(i) The plant was present for some years in the Zambezi system before it grew explosively. In the disturbed environmental conditions of the formative waters of the new Lake Kariba, the increase in available nutrient and the change in hydrological conditions favoured both the growth and spread of the plant. However, this indication of the beneficial importance of disturbance to the invading species has to be contrasted with the plant's rapid spread in the Sepik system where there was no apparent disturbance but where suitable habitats already existed.

(ii) The initial spread of the plant in favourable conditions was very rapid. Subsequent increases as part of the regular fluctuation in population size were much less marked. This may indicate that, with time, the ecosystem 'adapts' to the invading species in such a way as to diminish the rate of change and dampen the amplitude of the fluctuation.

(iii) The introduction of host-specific insects from the plant's native range appears to have been instrumental in bringing about a reduction in area. However, in Lake Kariba, there was little obvious sign of massive insect damage on the populations and, as other factors were also likely to have contributed to the decline, the exact nature of this effect in that system remains unclear.

(iv) Taxonomic studies have shown that *Salvinia molesta*, which was only described as a different species in 1972 (Mitchell 1972), is a member of a complex of closely-related species. Of these it is the only one to be reported as an invading plant causing weed problems.

This account of the invasion of *Salvinia molesta* on Lake Kariba and in the Sepik River suggests it is possible to distinguish two groups of factors that should be examined as possible explanations for the invasion phenomenon: plant factors, such as mode of reproduction, reproductive capacity, tolerance to stress, rate of vegetative growth and means of dispersal; and environmental factors, such as disturbance, nutrient availability, competition from native flora and the presence or absence of phytophagous insects. Further support for this differentiation is found in the summaries already given of adventive spread amongst the various representatives of other growth forms of aquatic plants.

PLANT FACTORS IN BIOLOGICAL INVASIONS OF AQUATIC PLANTS

Like many terrestrial weeds many notorious invading aquatic plants are taxonomically close to species which do not exhibit such behaviour and/or are morphologically very similar to other plants which often occupy the same habitat but do not grow aggressively in every case. Thus *Salvinia molesta* is the only invasive representative of a complex of four closely-related species. Herzog (1935) had distinguished this group of species from others in the genus by the characteristic nature of the hairs on the upper surface of the leaf and had amalgamated them into the species, *S. auriculata*. Four species can now be distinguished in terms of differences in the branching of sporocarp chains and numbers of chromosomes: *S. molesta* with 45 chromosomes, *S. auriculata* with 54 chromosomes, *S. herzogii* with 63 chromosomes and *S. biloba* (chromosome number unknown). *S. auriculata* is widely distributed in South and Central America from northern Argentina to Mexico, whilst the others all have relatively localised native distributions: *S. herzogii* in northern Argentina and southern Brazil, *S. biloba* in the vicinity of Rio de Janiero and *S. molesta* in southern Brazil. Indeed the native habitat for the latter species was only discovered by Forno and Harley (1979), five years after it had been described as a postulated garden hybrid by Mitchell (1972). Two of these species, *S. molesta* and *S. herzogii*, do not produce viable spores and depend on vegetative reproduction.

A series of experiments under controlled environmental conditions was carried out to compare the responses of *S. molesta, S. herzogii* and *S. auriculata* to different forms of nitrogen (NO_3^-, NH_4^+ and urea) at various levels (5 mg/l — 100 mg/l). These indicated that the first two species were generally capable of more rapid growth than the last. In one series of experiments, using nitrate as a source of nitrogen, *S. herzogii* grew significantly faster than *S. molesta* (Smith 1977). In another series all species were shown to grow better with urea as a nitrogen source (Palmer 1973). Cary and Weerts (1983), however, found that growth of *S. molesta* was significantly better with NH_4N than with NO_3N or urea. These and other results suggest that were *S. herzogii* introduced to 'new' environments it may be as successful as *S. molesta*. Both have the same capacity for high growth rates and dependence on vegetative reproduction in comparison with *S. auriculata*. The difference in modes of reproduction also offers an explanation for the marked difference in extent of native distribution ranges. It is probable that the presence of a complex of phytophagous insects feeding on the plants in South America has limited the natural spread of *S. herzogii* and *S. molesta* in the absence of sexual propagules and other dispersal mechanisms.

A second example of a pair of closely-related species that differ in their weediness is provided by *Eichhornia crassipes* and *E. azurea*. Although the latter species also has attractive flowers, only the former is a serious adventive weed. Both species have similar native distribution patterns and often occur in the same water body. Both have been introduced to a number of countries as ornamentals. However, *E. crassipes* is the only member of the genus to have a free-floating habit. By comparison with *E. azurea, E. crassipes* is simple to transport long distances and to propagate, even though both may have had a similar attraction to the plant collectors of the last century. Moreover, *E. azurea* is less specialised and vegetative reproduction occurs slowly by fragmentation rather than by the rapid production of offsets (Barrett 1978). The greater mobility, greater specialisation and more rapid vegetative reproduction would clearly favour the spread of *E. crassipes* rather than *E. azurea*, even though they may be similar in other respects.

Another group of plants which may usefully be compared are those members of the Hydrocharitaceae with a similar morphology of whorls of short sessile leaves on stems with short internodes. *Elodea canadensis, Hydrilla verticillata* and *Lagarosiphon major* are representative of a number of species that are superficially so similar in morphology that they are often confused. All three examples have markedly different native distributions but occupy rather similar habitats. *Hydrilla* grows mainly in tropical and subtropical waters whereas the other two grow in temperate to subtropical waters. However, beyond these rather general comparisons, there is little other relevant information to explain the massive invasion of *Hydrilla* in Florida, the spread of *Elodea* in Europe and Australia and the infestation of *Lagarosiphon* in New Zealand and the absence of major troublesome invasions of morphologically similar members of the family. However, in each invasion vegetative growth and reproduction have been responsible for the initial rapid growth of the plant population frequently resulting in the complete occupation of all the available habitat at a particular site without the need for recourse to sexual reproductive processes.

In most cases of biological invasion by plants, success in the initial stages depends on reproductive capacity and 'r' or 'R'-strategists (MacArthur and Wilson 1967; Grime 1977, 1979 respectively) are widely represented. Subsequent stages in the invasion of a particular habitat when the plants contend more with environmental stress may result in the failure of the invasion. However, plants at the aquatic end of the hydrosere continue to experience environmental conditions which favour the opportunist strategies and introduced species will continue to compete successfully with native species.

In addition, introduced species with efficient dispersal mechanisms ensure that the process of invasion of new areas continues until the plant is widely dispersed into all suitable habitats. This process is usually considered to be a characteristic component of a successful invasion, since, in its absence, the plant is considered as an 'escape' that is not truly naturalised. The absence of effective dispersal of viable reproductive propagules provides the most likely explanation for the failure of vigorous plants like *Cyperus papyrus* to spread widely and rapidly. In this regard the importance of humans as the main dispersal mechanism must not be overlooked.

ENVIRONMENTAL FACTORS IN BIOLOGICAL INVASIONS OF AQUATIC PLANTS

Successful biological invasions often occur where there has been recent marked disturbance of the normal ecosystem. The destruction of one system and its replacement with another, such as the impoundment of a river to form an artificial lake, removes existing plants and assists invasion by opportunist plants. Whether the invasion then succeeds will depend more on the plant largely in terms of its reproductive capacity, than on the environment. It is in such situations that the R-strategists are likely to be advantaged. The initial vegetation of disturbed environments is low in species diversity and with the return of stable conditions is usually succeeded by a more complex vegetation. Depending on the circumstances, invading species, which may have dominated the colonising vegetation, then experience competition from either K-strategists (MacArthur and Wilson 1967), or C-strategists (Grime 1977, 1979). It is probably this increased competition which is responsible for the impression that the ecosystem is 'adapting' to the invading plant and decreasing the fluxes in population numbers. The sequence in events described above seems to have taken place in the invasion of Lake Kariba by *Salvinia molesta*.

Occasionally, as occurred in the invasion of the Sepik River by *Salvinia molesta*, the introduced plant remains dominant. In such cases, the invader is usually an R or C-strategist that obtains additional competitive advantages from the absence of pests or diseases that evolved with the plant in its native range. Another possibility, as yet untested is the formation of allelopathic substances by the introduced plant (Szczepanski 1977).

FISH

Compared to the number of aquatic plant invaders in Australia, relatively few introduced fish have become established in the inland waters of the continent (Table 2). This difference no doubt reflects the fact that fish must be imported deliberately and with considerable care to have any chance of survival and establishment. However, the subsequent release of fish into aquatic habitats may be entirely accidental. Amongst the species now present in Australia there are some which are regarded as noxious because of their environmental effects (e.g. the carp and mosquitofish), and others of considerable value as sport fish (e.g. brown and rainbow trout). Weatherley and Lake (1967) and Tilzey (1977, 1980) have reviewed the distribution patterns and biology of species introduced for sport and provided insight into the factors involved in their successful establishment. There is a valuable series of reports on the carp (see Hume, Fletcher and Morrison 1983) and a growing literature on the mosquitofish and on species established through the aquarium trade (McKay 1977, 1984; Tilzey 1980; Arthington, Milton and McKay 1983; Milton and Arthington 1983; Arthington *et al.* 1984; Lloyd, Arthington and Milton in press). However, this is the first attempt to examine invasions of fish as an ecological process and to identify the array of factors of importance in the Australian context.

A MODEL OF SUCCESSFUL FISH INVASIONS

Successful establishment of an introduced fish species depends on both its biological attributes and the physicochemical and biological characteristics of the receiving environment. The interactions between these two sets of factors determine the effect of the introduced species on the ecosystem. A general model of the interacting 'fish' and environmental factors which commonly contribute to successful invasions is proposed in Figure 1. Collectively, the reproductive strategy and the fish factors constitute a biological strategy which allows introduced species to exploit and adapt readily to suitable alien systems. The ultimate result of the invasion may be the evolutionary development of new strains of the invading species which may, in turn, invade marginal habitats and contribute to further spread of the species.

Several introduced fish which have been particularly successful in Australia, notably brown and rainbow trout, the carp, the mosquitofish and other Poeciliidae, possess many attributes of the biological strategy described in the Invasion Model (Figure 1). Conversely, the lack of success of certain introduced species, e.g. Atlantic and chinook salmon and brook trout, can be explained, at least in part, in terms of components of this model. The model offers a framework within which to assess the probability of success and spread of recently established species such as representatives of the Cichlidae and other aquarium species. Finally, it should be possible to use the model as a basis for screening fish species proposed for importation.

COMPONENTS OF THE MODEL

Survival of a propagule

A species introduced to an area previously unoccupied by its own kind has no chance of becoming established unless the initial immigrants form part of a 'propagule', the minimum number of individuals able to found a reproducing population under favourable conditions (MacArthur and Wilson 1967). In theory, a single pregnant female of any poeciliid (live-bearing) species may give rise to a potential breeding population (Rosen and Bailey 1963). For example, female swordtail (*Xiphophorus helleri*) may produce broods of up to 240 living young. The distribution of this species in the Brisbane region, Queensland, and its inability to disperse via brackish waters such as the Brisbane River, indicate that there have been some 17 separate introductions to urban creeks (McKay 1978; Arthington, Milton and McKay 1983). Some of these may well have involved the release or escape of only a few pregnant females.

When humans deliberately set out to establish desirable introduced species for food and sport, one strategy is to release very large numbers, often as fry reared from imported eggs. This may, or may not, compensate for natural juvenile mortality in the new environment. Brown (*Salmo trutta*) and rainbow trout (*Salmo gairdneri*) were established in this way in Australia, but attempts to establish the Atlantic salmon (*Salmo salar*) and the chinook salmon (*Onchorhynchus tshawytscha*) failed.

Reproduction

Once a propagule is established the success of the introduction depends initially on the ability of the species to build up large populations. Reproductive strategies which guarantee high fecundity characterise many

TABLE 2. *Introduced freshwater fish which have established self-maintaining popula-tions in Australian inland waters. S = sport fish, A = aquarium fish, B = biological control agent.*

Families and species	Common name	Purpose of introduction
Salmonidae		
Salmo trutta	Brown trout	S
Salmo gairdneri	Rainbow trout	S
Salvelinus fontinalis	Brook trout	S
Percidae		
Perca fluviatilis	European perch or redfin	S
Cyprinidae		
Cyprinus carpio	European carp	S
Carassius auratus	Goldfish	A
Tinca tinca	Tench	S
Rutilus rutilus	Roach	S
Puntius conchonius	Rosy barb	A
Poeciliidae		
Gambusia affinis holbrooki	Mosquitofish	A and B
Xiphophorus helleri	Swordtail	A
Xiphophorus maculatus	Platy	A
Poecilia reticulata	Guppy	A
Poecilia latipinna	Sailfin molly	A
Phalloceros caudimaculatus	One-spot live-bearer	A
Cichlidae		
Oreochromis mossambicus	Mozambique mouth-brooder	A
Tilapia mariae	Black mangrove or Niger cichlid	A
Cichlasoma nigrofasciatum	Convict cichlid	
Aequidens pulcher	Blue acra	
Synbranchidae		
*Monopterus albus	Belut	?
Amphipnoidae		
*Amphipnous cuchia	Cuchia	?

Compiled from Weatherly and Lake (1967), Tilzey (1980), Cadwallader *et al.* (1980), Trendall and Johnson (1981), Arthington *et al.* (1983, 1984), Cadwallader and Backhouse (1983), McKay (1984), Merrick and Schmida (1984).

Notes:

1. Species marked * have almost certainly been introduced (Lake 1971).
2. All *Gambusia* in Australia have been shown to belong to the species *affinis*, subspecies *holbrooki* (Lloyd and Tomasov 1985).
3. A number of additional Salmonidae and aquarium species have been introduced but have not established self-maintaining populations.

successful introduced animals (Fox and Adamson 1979). Amongst the successful Australian introduced fish in Australia there are three fundamental reproductive strategies — oviparity (Salmonidae, Percidae and Cyprinidae), ovoviviparity (Poeciliidae) and mouth-brooding (Cichlidae).

Oviparity. Oviparous species offset losses due to juvenile mortality by producing large numbers of eggs. Female carp (*Cyprinus carpio*) weighing 5 kg may produce up to one million oocytes (Merrick and Schmida 1984), and large females may spawn more than once per season (Cadwallader and Backhouse 1983). On the other hand, brown and rainbow trout have a much lower fecundity. Female rainbow trout weighing 1 kg produce about 1500 oocytes. Tilzey (1977) attributes the rapid expansion of the initial trout stocks established in Australia to unusually high fecundity due to the relatively large body sizes of mature females. Several factors contributed to the high growth rates and large sizes of these fish. High individual food availability, low trout population densities and an extended growing season were probably the crucial factors, although inherent growth characteristics may also have influenced growth rates (Tilzey 1977).

Ovoviviparity. Ovoviviparity in pest Poeciliidae involves the production of successive broods of living young that are nourished by yolk, with minimal dependence on nutrients from the female (Thibault and Schultz 1978). The advantages of producing young in a relatively advanced state of development are particularly evident in the mosquitofish (*Gambusia affinis*). Females mature after only 4–6 weeks and may produce a

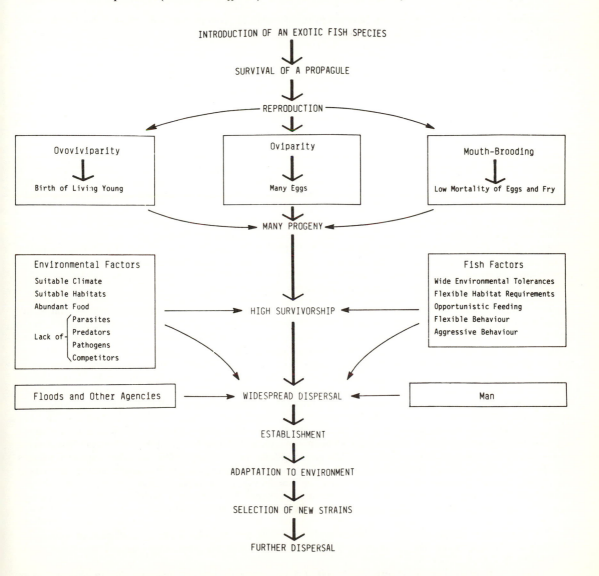

Fig. 1. Diagrammatic representation of a model for the stages in invasion of an introduced fish species.

brood of young every 3–4 weeks (Krumholz 1948). Brood size varies with the size of the female and can be as high as 428 (Motobar 1978), although the average brood contains up to 50 (Krumholz 1948). Photoperiod and temperature govern the timing and length of the breeding season, which lasts from August to May in Queensland, thereby enabling individual females to produce up to 9 broods (Milton and Arthington 1983). Thus large populations can be established in a single breeding season in spite of natural mortality. Johnson (1975) recorded an increase from 7,000 to 102,000 mosquitofish in 5 months in small ponds.

Mouth-brooding. Mouth-brooding Cichlidae typically have low fecundity but this is offset by efficient protection of eggs and fry against predation. Female cichlids undergo successive breeding cycles and may produce new broods every 4–6 weeks. The breeding season of the Mozambique mouth-brooder (*Oreochromis mossambicus*) extends from September/October to March/April in Queensland, allowing the production of four broods. Females of this species weighing 100 g may produce up to 600 eggs but brood sizes are much smaller, at most 250 fry (Bruton and Boltt 1975). This cichlid, like many others has a capacity for precocious sexual maturation at 3-4 months. This may lead, in situations of food competition, to very dense populations of small ('stunted') fish. When favourable conditions are restored, maturation is delayed until females are 12–15 months old. Sexual precocity allows reproduction and population growth to continue even in adverse circumstances, a valuable attribute for an invading species.

High survivorship of progeny

A suite of inherent biological factors determines survivorship of progeny and their availability for dispersal beyond the site of the initial introduction (Figure 1).

Biological factors

Environmental tolerances. Environmental tolerances are wide in most fish introduced successfully to Australia, although the Salmonidae are stenotherms (i.e. the upper lethal temperature lies below 28°C, Varley 1967) requiring at least 4 mg/l dissolved oxygen for normal activity (Graham 1949). By contrast, carp can survive temperatures from 5°C to over 32°C and tolerate low dissolved oxygen concentrations (Merrick and Schmida 1984).

Poeciliidae are generally a very hardy group of fishes, a feature which has enhanced their appeal as aquarium species. The world's most widespread poeciliid, the mosquitofish, has extraordinary physiological tolerances. Naturally eurythermal, mosquitofish have been reported to survive in ice-covered waters and in thermal effluents up to 44°C for short periods (Krumholz 1948; Ferens and Murphy 1974; Hirose 1976). The 96 LC_{50} for dissolved oxygen is 0.2 mg/l (Ahuja 1964; Sjogren 1972) and for salinity is 50 g/l (Ahuja 1964). Mosquitofish are also tolerant of a wide range of pollutants.

The Mozambique mouth-brooder is also a hardy species which can tolerate temperatures of 14–39°C in natural habitats and in pond cultures (Balarin and Hatton 1979). It is euryhaline, able to adapt gradually to salinities of 0–120 g/l (Whitfield and Blaber 1979). Low dissolved oxygen ($\pm$ 1 mg/l) and high turbidity tolerance allow this cichlid to live in silty lagoons and shallow lakes where severe deoxygenation occurs from time to time (Maruyama 1958; Bardach, Ryther and McLarney 1972). These attributes have contributed to its suitability for pond culture and its success in many areas of introduction.

Habitat requirements. Given their wide physiological tolerances it is not surprising to find that many successful introduced fish have very flexible habitat requirements. Trout, for example, occur naturally in aquatic habitats ranging from torrential lotic to still lentic waters. Euryhalinity allows them to migrate to cool marine waters but marine and lentic populations must undergo annual spawning migrations to fast-flowing, oxygen-rich streams with stony or gravelly substrates (Tilzey 1977). Thus maximum water temperatures and spawning requirements are the major barriers to trout distributions in Australia (Weatherley and Lake 1967).

Carp are found in sluggish tableland streams, dams, shallow lakes and lagoons (Weatherley and Lake 1967). Although they are more active than previously thought (Merrick and Schmida 1984), the torrential waters and coarse substrates of river headwaters are barriers to upstream spread of carp (Hume, Fletcher and Morison 1983). Shallow lentic waters provide muddy benthic and littoral substrates suitable for feeding, and submerged vegetation for spawning sites. The mosquitofish occurs in similar habitats but is unable to tolerate fast-flowing waters, partly because predatory efficiency is low and long-term survival impossible at higher current velocities (Reddy and Pandian 1974). In Australia the mosquitofish is common in the turbid lower reaches of coastal drainages, swamps, lagoons, billabongs, salt lakes, and ponds, lakes and dams of all sizes. Disturbed habitats, particularly those infested with floating plants, such as water hyacinth and *Salvinia*, seem particularly susceptible to invasion by the mosquitofish (Arthington, Milton and McKay 1983).

Feeding behaviour. Opportunistic predation and omnivory are typical feeding strategies in successful introduced fish, and even the predominantly herbivorous Cichlidae switch to animal foods in some circumstances.

Trout feed mainly on benthic invertebrates and surface terrestrial insects, selecting the largest and most accessible prey. Tilzey (1977) concludes that the availability of suitable prey species was probably a major factor favouring the success of initial trout stocks released in Australia. The carp is a bottom-feeding omnivore favouring animal foods (Lake 1959). Bottom muds or small insects and plants at the surface are ingested by suction and crushed by the pharyngeal teeth. The entire masticatory apparatus is adapted for polyphagy (Sibbing 1982), but there is an overall preference for chironomid larvae and then microcrustaceans (Hume, Fletcher and Morison 1983). The mosquitofish also exhibits flexible omnivory with a preference for animal foods. Terrestrial insects taken at the surface often comprise 80–90% of the diet (Cadwallader 1979; Arthington, unpublished data). As in trout and carp, prey preferences are governed by prey size and availability (Farley 1980; Wurtsbaugh, Cech and Compton 1980).

Fry and early juveniles of the Mozambique mouth-brooder feed on small invertebrates, especially Crustacea (Le Roux 1956), whereas adult fish graze on phytoplankton, filamentous algae, aquatic plants and detritus of plant origin (Bardach, Ryther and McLarney 1972; Lowe-McConnell 1975). Although animal foods such as zooplankton, fish eggs and small fish are eaten, the significance of animal food in the diet of adults is uncertain (Bowen 1980).

Behavioural flexibility. Flexibility in the exploitation of food resources clearly favours the establishment of introduced species. It offers a strategy for survival when the preferred foods are in short supply and a means of optimising net energy gain when food is abundant. Flexible predator avoidance behaviour also enhances the survival of introduced species exposed to unfamiliar piscivores. Mosquitofish which encounter a predator exhibit a fright response, remain motionless momentarily, then flee quickly and accurately to a home shore using a sun-compass orientation (Goodyear and Ferguson 1969). These behavioural responses are reinforced by schooling and are particularly well-developed at high predator densities (Goodyear 1973). Trout also have very effective predator escape behaviour (Tilzey 1977). Mouth-brooding in cichlids ensures high survivorship of alevins, which remain close to the brooding parent and take refuge in its mouth at the slightest disturbance. Schooling in older fish helps to reduce losses due to predation (Bruton and Boltt 1975).

Aggressive behaviour. Interspecific and intraspecific aggression may contribute to the ease of establishment and proliferation of introduced fish. Mosquitofish nip the fins and generally harass other species in their immediate environment, sometimes causing so much physiological stress that reproduction is completely inhibited (Schoenherr 1981). At least 25 indigenous fish species have been affected by introductions of the mosquitofish around the world (Myers 1965; Schoenherr 1981), probably as a result of aggressive interference and predation on eggs and fry.

Amongst mouth-brooding cichlids only the most aggressive males reproduce, thereby enhancing the inherent vigor of progeny. Less aggressive and younger males are pushed to the margins of spawning grounds or fail to establish nesting territories. Such aggression is a factor taken into consideration during deliberate introductions of cichlids for single species and mixed species aquaculture (Philippart and Ruwet 1982).

Environmental Factors

Suitable climate. The interplay of physiological tolerances and physical environmental variables such as photoperiod and temperature sets limits to the distribution of any species. An introduced species must encounter conditions within these limits to survive and become established. Browning (1977) mentions the "initial barrier of the seasons" which confronts any species arriving in Australia from the northern hemisphere. This is probably not a problem for introduced fish because they are usually protected from seasonal shock by a period of acclimation under hatchery or aquarium conditions prior to release.

The sophisticated techniques of 'bioclimatic matching' (Nix and Wapshere, this volume) have not yet been applied systematically to the analysis of introduced fish distributions although the potential value of this approach is obvious. However, Weatherley and Lake (1967) and Tilzey (1977) concluded that the success of trout in Australia is largely determined by the physicochemical similarity of Australian and northern hemisphere trout habitats. Maximum seasonal water temperatures greater than 27°C are one of the major barriers limiting trout distributions in Australia. Conversely, minimum seasonal water temperatures determine the southern distributional limits of tropical and subtropical aquarium species. Swordtail suffer considerable winter mortality in southeastern Queensland but there have been isolated sightings in northern New South Wales (McKay, in Tilzey 1980). In some cichlids thermal resistance is affected by salinity. Thus the Mozambique mouth-brooder can tolerate low temperatures in saline water better than in fresh water. This interaction explains the southern limit of this species in South Africa, where the winter temperature drops to 12°C (Allanson, Bok and Van Wyk 1971).

Swincer (this volume) maintains that climatic certainty may be a critical factor in successful animal invasions. For poikilothermic introduced species the predictability of the thermal regime is particularly important. However, some introduced fish have the capacity to survive temperatures far beyond their normal thermal limits for short periods (e.g. the mosquitofish and various cichlids). This may allow an invading species to survive, perhaps without breeding, before colonising more favourable habitats, or to persist in spite of climatic certainty.

When bioclimatic 'distance' is very large an introduced species may be able to survive only in close association with humans and habitats created by humans. This is certainly true of fish, e.g. the two cichlids which breed in the heated waters of the Hazelwood cooling pondage in Victoria (Cadwallader, Backhouse and Fallu 1980). Cichlids and mosquitofish have also survived in Great Britain and parts of Europe in heated effluents from power plants.

Suitable habitats. The general habitat requirements of many successful introduced fish are often so broad that there is high probability of encounter with suitable environments. For some, the requirement for specific spawning habitat is a more significant limiting factor. Trout have been unable to establish in many slow-moving Australian rivers within their thermal tolerance limits because of the paucity of suitable spawning substrates (Tilzey 1977). The spawning success of carp in floodplain billabongs is associated with flood-induced changes in the availability of suitable spawning habitat. In rivers, rapidly fluctuating water levels during spawning may cause mass mortality of carp eggs through exposure (Hume, Fletcher and Morison 1983). The breeding arenas of mouth-brooding cichlids have quite specific characteristics with respect to substrate, depth and density of vegetation, and females need a special brooding zone sheltered by vegetation when they are caring for eggs and alevins (Bruton and Boltt 1975).

Food. Browning (1977) states that the likelihood of successful invasion may be determined by the capacity of species to utilise a resource not already fully exploited, or to exploit a resource more efficiently than indigenous species. Trout initially flourished in Australia partly because indigenous predatory fishes incompletely utilised the available food resources (Tilzey 1977). The concept of a completely unoccupied food niche is difficult to substantiate except with respect to certain microphagous and macrophagous cichlids, e.g. the Mozambique mouth-brooder, which has been widely introduced in order to develop new fisheries based on unutilised phytoplankton production. Other cichlids have been introduced for biological control of nuisance macrophytes in systems lacking indigenous grazers (Philippart and Ruwet 1982). Similarly, *Ctenopharyngodon idella* (Chinese grass carp), a cyprinid, has been widely introduced in North America, Egypt, Europe and Southeast Asia for this purpose (van Zon 1981).

Lack of biotic control agents. A key factor in the establishment of introduced species throughout the world has been their release from the natural biotic agencies of population control, i.e. parasites, predators, pathogens and competitors. Although indigenous trout host a multitude of parasites and diseases, very few have been recorded in wild Australian stocks. Similarly, the mosquitofish is host to 22 parasites in North America but so far there is only one record of parasitism from Australia (Lloyd 1984). The spring viraemia virus, which causes high mortality in carp under culture, has yet to be found in Australia, which led to its consideration as a biological control agent. This proposition was abandoned for practical and scientific reasons (Hume, Fletcher and Morison 1983).

Quantitative data on the effects of predators on introduced fish are very limited but information from dietary studies indicates minimal impact on species established in Australia. Tilzey (1977) has shown that there are only three or four indigenous predatory fish large enough to prey on trout throughout most of their range. Two indigenous predators occur with carp in Victorian waters and these, as well as introduced redfin (*Perca fluviatilis*), eat carp but their effect on populations is not known (Hume, Fletcher and Morison 1983).

Mosquitofish are small and therefore vulnerable to birds, other fish and even predatory water spiders of the genus *Dolomedes* (Suhr and Davis 1974; Main 1976). They have been found in the guts of several indigenous fish which are common in southeastern Queensland (*Mogurnda, Leiopotherapon* and *Glossamia*) but these are isolated records only, and quantitative data are not available.

Interspecific competition between introduced and indigenous species is, like the concept of a vacant niche, difficult to substantiate. Flick and Webster (1975) removed non-trout species from a mountain stream over a 13–year period but were unable to show any effects on growth and survival of brook trout (*Salvelinus fontinalis*). Jackson (1975) suggested that river blackfish (*Gadopsis marmoratus*) may avoid direct competition with trout by feeding in a different part of the habitat. Tilzey (1977) concluded that competition for food between indigenous fish species and trout has been insignificant in Australia. However, the limited success of brook trout in Australia is thought to be the result of competition with brown and rainbow trout (Tilzey 1980).

Lack of competition may partly explain the success of the mosquitofish in disturbed waterbodies unsuited to indigenous species (Arthington, Milton and McKay 1983). Co-existing populations of mosquitofish and several small indigenous species share habitats and food resources and may compete when resources are scarce, but it is usually the indigenous species which show declines in abundance (Arthington, Milton and McKay 1983; Lloyd 1984). The pigmy perch (*Nannoperca australis*) has declined in the Murray River since 1950, when the mosquitofish became established. In this instance there is no clear-cut evidence of environmental disturbances which could have affected the pigmy perch (Lloyd 1984), although the construction of Lake Hume might have brought about changes downstream of the dam that were detrimental to native fish. Hume, Fletcher and Morison (1983) found no evidence of competition between the mosquitofish and small indigenous species in Victorian waters in spite of dietary overlaps.

DISPERSAL

Inherent biological attributes and environmental factors which influence survivorship also influence the way introduced species expand their geographic range through natural dispersal (Figure 1). Extensive flooding has undoubtedly contributed to the spread of introduced fish in Australia and explains the presence of carp and mosquitofish in some isolated waterbodies. However, the deliberate efforts of humans have played a decisive role in spreading angling species and mosquitofish. Trout were introduced into most suitable river catchments before 1900, and into lotic waters upstream of natural barriers, as well as inaccessible lentic waters (Tilzey 1977). Creation of large, inland impoundments is still providing new habitats for trout and slowly extending their range in southeastern Australia (Tilzey 1980).

The most spectacular Australian example of rapid establishment and spread of an introduced fish is provided by the carp, and in this instance the genetic strain has been of paramount importance. Carp in Australia belong to three genetically distinct strains (Shearer and Mulley 1978). The 'Prospect' strain was introduced into the Prospect Reservoir near Sydney and has remained confined to that area (Pollard, Llewellyn and Tilzey 1980). A 'Singapore' strain, called koi carp in other countries, was introduced into canals in the Murrumbidgee Irrigation Area and has also shown little tendency to spread (Pollard, Llewellyn and Tilzey 1980; Hume, Fletcher and Morison 1983). The third strain, the 'Boolara', was released in Lake Hawthorn near Mildura in 1964 and spread from there throughout the entire Murray-Darling system in just over ten years (Pollard, Llewellyn and Tilzey 1980). This strain is believed to be a hybrid between an imported mirror variety and a fully scaled variety of unknown origin. Its spectacularly rapid increase in abundance and spread are assumed to be consequences of inherent hybrid vigour (Hume, Fletcher and Morison 1983). However, recent evidence suggests that Boolara carp are no longer expanding their range appreciably in the Murray and Gippsland Lakes catchments, and are declining in abundance in the Goulburn River and elsewhere. In floodplain waters this may be because of an overall decline in flooding frequency affecting food supplies, spawning success and growth of carp. Genetic factors may also be involved (Hume, Fletcher and Morison 1983).

Establishment, adaptation and development of new strains

An introduced species dispersed widely into geographically isolated areas is likely to be subjected to different selection pressures in different parts of its range (Weir 1977). Selection may result in the development of several genetically distinct populations with different phenotypic characteristics. For instance, the mosquitofish exists as 'warm-adapted' and 'cold-adapted' strains in parts of the United States (Otto 1973). A hatchery population of rainbow trout from Western Australia, consistently exposed to high summer water temperatures, has been shown to have higher summer heat tolerance than stocks from cooler regions (Morrissy 1973). Such warm-adapted fish could spread slowly as they reproduce and undergo further selection in marginal trout habitats (Tilzey 1977; Pollard, Llewellyn and Tilzey 1980). However, genetic differences between these strains have yet to be determined.

Many introduced species subjected to intensive culture and selective breeding programs already exist in a host of different strains and varieties. Such intraspecific variation introduces an additional level of uncertainty as to the possible ecological and evolutionary outcome of any biological invasion. In Australia the importance of genetic differences within a species has been dramatically demonstrated by the history of carp invasions. Experience with this species highlights the need to know the genetic identity of introduced species entering any foreign country and the associated phenotypic attributes which may predispose the species for success as an invader. This knowledge could prevent needless expenditure on costly research and eradication programs in the future, but the likelihood of obtaining basic information on genetic characteristics of strains prior to their introduction seems slight, except when the introduction is deliberate and the species involved are deemed to be valuable to humans.

SIMILARITIES IN AQUATIC PLANT AND FISH INVASIONS

The preceding accounts have established that three main stages characterise biological invasions of ecosystems by aquatic plants and fish: namely, introduction of species; establishment of the population through reproduction; and dispersal.

At each stage of a biological invasion two sets of factors interact to determine the success or failure of the species and its transition to the next stage. These factors can be identified as the biological attributes of the invading species and the physical, chemical and biological features of the alien environment (Figure 1).

Introduction of species

An extension to the geographic range of a plant or animal species is brought about by the dispersal of breeding populations. Plants have the benefit of dormant stages in the life cycle, such as seeds, that are often especially adapted for dispersal. Even so, freshwater macrophytes are seldom readily dispersed between distant unconnected water bodies and this is even more marked for freshwater fish. Consequently, there is a relatively high proportion of species with natural, restricted geographic ranges. However, the increasing ease of movement around the world has meant that introduction of aquatic species to alien environments has become more frequent. For the most part, initial introductions of plants and fish to alien continents have almost always been deliberate and the species introduced have usually had some special attraction and/or intended use for humans. Accidental introductions have occurred mainly through the aquarium trade when unwanted fish stocks and associated aquarium plants or propagules have been discarded or allowed to escape into water bodies. Alligator weed seems to be the notable exception amongst introduced aquatic plants, having been spread between continents accidentally.

Establishment of the population through reproduction

Biological factors. In most cases of biological invasions by aquatic plants and fish, success in the initial stages is dependent on reproductive capacity, provided that there is a fundamental bioclimatic match with the alien environment. Opportunist R- or r- strategists (MacArthur and Wilson 1967; Grime 1977, 1979) with high reproductive rates are well represented amongst both plants (e.g. water hyacinth and *Salvinia*) and fish (e.g. mosquitofish and other Poeciliidae). Plants capable of prolific vegetative reproduction are at a special advantage as one viable propagule is sufficient to start a new colony. During subsequent stages in the invasion process other biological attributes, such as flexible habitat requirements and ability to tolerate environmental fluctuations and extremes, become more important. Similarly, the world's most successful fish invaders (i.e. the mosquitofish, the Mozambique mouth-brooder and the European carp) have unusually wide physiological tolerances, ability to live in a variety of habitats and omnivorous feeding behaviour. These attributes, coupled with high reproductive capacity, constitute a biological strategy which predisposes these species for success as invaders.

Environmental factors. A suite of environmental factors and a variety of organism-environment interactions may contribute to the success or failure of plant and fish invasions. It is evident, however, that disturbed ecosystems are particularly vulnerable to plant invasions, for reasons previously described. Floating aquatic plants such as water hyacinth and *Salvinia* profoundly alter the character of water bodies by reducing the habitat available to indigenous fish which forage at the surface in open water. Aquatic systems invaded by plants of this growth habit may then be colonised by introduced fish with broad habitat requirements and more flexible feeding behaviour. Thus it is common to find the mosquitofish and swordtail flourishing in water bodies with serious infestations of introduced aquatic weeds (Arthington, Milton and McKay 1983).

Both introduced plants and fish have displayed considerable success in new ecosystems where there was no apparent disturbance but where suitable habitats and other necessary resources already existed, e.g. *Salvinia* in the Sepik River, and trout, carp and mosquitofish in Australia. In these circumstances, successful introduced plants are usually R-strategists or C-strategists with the additional competitive advantage of freedom from pests and diseases characteristic of their native range. Most introduced plants and fish that are now well established in Australia are thought to be relatively free of parasites and diseases and probably experience considerably lower grazing and predator pressure than in waters where they are indigenous. They are thus at a competitive advantage over the species that are native to the environments they have invaded.

Dispersal

The third stage of every successful biological invasion is the dispersal of the organism into all suitable habitats. In the absence of this phase an introduced organism is properly considered as an 'escape' that is not truly naturalised. Efficient dispersal mechanisms, such as the possession of sexual or asexual propagules, or the capacity to disperse widely on flood waters, characterise the successful introduced plants and fish. However, the decisive influence of humans in the inter-continental dispersal of many troublesome aquatic plants and animals also operates in the widespread dispersal of many of the aquatic plants and sport fish and the mosquitofish within Australia and other countries. Indeed, the aquarium species now established in Australia and other tropical and subtropical regions owe their major patterns of distribution to human actions.

CONCLUSIONS AND RECOMMENDATIONS

In spite of the obvious differences between the two groups of aquatic invaders we have been able to identify a common framework for the invasion process in aquatic ecosystems and several important biological attributes characteristic of successful invasive plants and fish. The similarities between plant and animal aquatic invaders which have established readily and dispersed widely are such that it is possible to suggest preventive measures directed at the most likely source of future undesirable introductions. We also briefly discuss areas of research and approaches to management which may help alleviate problems due to undesirable introduced organisms in aquatic ecosystems.

Preventive measures

Plants. There are two main components to an effective system for avoiding the establishment of introduced aquatic plants: namely, prevention of entry; and restriction of spread. Current procedures in force in Australia operate in both these areas. The National Co-ordinating Committee on Aquatic Weeds, which reports to both the Australian Water Resources Council and the Australian Weeds Committee, provides a major source of advice to the government agencies responsible for carrying out these procedures. A list of plant species that may be imported has been drawn up and a similar list of non-permissible plants has been promulgated. All approved imports are examined for disease, for cleanliness and to verify identification. They are then kept in quarantine for a period before release to the importer. However, these measures cannot prevent unauthorised or accidental importation of unwanted plants.

Restriction of spread throughout the country of an introduced invader that has become successfully established is only feasible when humans are the main if not the only, dispersal agent. Promulgation of dangerous introduced aquatic plants as noxious plants, public awareness campaigns, illustrated posters and the like are used to enforce and promote control of the weeds.

Fish. Although other routes of entry are possible, the major source of introduced fish entering Australia in recent years has been the aquarium industry, and it is in this area that more stringent preventive measures are most needed. The procedures currently in force and the important role of the quarantine system have been reviewed by McKay (1984), but the following points are relevant to this chapter.

1. Species proposed for importation, and those currently entering Australia regularly through the aquarium trade, could be screened for their propensity towards high reproductive capacity, high survivorship under Australian conditions, and rapid dispersal by natural mechanisms. The Invasion Model (Figure 1) provides a framework for the screening process. It is noteworthy that a screening approach over several years has led to the elimination of a few species from the legal imports list (see McKay 1984), but a more rigorous screening could limit importations to species which are both attractive to aquarists and easy to maintain yet unlikely to reproduce and spread under Australian conditions. Some of the necessary biological information is available but basic research would be needed on many species.
2. More stringent controls and improved inspection procedures are needed at ports of entry of aquarium stocks to ensure that species are identified accurately and prohibited species are not imported accidentally. To achieve this will be extremely difficult with the present rate of entry of aquarium fish, estimated to be around 10 million fish annually.
3. Quarantine measures and inspection procedures are being improved to reduce the risk of importation of introduced pathogens and parasites. The present mandatory holding period of 2 weeks is insufficient, however to detect diseases with longer incubation periods and those which are asymptomatic. Many parasitic infections, particularly internal parasites, are not detectable upon external examination, and are difficult to identify even in dissected fish. Although quarantine procedures have improved markedly recently there nevertheless remains a possibility of introducing organisms which could endanger indigenous fish and threaten valuable recreational fisheries.
4. Water brought into Australia with imported fish stocks should not be allowed to contaminate natural water bodies because of the risk of releasing alien parasites, pathogens, fish eggs and minute plant propagules as well as human pathogens with aquatic vectors.

Research

Plants. Introduced aquatic weeds have provided significant economic problems in Australia, and their control by mechanical, chemical and biological means has been the subject of considerable research (Mitchell 1978). Whilst effective means of control exist, research should continue in order to refine and extend control measures and to make them more cost-effective. Research on the ecology and biology of the weeds in relation to their control has also been carried out (e.g. Cary and Weerts 1983; Bowmer, Mitchell and Short 1984), but knowledge in this field is deficient in many areas. Of particular importance are germination requirements of propagules; capacity of plants, or portions of plants, to survive stress such as desiccation, mechanical damage from floods, etc; nature and effect of environmental factors that promote growth and increase rate of reproduction; general habitat requirements for some of the less well-known plants such as *Lagarosiphon* spp.; and reproductive capacity and other factors affecting further dispersal of plants, such as *Cyperus papyrus* which currently establish successfully but do not disperse.

Fish. The most urgent research questions relate to the proposal to introduce the Nile perch (*Lates niloticus*) into tropical water bodies to establish recreational fisheries (see Barlow 1984). It is estimated that the research program currently underway to investigate the potential for spread of this species in Australia, and the potential for detrimental effects on indigenous species, will take 8–11 years to complete, whereupon a decision will be made on its introduction into this country. This research program will also yield information on the reproductive biology of indigenous fish suitable for stocking into rivers and impoundments, particularly the congeneric *Lates calcarifer* or barramundi. The extensive stocking of tropical impoundments with either of these species will raise a number of further matters requiring research, and in particular, the effect of introducing a large carnivorous species into waters to which it is alien, and which offer limited food supplies in the form of forage fish and crustaceans.

Research is urgently needed on tropical and subtropical aquarium fish which have established self-maintaining populations in Australia and which have a record of undesirable effects in other parts of the world.

The species of most concern in this category is the Mozambique mouth-brooder or tilapia. Many of the biological attributes of this species which contribute to its success as an invader also render it ideal as a forage and food fish, and it seems probable that it will be dispersed widely and harvested by humans, or used as a forage fish in association with recreational fisheries. Research on its long-term effects both detrimental and beneficial on aquatic ecosystems, on breeding behaviour and growth rates under Australian conditions, on the phenomenon of stunting, and on population regulation will contribute to an increased understanding of this species in alien environments.

Management of undesirable biological invasions

Plants. Once an introduced plant has successfully invaded and established itself and is found to have adverse ecological and economic effects, every attempt must be made to prevent its further spread. Eradication of plants, such as *Salvinia*, which are incapable of producing viable spores or seeds, is possible, if the infestation is vigorously and persistently controlled at an early stage of the invasion of a relatively small, confined water body. Often, however, the water body is too large with parts that may be inaccessible, or the infestation is too well established. In either case it is critically important that control attempts are well planned and thorough and that they are persistently carried out. Regular surveys and follow-up control of outbreaks from surviving plants are required for a number of years. The necessity for such a sustained and consequently expensive program serves to emphasise the benefit of biological control measures which, if successful, are self-sustaining.

These management procedures must be complemented with the preventive measures described earlier. Noxious plant legislation is particularly important as it provides the means to enforce the rigour of control measures. Whilst it is unlikely that the introduced plants that are now well established can be eradicated from the Australian continent, or that further invasions of undesirable introduced plants can be prevented, the continued surveillance and rigorous control outlined here, backed by continuing research, will certainly ameliorate the problem and minimise its adverse effects.

Fish. There have been several approaches to the management of undesirable introduced fish (e.g. carp) in Australia, including enactment of legislation declaring the species a noxious fish and prohibiting the possession, handling or release of live fish. Legislation of this type is difficult to enforce and fraught with problems when the species is perceived by some to be useful. Attempts to eradicate carp from Victorian waters have been unsuccessful, and eradication will normally be impractical when extensive areas and many water bodies are infested with fish. Biological methods of population control are usually very expensive to research and develop, and the outcomes are often unpredictable. However, biological methods with potential are the use of specific pathogens and parasites and genetic manipulations of species.

ACKNOWLEDGMENTS

Angela Arthington wishes to thank the Australian National Parks and Wildlife Service, Canberra, for initiating and funding research on introduced fish in Queensland and David Milton for many forms of assistance throughout the studies.

REFERENCES

Ahuja, S.K. (1964). Salinity tolerance of *Gambusia affinis*. *Indian Journal of Experimental Biology 2*, 9–11.

Allanson, B.R., Bok, A., and Van Wyk, N.I. (1971). The influences of exposure to low temperature on *Tilapia mossambica* Peters (Cichlidae). II. Changes in serum osmolarity, sodium and chloride concentrations. *Journal of Fish Biology 3*, 181–185.

Arthington, A.H., Milton, D.A., and McKay, R.J. (1983). Effects of urban development and habitat alterations on the distribution and abundance of native and exotic freshwater fish in the Brisbane region, Queensland. *Australian Journal of Ecology, 8*, 87–101.

Arthington, A.H., McKay, R.J., Russell, D.J., and Milton, D.A. (1984). Occurrence of the introduced cichlid *Oreochromis mossambicus* (Peters) in Queensland. *Australian Journal of Marine and Freshwater Research 35*, 367–372.

Aston, H.I. (1973). *Aquatic Plants of Australia*, Melbourne University Press, Melbourne.

Aston, H.I. (1977). Supplement to *Aquatic Plants of Australia*, Melbourne University Press, Melbourne.

Bagnall, L.O., Furman, T. de S., Hentges, J.F., Nolan, W.J., and Shirley, R.L. (1974). Weed and fiber from effluent-grown water hyacinth. In *Wastewater Use in the Production of Food and Fiber — Proceedings*, EPA 660/2–74–041, Environmental Protection Agency, Washington.

Balarin, J.D., and Hatton, J.P. (1979). *Tilapia. A Guide to Their Biology and Culture in Africa*, Unit of Aquatic Pathobiology, University of Stirling, Scotland.

Bardach, J.E., Ryther, J.H., and McLarney, W.O. (1972). *Aquaculture: The Farming and Husbandry of Freshwater and Marine Organisms*, Wiley-Interscience, New York.

Barlow, C.G. (1984). The nile perch project: progress and plans. *Search 15*, 88–91.

Barrett, S.C.H. (1978). Floral biology of *Eichhornia azurea* (Swartz) Kunth (Pontederiaceae). *Aquatic Botany* 5, 217–228.

Bowen, S.H. (1980). Detrital nonprotein amino acids are the key to rapid growth of tilapia in Lake Valencia, Venezuela. *Science 207*, 1216–1218.

Bowmer, K.H., Mitchell, D.S., and Short, D.L. (1984). Biology of *Elodea canadensis* Mich. and its management in Australian irrigation systems. *Aquatic Botany 18*, 231–238.

Browning, T.O. (1977). Processes that contribute to the establishment and success of exotic animal species in Australia. *Proceedings of the Ecological Society of Australia 10*, 27–38.

Bruton, M.N., and Boltt, R.E. (1975). Aspects of the biology of *Tilapia mossambica* Peters (Pisces: Cichlidae) in a natural freshwater lake (Lake Sibaya, South Africa). *Journal of Fish Biology 7*, 423–446.

Cadwallader, P.L. (1979). Distribution of native and introduced fish in the Seven Creeks River system, Victoria. *Australian Journal of Ecology 4*, 361–385.

Cadwallader, P.L., and Backhouse, G.N. (1983). *A Guide to the Freshwater Fish of Victoria*, Victorian Government Printing Office, Melbourne.

Cadwallader, P.L., Backhouse, G.N., and Fallu, R. (1980). Occurrence of exotic tropical fish in the cooling pondage of a power station in temperate south-eastern Australia. *Australian Journal of Marine and Freshwater Research 31*, 541–546.

Cary, P.R., and Weerts, P.G.J. (1983). Growth of *Salvinia molesta* as affected by water temperature and nutrition. I. Effects of nitrogen level and nitrogen compounds. *Aquatic Botany 16*, 163–172.

Chapman, V.J., Brown, J.M.A., Hill, C.F., and Carr, J.L. (1974). Biology of excessive weed growth in the hydro-electric lakes of the Waikato River, New Zealand. *Hydrobiologia 44*, 349–363.

Elton, C.S. (1958). *The Ecology of Invasions by Animals and Plants*, Methuen, London.

Farley, D.G. (1980). Prey selection by the mosquitofish, *Gambusia affinis* in Fresno County rice fields. *Proceedings and Papers A. Conference of the Californian Mosquito Vector Control Association 48*, 51–55.

Ferens, M.C., and Murphy, T.M. (1974). Effects of thermal effluents on populations of mosquitofish. In *Thermal Ecology* (ed G.W. Esch and R.W. McFarlane) pp.237–245, A.E.C. Symposium Series, Augusta, Georgia.

Finlayson, C.M., and Mitchell, D.S. (1983). Management of salvinia (*Salvinia molesta*) in Australia. *Australian Weeds 2*, 71–76.

Flick, W.A., and Webster, D.A. (1975). Movement, growth and survival in a stream population of wild brook trout (*Salvelinus fontinalis*) during a period of removal of non trout species. *Journal of the Fisheries Research Board of Canada 32*, 1359–1367.

Forno, I.W., and Harley, K.L.S. (1979). The occurrence of *Salvinia molesta* in Brazil. *Aquatic Botany 6*, 185–187.

Fox, M.D., and Adamson, D. (1979). The ecology of invasions. In *A Natural Legacy — Ecology in Australia* (eds H.F. Recher, D. Lunney and E. Dunn) pp. 135–151, Pergamon Press, Oxford.

Goodyear, C.P. (1973). Learned orientation in the predator avoidance behaviour of the mosquitofish, *Gambusia affinis*. *Behaviour 65*, 212–223.

Goodyear, C.P., and Ferguson, D.E. (1969). Sun-compass orientation in the mosquitofish, *Gambusia affinis*. *Animal Behaviour 17*, 636–640.

Gopal, B., and Sharma, K.P. (1981). *Water-Hyacinth : The Most Troublesome Weed in the World*, Hindasia Publishers, Delhi.

Graham, J.M. (1949). Some effects of temperature and oxygen pressure on the metabolism and activity of the speckled trout (*Salvelinus fontinalis*). *Canadian Journal of Research 27*, 270–288.

Grime, J.P. (1977). Evidence for the existence of three primary strategies in plants and its relevance to ecological and evolutionary theory. *American Naturalist 111*, 1169–1194.

Grime, J.P. (1979). *Plant Strategies and Vegetation Processes*, John Wiley and Sons, Chichester.

Harley, K.L.S., and Mitchell, D.S. (1981). The biology of Australian weeds. 6. *Salvinia molesta* D.S. Mitchell. *Journal of the Australian Institute of Agricultural Science 47*, 67–76.

Herzog, R. (1935). Ein beitrag zur systematik der gattung *Salvinia*. *Hedwigia 74*, 257–284.

Hirose, Y. (1976). Observations on the overwintering of mosquitofish, *Gambusia affinis*, in Tokushima City, Japan. *Japanese Journal of Sanitation Zoology 27*, 311–312.

Hockley, J. (1974)...... and alligator weed spreads in Australia. *Nature 250*, 704.

Holm, L.G., Plucknett, D.L., Pancho, J.V., and Herberger, J.P. (1977). *The World's Worst Weeds*, University Press of Hawaii, Honolulu.

Hume, D.J., Fletcher, A.R., and Morison, A.K. (1983). *Carp Program Final Report*, Carp Program Publication No. 10, Fisheries and Wildlife Division, Ministry for Conservation, Victoria.

Jackson, P.D. (1975). Bionomics of brown trout (*Salmo trutta L.*) in a Victorian stream with notes on interactions with native fishes. Ph.D thesis, Monash University (cited in Tilzey 1977).

Johnson, C.R. (1975). Investigations into the culture and winter maintenance of *Gambusia affinis*. *Proceedings and Papers A. Conference of Californian Mosquito Control Association 43*, 44.

Krumholz, L.A. (1948). Reproduction in the western mosquitofish *Gambusia affinis* and its use in mosquito control. *Ecological Monographs 18*, 1–43.

Lake, J.S. (1959). The freshwater fishes of New South Wales. *New South Wales State Fisheries Research Bulletin* No. 5 (cited in Tilzey 1977).

Lake, J.S. (1971). *Freshwater Fishes and Rivers of Australia,* Thomas Nelson, Melbourne.

Le Roux, P.J. (1956). Feeding habits of young of four species of *Tilapia. South African Journal of Science 53*, 33–37.

Lloyd, L. (1984). Exotic fish: useful additions or 'animal weeds', *Fishes of Sahul 1*, 31–34, 39–43.

Lloyd, L., Arthington, A.H., and Milton, D.A. (in press). The mosquitofish — a valuable mosquito control agent or a pest? In *The Ecology of Exotic Plants and Animals in Australasia,* (ed R.L. Kitching) pp. 1–35 Jacaranda Press, Brisbane.

Lloyd, L., and Tomasov, J. (1985). The status of the genus *Gambusia* in Australia. *Australian Journal of Marine and Freshwater Research 36*, 1–6.

Lowe-McConnell, R.H. (1975). *Fish Communities in Tropical Freshwaters: Their Distribution, Ecology, and Evolution*, Longman, London.

MacArthur, R.H., and Wilson, E.O. (1967). *The Theory of Island Biogeography*, Princeton University Press, New Jersey.

Maddox, D.M., Andres, L.A., Hennessey, R.D., Blackburn, R.D., and Spencer, N.R. (1971). Insects to control alligator weed. *Bioscience 21*, 985–991.

Main, B.Y. (1976). *Spiders*, Collins, Sydney.

Marshall, B.E., and Junor, F.J.R. (1981). The decline of *Salvinia molesta* on Lake Kariba. *Hydrobiologia 83*, 477–484.

Maruyama, T. (1958). An observation on *Tilapia mossambica* in ponds referring to the diurnal movement with temperature change. *Bulletin Freshwater Fisheries Research Laboratory, Tokyo 8*, 25–32.

Mason, R. (1960). Three waterweeds of the family Hydrocharitaceae in New Zealand. *New Zealand Journal of Science, 3*, 382–395.

McKay, R.J. (1977). *The Australian aquarium fish industry and the possibility of the introduction of exotic fish species and diseases*, Dept. of Primary Industry, Fisheries Division, Fisheries Paper No. 25, Australian Government Publishing Service, Canberra.

McKay, R.J. (1978). *The Exotic Freshwater Fishes of Queensland*. Report to the Australian National Parks and Wildlife Service, Canberra.

McKay, R.J. (1984). Introductions of exotic fishes in Australia. In *Distribution, Biology and Management of Exotic Fishes* (eds W.R. Courtenay and J.R. Stauffer) pp. 177–199, Johns Hopkins University Press, Baltimore.

Merrick, J.R., and Schmida, G.E. (1984). *Australian Freshwater Fishes: Biology and Management,* Griffin Press, Adelaide.

Milton, D.A., and Arthington, A.H. (1983). Reproductive biology of *Gambusia affinis holbrooki* Baird and Girard, *Xiphophorus helleri* (Gunther) and *X. maculatus* (Heckel) (Pisces; Poeciliidae) in Queensland, Australia. *Journal of Fish Biology 23*, 23–41.

Mitchell, D.S. (1972). The Kariba weed: *Salvinia molesta. British Fern Gazette 10*, 251–252.

Mitchell, D.S. (1978). *Aquatic Weeds in Australian Inland Waters*, Australian Government Publishing Service, Canberra.

Mitchell, D.S. (1979). *The Incidence and Management of* Salvinia molesta *in Papua New Guinea*, Office of Environment and Conservation and Department of Primary Industry, Port Moresby.

Mitchell, D.S., and Rose, D.J.W. (1979). Factors affecting fluctuations in extent of *Salvinia molesta* on Lake Kariba. *PANS 25*, 171–177.

Morrissy, N.M. (1973). Comparison of strains of *Salmo gairdneri* Richardson from New South Wales, Victoria and Western Australia. *Bulletin of the Australian Society for Limnology 5*, 11–20.

Motobar, N.M. (1978). Larvivorous fish, *Gambusia affinis* — a review. *W.H.O. Vector Biology and Control 703*, 1–5.

Myers, G.S. (1965). *Gambusia*, the fish destroyer. *Australian Zoologist 13*, 102.

Otto, R.G. (1973). Temperature tolerance of the mosquitofish, *Gambusia affinis* (Baird and Girard). *Journal of Fish Biology 5*, 575–585.

Palmer, C.A. (1973). A comparative study of the growth of *Salvinia molesta* and *Salvinia herzogii* in three different forms of nitrogen. B.Sc. (Hons) thesis, University of Rhodesia, Salisbury.

Pettet, A. (1964). Seedlings of *Eichhornia crassipes* : a possible complication to control measures in the Sudan. *Nature 210*, 516–517.

Philippart, J.C., and Ruwet, J.C. (1982). Ecology and distribution of tilapias. In *The Biology and Culture of Tilapias* (eds R.S.V. Pullin and R.H. Lowe-McConnell) pp. 15–59, ICLARM Conference Proceedings 7, International Center for Living Aquatic Resources Management, Manila.

Pollard, D.A., Llewellyn, L.C., and Tilzey, R.D.J. (1980). Management of freshwater fish and fisheries. In *An Ecological Basis for Water Resource Management* (ed. W.D. Williams) pp. 227–270, Australian National University Press, Canberra.

Reddy, S.R., and Pandian, T.J. (1974). Effect of running water on the predatory efficiency of the larvivorous fish, *Gambusia affinis*. *Oecologia 16*, 253–256.

Robson, T.O. (1976). A review of the distribution of aquatic weeds in the tropics and sub-tropics. In *Aquatic Weeds in South East Asia* (ed. C.K. Varshney and J. Rzoska) pp. 25–30, Dr W. Junk, The Hague.

Rosen, D.E., and Bailey, R.M. (1963). The poeciliid fishes (Cyprinodontiformes), their structure, zoogeography and systematics. *Bulletin of the American Museum of Natural History 126*, 1–176.

Sainty, G.R., and Jacobs, S.W.L. (1981). *Waterplants of New South Wales*, Water Resources Commission of New South Wales, Sydney.

Salisbury, E.J. (1961). *Weeds and Aliens*, Collins, London.

Schoenherr, A.A. (1981). The role of competition in the displacement of native fishes by introduced species. In *Fishes in North American Deserts* (ed. R.J. Naiman and D.L. Soltz) pp. 173–203, Wiley–Interscience, New York.

Sculthorpe, C.D. (1967). *The Biology of Aquatic Vascular Plants*, Edward Arnold, London.

Seneratna, J.E. (1943). *Salvinia auriculata* Aublet — a recently introduced, free-floating water weed. *Tropical Agriculture Magazine, Ceylon, Agricultural Society 99*, 146–149.

Shearer, K.D., and Mulley, J.C. (1978). The introduction and distribution of the carp, *Cyprinus carpio* Linnaeus, in Australia. *Australian Journal of Marine and Freshwater Research 29*, 551–563.

Sibbing, F.A. (1982). Pharyngeal mastication and food transport in the carp (*Cyprinus carpio* L.): a cineradiographic and electromyographic study. *Journal of Morphology 172*, 223–258.

Sjogren, J.D. (1972). Minimum oxygen thresholds of *Gambusia affinis* and *Poecilia reticulata*. *Proceedings and Papers A. Conference of California Mosquito Control Association 40*, 124–126.

Smith, F.H.C. (1977). A comparative study of the response of *Salvinia* species to nitrogen. B.Sc. (Hons) thesis, University of Rhodesia, Salisbury.

Suhr, J.M., and Davis, J.D. (1974). The spider, *Dolomedes sexpunctatus* as a predator on mosquitofish, *Gambusia affinis*, in Mississippi. *A.S.B. Bulletin 21*, 87.

Swarbrick, J.T., Finlayson, C.M., and Cauldwell, A.J. (1981). The biology of Australian weeds. 7. *Hydrilla verticillata* (L.f.) Royle. *Journal of the Australian Institute of Agricultural Science 47*, 183–190.

Szczepanski, A.J. (1977). Allelopathy as a means of biological control of water weeds. *Aquatic Botany 3*, 193–197.

Thibault, R.E., and Schultz, R.J. (1978). Reproductive adaptations among viviparous fishes (Cyprinodontiformes: Poeciliidae). *Evolution 32*, 320–333.

Tilzey, R.D.J. (1977). Key factors in the establishment and success of trout in Australia. *Proceedings of the Ecological Society of Australia 10*, 97–105.

Tilzey, R.D.J. (1980). Introduced fish. In *An Ecological Basis for Water Resource Management* (ed. W.D. Williams) pp. 271–279, Australian National University Press, Canberra.

Trendall, J.T., and Johnson, M.S. (1981). Identification by anatomy and gel electrophoresis of *Phalloceros caudimaculatus* (Poeciliidae) previously mistaken for *Gambusia affinis holbrooki* (Poecillidae). *Australian Journal of Marine and Freshwater Research 32*, 993–996.

Van Zon, J.C.J. (1981). Status of the use of grass carp (*Ctenopharyngodon idella* Val.). In *Proceedings of the Fifth International Symposium on Biological Control of Weeds, Brisbane, Australia, 22–29 July 1980* (ed. E.S. DelFosse) pp. 249–260, CSIRO, Melbourne.

Varley, M.E. (1967). *British Freshwater Fishes : Factors Affecting Their Distribution*, Fishing News (Books) Ltd., London.

Weatherley, A.H., and Lake, J.S. (1967). Introduced fish species in Australian waters. In *Australian Inland Waters and Their Fauna* (ed. A. Weatherley) pp. 217–239, Australian National University Press, Canberra.

Weir, J.S. (1977). Exotics: past, present and future. *Proceedings of the Ecological Society of Australia 10*, 4–13.

Whitfield, A.K., and Blaber, S.J.M. (1979). The distribution of the freshwater cichlid *Sarotherodon mossambicus* in estuarine systems. *Environmental Biology of Fishes 4*, 77–81.

Wurstbaugh, W., Cech, J.J., and Compton, J. (1980). Effect of fish size on prey selection in *Gambusia affinis*. *Proceedings and Papers A. Conference Californian Mosquito Vector Control Association 48*, 48–51.

INVADED COMMUNITIES

We may conclude from the previous three chapters that invasive species as a group show certain attributes in common which predispose them to be invasive, but that no one species possesses all these attributes. Rather, it seems that different invasive species have differing combinations of attributes which make them potentially invasive. But what about the communities of plants and animals in Australia which are being invaded? Do some of these biotic assemblages have characteristic properties — physical or biological — which more readily allow for invasion of introduced species? The next two chapters attempt to answer this question for Australian natural and agricultural communities in terms of introduced plants, vertebrates and invertebrates.

THE SUSCEPTIBILITY OF NATURAL COMMUNITIES TO INVASION

Marilyn D. Fox[1] and Barry J. Fox[2]

There have been two recent comprehensive reviews of introduced species in Australia (Anderson 1977; Kitching and Jones 1981). These reviews emphasise the autecology of successful invading species, often in environments highly disturbed by humans. Less has been written about the invasion of natural communities by introduced species. Simberloff (1981) addressed some of the theoretical considerations of the community response to invasions, in particular the community models of equilibrium island biogeography and limiting similarity. From his extensive survey of the literature concerning introductions, Simberloff found little support for either model.

It is part of the modern ethos to reserve areas of natural environment for our present enjoyment and for the long-term conservation of species and habitats. The question of invasion of natural communities by introduced species is therefore an urgent one. Are such conservation areas safe from invasion? If not, what are the management practices that should be implemented to minimise invasion?

In this chapter we outline a theoretical framework within which invasions may be viewed, we erect a number of hypotheses regarding factors affecting the invasion of natural communities and we review the evidence, from Australia and elsewhere, that may support or refute them. Some of these hypotheses were also considered for the fynbos biome of South Africa by Macdonald and Jarman (1984). We then suggest broad management objectives to minimise invasions into conservation areas.

THE RESOURCE BASE

Natural communities comprise a number of coexisting species which utilise a common resource base. As a result of interactions through evolutionary and ecological time they have come to form an inter-connected framework within which available resources are (presumably) fully utilised. For the most part, natural communities maintain a continuity of composition through time which results from their resilience following disturbance.

The types of disturbance to which communities have been repeatedly exposed through evolutionary time have been termed endogenous disturbance (Westman 1985). Examples of endogenous disturbances are periodic flooding, cyclonic damage, wildfire or herbivore irruptions. Natural communities have mechanisms to survive such disturbances in the form of individual species' adaptations which culminate in the re-establishment of the pre-disturbance community. This may occur through direct replacement of pre-existing species or by the more usual process of succession. Exogenous disturbance is essentially human-induced disturbance, and may be produced by alteration of an endogenous disturbance, such as altered fire regime, flood control, or drainage; or it may be a novel event such as removal of topsoil, addition of fertiliser or the removal of native animals.

Disturbances affect the resource base of a community in a number of ways, the most radical being the creation of new resource or the destruction of existing resources. New resources may be utilised by native species in the community, or may be exploited by new species, either native or introduced. The outcome of total resource loss will be local extinction.

Disturbance may also modify an existing resource by either adding more of the same resource, or by shifting the resource. The creation of spare resource by the modification of an existing resource is depicted in Figure 1. In the case of 'resource amplification' (Figure 1a), disturbance amplifies an existing resource; for example, disturbance may create more open space or allow more light to reach the soil surface; this additional resource

---

[1] National Herbarium of New South Wales, Royal Botanic Gardens, Sydney, N.S.W. 2000
[2] School of Zoology, University of New South Wales, Kensington, N.S.W. 2033

can be utilised by existing components of the community, or new species can invade to use it. In the case of 'resource shift' (Figure 1b), the existing pattern of resource distribution is shifted such that there is loss of some resource, with concomitant local extinction, and the creation of new resource that may be exploited by a new species.

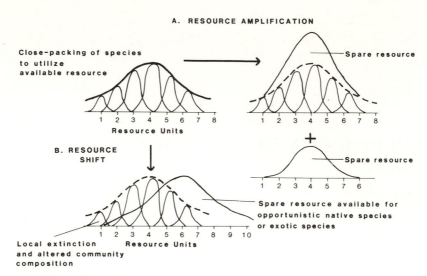

Fig. 1. Creation of spare resource by disturbance, either by (a) resource amplification, or (b) resource shift.

A simple example serves to illustrate these aspects of disturbance ecology. Pockets of bushland have been retained within the urban spread of many Australian cities. These were once contiguous with extensive bushland that was subject to particular drainage patterns and fire regimes. As a small, isolated fragment the bushland reserve is now subject to altered drainage and is often protected from fire. As a result, the natural composition of such bushland is being altered, with more shade-tolerant, mesic species dominating and the species that require the more open, post-fire conditions in danger of becoming locally extinct. These situations exemplify both resource amplification (the mesic, late pyric successional stages) and resource shift (the altered fire regime). Added to these alterations to an endogenous disturbance, is the exogenous disturbance resulting from enriched run-off from adjacent streets and properties. This leads to plumes of moist, nutrient-rich soil in which additional naturalised species may establish.

The house mouse (*Mus musculus*) in Australia represents a faunal example of an introduced species utilising spare resource; it is an extremely opportunistic animal with a plasticity of diet, habitat requirements,

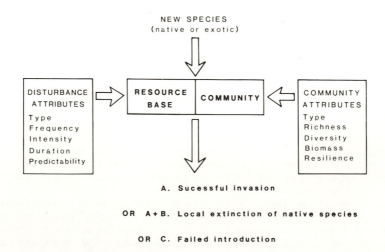

Fig. 2. The outcome of disturbance to a community may be: (a) successful invasion by an additional species (native or introduced); (b) invasion with the local extinction of the native species; (c) failed introduction.

reproduction and behaviour that allows extremely rapid response to any form of disturbance. The result is that the house mouse utilises the spare resource until a native species is able to respond and then to competitively exclude the house mouse (Fox and Fox 1984; Fox and Pople 1984). In this way the house mouse makes use of what can be seen as a 'new resource' that was otherwise unused by the rest of the community. In an extreme case the house mouse might maintain a successful invasion of that community if no native species is able to cope with the altered disturbance conditions.

The resource base and the community are intimately linked (Figure 2) with three possible outcomes of the introduction of a new species to the community. The new species may establish, use spare or new resource, and constitute a successful invasion. This may occur with or without the local extinction of a native species, either as a result of loss of suitable resource or by competition with the new species. The third outcome, and one which is given little attention in the literature, is that the introduction may fail.

It must be emphasised that the new or spare resource utilised by the species results from disturbance. This leads to some hypotheses linking invasion and disturbance.

THE DISTURBANCE HYPOTHESES
"It will be noticed that invasions most often come to cultivated land, or land much modified by human practice" (Elton 1958).

Hypothesis 1. Invasion is independent of disturbance
There are abundant data to reject this hypothesis. Moore (1959) demonstrated this for the occurrence of introduced species in grazed and ungrazed pastures. In the absence of grazing there are no introduced species whilst under grazing three native grasses, previously dominant in the pasture, are lost and the pasture comprises largely native *Danthonia* species and introduced species.

Wherever introduced species have become conspicuous parts of natural communities there have been alterations to the endogenous disturbances of the community, or exogenous disturbance has occurred. Prickly pear (*Opuntia stricta*) invaded woodlands subjected to an altered fire regime, introduced grazing and clearing. Trees of camphor laurel (*Cinnamomum camphora*) establish in rainforest margins subjected to clearing and a changed fire regime.

Animal invaders may appear to be invading undisturbed communities, but subtle alterations to endogenous disturbance have usually occurred and disturbance may have led to the competitive extinction of native species. The spread of feral rabbits (*Oryctolagus cuniculus*) across temperate Australia followed massive habitat

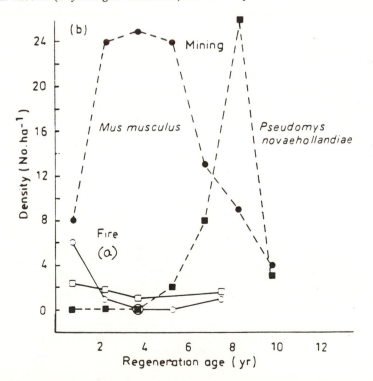

Fig. 3. Small mammal succession after (a) an endogenous disturbance (fire), and (b) an exogenous disturbance (mining) (from Fox and Fox 1984).

alteration, with the provision of supplementary water, suppression of predators and the early extinction of many similarly sized native species such as bandicoots, small wallabies and rat-kangaroos which occupied similar ecological roles.

A possible exception to this hypothesis is the success of the cane toad (*Bufo marinus*), currently spreading through the apparently undisturbed extensive wetlands of northern Australia. This species represents the exceptional case of an introduction to a new habitat of a species which effectively has no competitors. Having evolved elsewhere, it also benefits from the absence of the predators, parasites and disease organisms that may keep its population in check in its native habitat. Such a species exemplifies the 'weedy' characteristics outlined by Baker (1965).

Hypothesis 2. There is no relationship between degree of invasion and degree of disturbance

The seral responses in a community of small mammals to both an endogenous and exogenous disturbance are illustrated in Figure 3a and 3b respectively. In Figure 3a, the post-fire succession includes the introduced species *Mus musculus* which occurs in sympatry with the native New Holland mouse (*Pseudomys novaehollandiae*). The two ecologically similar species are separated principally by their micro-habitat requirements. The inclusion of the introduced species results from presumed alteration to the fire regime.

In the second case (Figure 3b), the disturbance results from mining for heavy minerals in the sand which is the substrate for this forest. This disturbance, incorporating the clearance of vegetation and disruption of the soil horizons, followed by regeneration procedures including substantial addition of fertiliser, effectively stretches the time axis of the small mammal succession. This is a form of habitat shift with amplification of the early seral stages enhanced by the nutrient enrichment. These are exploited by the introduced *M. musculus* which is only replaced by the native *P. novaehollandiae* after four years from initial disturbance. The more intense disturbance of sand-mining leads to more prolonged invasion.

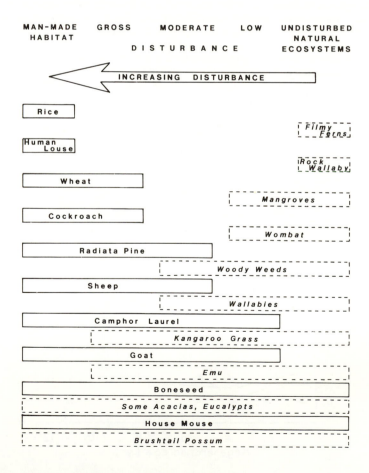

Fig. 4. The range of responses to different degrees of disturbance by some introduced species (solid boxes) and native species (open boxes).

There is a range of species responses to levels of disturbance (Figure 4) shown by a number of native and introduced species. There are some introduced species such as mice and the human louse that are restricted to commensal habitats, whilst others require gross disturbance, and some exceptionally weedy species can invade natural ecosystems. There are some native species that are as plastic as these weeds. For instance, the brushtail possum (*Trichosurus vulpecula*) still lives in Hyde Park in the middle of Sydney as well as throughout its natural habitat, where it may occupy the roofs of dwellings. At the other end of the spectrum some native species can occur only in undisturbed natural habitats, such as the filmy ferns of the rainforests and some of the rock wallabies.

Two examples of introduced species capable of invading natural ecosystems, namely boneseed (*Chrysanthemoides monilifera*) and the house mouse (*Mus musculus*), enter communities subjected to altered fire regimes but which may be considered 'undisturbed' in other respects.

As well as the connections between invasions and disturbance there is an hypothesis linking the richness (and diversity) of communities and their susceptibility to invasion.

THE RICHNESS HYPOTHESIS

Hypothesis 3. There is no connection between community richness and invasion

Two data sets (Abbott 1980; Aplin, Rhodes and King 1983a,b), for shrublands in Western Australia, both show highly significant exponential decay curves for introduced species as a percentage of total species when plotted against the number of native species (Figure 5). The figures of Aplin, Rhodes and King are for an experimental area that has been grazed and all plots have at least 20% of introduced species. Abbott's data are for heathlands on islands and mainland sites. In general, the islands are more weedy, and the richer mainland sites generally have less than 10% introduced species. These data reject both the hypothesis that there is no connection between community richness and invasion, as well as the disturbance hypotheses (see earlier).

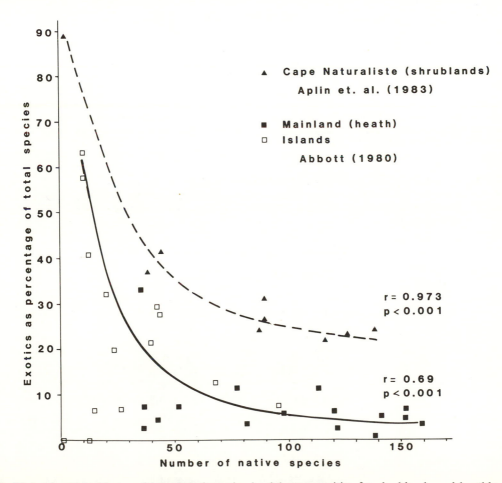

Fig. 5. The reduced incidence of introduced species in rich communities for shrublands and heathlands in Western Australia (from Abbott 1980; Aplin, Rhodes and King 1983a, b).

A survey of the composition of small mammal communities on heathlands in eastern Australia (data from Posamentier 1976; Braithwaite, Cockburn and Lee 1978; Fox 1983) also does not support this hypothesis (Figure 6). Those eight communities that contain two introduced species have both the mode and median richness of two native species (range 0-4 species), for the twelve communities where there is one introduced

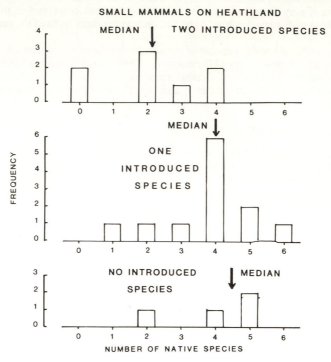

Fig. 6. Increasing median number of native species in small mammal communities with two, one or no introduced species (data presented in Fox 1983, with additional data derived from Posamentier 1976; Braithwaite, Cockburn and Lee 1978).

TABLE 1. *Summary of the percentage of introduced species in 92 plant communities (n is the number of sites), classified into six structural formations and into those that are relatively undisturbed compared to disturbed sites.*

	Percentage of introduced in plant species list	
Formation	Undisturbed	Disturbed
Closed-forest	*n* = 3 1.9 ± 1.0	*n* = 2 29.9 ± 2.6
Open-forest	*n* = 15 1.6 ± 0.5	*n* = 4 8.3 ± 2.0
Woodland	*n* = 10 0.7 ± 0.3	*n* = 6 27.0 ± 4.3
Shrubland	*n* = 7 0.3 ± 0.3	*n* = 5 17.3 ± 3.3
Heathland	*n* = 18 7.1 ± 1.8	*n* = 16 22.7 ± 4.7
Grassland and others	*n* = 5 2.1 ± 2.1	*n* = 1 17.2
Total	*n* = 58 3.1 ± 0.7	*n* = 34 21.2 ± 2.6

species present the mode and median richness is four native species (1-6 species) and, of four communities that had no introduced species the mode is five and the median richness of native species was between four and five (2-5 species). Richer small mammal communities contain fewer introduced species.

Presumably a community with many interacting species is better able to utilise any spare resource and thereby better able to prevent new species becoming established. Does it follow then that communities such as rainforest that are richer than other plant formations, are less susceptible to invasion?

THE PLANT FORMATION HYPOTHESES

Hypothesis 4. All structural formations are equally susceptible to invasion

The results of an analysis of the occurrence of introduced species in 92 floristically based surveys of a range of plant formations conducted by the Ecology Section of the Royal Botanic Gardens, Sydney (Table 1) support this hypothesis. Within each formation there can be as great a range of values as for all formations combined. In such cases this relates to the degree of disturbance of the sites.

Of the undisturbed sites most communities include fewer than 2% introduced species. The exception is heathland where the average value is 7.1%. Heathlands, because of their oligotrophic soils and increased fire frequency, may have been disturbed but were considered 'undisturbed' in this survey. This supports the results of a similar comparison for South African biomes (Macdonald 1984) which indicated that the fynbos (heathland) biome is currently more severely infested by introduced plant species than are the other biomes. The mean value for disturbed heathland sites is not, however, as great as that for closed forest (30%) or woodland (27%). Overall, the undisturbed sites have an average percentage of introduced species of only 3.1%, whilst for the disturbed sites it is 21.2%.

It is possible that some plant formations are more susceptible to disturbance, and because of this are more susceptible to invasion.

Hypothesis 5. All plant formations are equally susceptible to disturbance

The degree of disturbance and typical animal and plant invaders for the major structural formations and aquatic ecosystems are summarised in Table 2. Under the column for 'degree of disturbance' the endogenous disturbance is given first and then the most prevalent exogenous disturbance. The column 'typical animal invaders' lists the principal mammalian pests and the cane toad (a quasi-mammal). There are relatively few avian or reptilian pests. The final column notes the incidence of plant invasion. Exceptionally successful weed species are named.

TABLE 2. *Summary of the major plant formations, the degree to which they are disturbed by both endogenous and exogenous disturbances and the typical animal and plant invaders.*

Degree of disturbance	Typical animal invaders	Incidence of plant invasion
Closed-forest		
Endogenous: *wind-throws*	No: *Mus*, cats, foxes	Success of climbers, weeds in gaps
Exogenous: limited logging, clearing	Yes: cane toad	and margins
Tall Open-forest		
infrequent fire	No: *Mus*	Very few successful tree weeds, most
clearing, logging, erosion	Yes: cats, foxes, cane toad	in understorey
Open-forest		
frequent fire	No: cane toad, rabbit	Very few successful tree weeds, most
increased fire, logging, clearing, grazing	Yes: *Mus, R. rattus,* cats, foxes	in understorey
Woodland		
fire	No: cane toad	*Opuntia* spp., introduced grasses
increased fire, clearing, grazing	Yes: rabbit, fox, cat, goat etc.	
Shrubland		
fire	No: cane toad	Semi-arid and arid, not many weeds
clearing	Yes: hares, rabbit, foxes, goats, camels etc.	
Heathland		
fire	No: cane toad	Coastal *Chrysanthemoides,* many
clearing, eutrophication	Yes: *Mus*, foxes	with eutrophication

TABLE 2. (continued)

Degree of disturbance	Typical animal invaders	Incidence of plant invasion
Grasslands		
fire	No: —	Many intentional to 'improve' pasture
grazing	Yes: cane toad, pigs, etc.	
Swamps		
flooding/drying	No: —	Many with eutrophication
draining, eutrophication	Yes: cane toad	
Aquatic ecosystems		
Lakes		
—	Introduced fish	Aquatic weeds
eutrophication		
Rivers		
floods	Introduced fish	Can be high
flood control, salt		
Estuaries		
floods	Introduced fish and crabs	Can be high
salting		

Communities subject to recurrent disturbance are more prone to invasion. Communities that are subject to irregular massive disturbance such as flooding of coastal rivers, estuaries and harbours are, for that time, very susceptible to invasion. Communities free of disturbance or subject to regular, low-intensity disturbance are relatively free of invasions.

THE GRADIENT HYPOTHESIS

Hypothesis 6. Communities will be equally susceptible to invasion across an environmental gradient
   This hypothesis has not yet been tested adequately in the literature. Forcella and Harvey (1983) considered plant cover of plots both in roadside and in native vegetation on an elevational gradient in Montana (Figure 7). The gradient, from 1040m to 1700m, encompassed grassland, low- and mid-montane forest and subalpine vegetation, and went from warm dry conditions to cool moist conditions. In both roadside and native vegetation plots, introduced plants had their greater cover at low elevations, dropping off steadily at higher elevations; native plants had relatively higher cover at higher elevations. Overall, the greatest plant cover (both native and introduced) was greater at lower elevations (70 – 120% versus 6 – 20%).

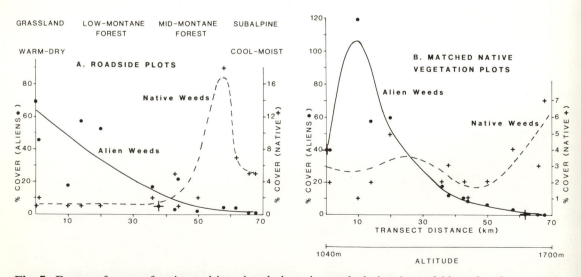

Fig. 7. Degree of cover of native and introduced plants in matched plots in roadside and native vegetation along an altitudinal gradient in Montana, USA (from Forcella and Harvey 1983).

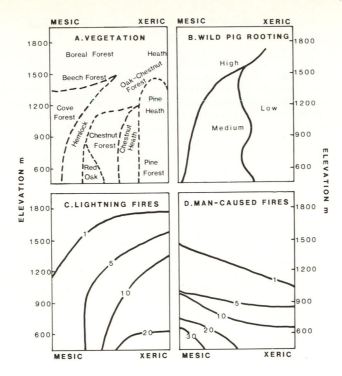

Fig. 8. Vegetation and disturbance gradients in the Great Smoky Mountains, USA: (a) from Whittaker 1956; (b) from Harmon 1981; (c) and (d) from Harmon, Bratton and White 1983).

These data appear to reject this hypothesis. However, is this altered susceptibility because of the environmental gradient, or the result of a disturbance gradient? Results from the Great Smoky Mountains (Figure 8) suggest that disturbances have gradients independent of vegetation patterns and of other disturbance gradients (Harmon, Bratton and White 1983). Bratton, Harmon and White (1982) documented the percentage of soil disturbance by wild pigs (*Sus scrofa*) This was found to be highest in the northern hardwoods and lower elevation successional hardwoods and ranged across both the moisture gradient and elevation gradient. The pig is an introduced species and hence this is an exogenous disturbance. The gradient for lightning fires (an endogenous disturbance) is greatest in the low elevation, xeric sites and diminishes in sites at higher elevation and more mesic sites (Harmon 1981). By comparison, fires originating from human causes are greatest in the low elevation mesic cove forests and diminish in drier and higher sites.

This is a fertile field for future research — we could find no specific study of degree of invasions across environmental gradients from the Australian literature. Our own unpublished data of matched vegetation types across a rainfall gradient in southwestern New South Wales suggest that the incidence of invasion is higher in sites with a higher rainfall. However, habitat modification is also more intense and has a longer history in these sites as well. The sites were selected to minimise the impact of current grazing but all had a history of domestic and feral grazing. Again, these results may reflect rejection of the disturbance and richness hypotheses rather than characteristics of the gradient.

CONCLUSIONS

There is no invasion of natural communities without disturbance. Where there has been successful invasion of natural communities by introduced species we contend that there has been subtle alteration of endogenous disturbance regimes. The principal characteristic of disturbance is the creation of spare resource. There is a trend to greater invasion with more prolonged, repeated or more intense disturbance. Rich communities are less susceptible to invasion. All plant structural formations are susceptible to invasion, although some are more likely to be disturbed and therefore more likely to be invaded, thereby illustrating an interactive effect. Communities are more susceptible to invasion at particular zones on an environmental gradient and different communities differ in their susceptibility along gradients; however, this too is related to disturbance gradients, independent of vegetation patterns.

Considering the success of individual plant and animal invaders (dealt with in depth elsewhere in this volume), the success of a plant invader may depend more on climate and other physical variables than on the susceptibility of the original plant community. The success of an animal invader may depend more on the plant community than on the susceptibility of the original animal community.

In general terms, the principal management policy which minimises invasion of conservation areas is to minimise disturbance of all kinds. Maintenance of a high level of species richness (one of the main conservation objectives) will also increase the community's resistance to invasion. However, there is an interaction between these objectives, although the maintenance of high species richness is often achieved as a result of a degree of disturbance that creates habitat mosaics (Fox 1984). A fine balance is then required between the degree and the type of disturbance required to maintain a high value for native species richness, and that which may result in successful invasion by introduced species. Such a balance can only be achieved if the objectives for each conservation area are clearly stated so that they can be assessed and ranked in terms of priority of efforts to exclude invasions (from different species). In the absence of the necessary information to make such decisions, we feel the available data indicate strongly that one should minimise disturbance as much as possible until such information becomes available.

REFERENCES

Abbott, I. (1980). The transition from mainland to island, illustrated by the flora and landbird fauna of headlands, peninsulas and islands near Albany, Western Australia. *Journal of the Royal Society of Western Australia 63*, 79–92.

Anderson, D. (ed.) (1977). Exotic species in Australia — their establishment and success. *Proceedings of the Ecological Society of Australia 10*, 1–186.

Aplin, T.E.H., Rhodes, L., and King, D.R. (1983a). A botanical survey of a rabbit study area, Cape Naturaliste, Australia. *Western Australia Herbarium Research Notes 0(9)*, 1–14.

Aplin, T.E.H., Rhodes, L., and King, D.R. (1983b). A botanical survey of a rabbit study area, Chidlow, Australia. *Western Australia Herbarium Research Notes 0(9)*, 15–26.

Baker, H.G. (1965). Characteristics and modes of origin of weeds. In *The Genetics of Colonizing Species* (eds H.G. Baker and G.L. Stebbins) pp. 147–172, Academic Press, London.

Braithwaite, R.W., Cockburn, A., and Lee, A.K. (1978). Resource partitioning by small mammals in lowland heath communities of south-eastern Australia. *Australian Journal of Ecology 3*, 423–445.

Bratton S.P., Harmon, M.E., and White, P.S. (1982). Rooting impacts of the European wild boar on the vegetation of Great Smoky Mountains National Park during a year of mast failure. *Castanea 47*, 230–242.

Elton, C.S. (1958). *The Ecology of Invasions by Animals and Plants,* Methuen, London.

Forcella, F., and Harvey, S.J. (1983). Eurasian weed infestation in western Montana in relation to vegetation and disturbance. *Madrono 30*, 102–109.

Fox, B.J. (1983). Mammal species diversity in Australian heathlands: the importance of pyric succession and habitat diversity. In *Mediterranean-type Ecosystems: The Role of Nutrients* (eds F.J. Kruger, D.T. Mitchell and J.U.M. Jarvis) pp. 473–489, Springer Verlag, Berlin.

Fox, B.J. (1984). Small scale patchiness and its influence on our perception of animal species' habitat requirements. In *Survey Methods for Nature Conservation*, Volume I (eds K. Myers, C.R. Margules and I. Musto) pp. 162–178, CSIRO, Melbourne.

Fox, B.J., and Fox, M.D. (1984). Small-mammal recolonisation of open-forest following sand mining. *Australian Journal of Ecology 9*, 241–252.

Fox, B.J., and Pople, A.R. (1984). Confirmation of interspecific competition between native and introduced mice. *Australian Journal of Ecology 9*, 323–334.

Harmon, M.E. (1981). Fire history of Great Smoky Mountains National Park 1940 — 1979. *Uplands Field Research Laboratory Research/Resource Management Report* No. 46.

Harmon, M.E., Bratton, S.P., and White, P.S. (1983). Disturbance and vegetation response in relation to environmental gradients in the Great Smoky Mountains. *Vegetatio 55*, 129–139.

Kitching, R.L., and Jones, R.E. (eds) (1981). *The Ecology of Pests*, CSIRO, Melbourne.

Macdonald, I.A.W. (1984). Is the fynbos biome especially susceptible to invasion by alien plants? — a re-analysis of available data. *South African Journal of Science 80*, 369–377.

Macdonald, I.A.W., and Jarman, M.L. (eds) (1984). Invasive alien organisms in the terrestrial ecosystems of the fynbos biome, South Africa. *South African National Scientific Programmes* Report No. 85.

Moore, R.M. (1959). Some ecological aspects of the weeds problem in Australia. *Proceedings of the IVth International Congress of Crop Protection*, Hamburg, Volume I, pp. 447–449.

Posamentier, H.G. (1976). Habitat requirements of small mammals in coastal heathlands of N.S.W. M.Sc. thesis, University of Sydney.

Simberloff, D. (1981). Community effects of introduced species. In *Biotic Crises in Ecological and Evolutionary Time* (ed. M.H. Nitecki) pp. 53–82, Academic Press, New York.

Westman, W.E. (1985). The concept of resilience. In *Resilience in Mediterranean Ecosystems* (ed. B. Dell) (in press), Dr W. Junk, The Hague.

Whittaker, R.H. (1956). Vegetation of the Great Smoky Mountains. *Ecological Monographs 26*, 1–80.

PHYSICAL CHARACTERISTICS OF SITES IN RELATION TO INVASIONS

D.E. Swincer[1]

Australia presents a unique opportunity to study biological invasions. Its land mass is large with a diversity of climate and habitats, and yet potential invaders inevitably must cross a surrounding ocean, which in most cases acts as an important barrier. With respect to insects and related groups, few species seem to have arrived prior to the 1960s other than those directly imported. The last two decades have been accompanied by an increase in the number of biological invasions by invertebrates with some of major agricultural importance. For instance, five aphids, two Hymenoptera, one *Trogoderma* species, two mite species, and two species of snail have all entered Australia since 1960, as well as some others of lower pest status. Once an organism has arrived, it encounters and must overcome two physical obstacles before becoming established in the new region. Firstly, it must be able to survive in the climate of the new region; and secondly, it must find a place in which to live — a habitat. These two factors are interconnected and at times inseparable because they may ameliorate each other. Further, if the invader is not only to survive in the new region but also to establish itself, it must be part of a 'propagule', i.e. the minimum number of individuals capable of founding a reproducing population. For the purposes of this chapter I shall assume this latter point to be the case, since I am considering only the physical characteristics of sites in relation to invasion.

ASSESSMENT OF THE INVADER

Undoubtedly many species have arrived in Australia and either been transient in nature or else they have survived and maintained only low population levels. Such new arrivals are seldom noticed or perhaps only recorded after they have been present for some time. Some biological invaders may have been recognised pests in some other country; some rapidly create a problem in their new location to make them noticed. For some invaders it may not be the primary site of invasion that is noticed first, but rather the subsequent area or areas invaded. Even if an invader is discovered in its earliest phase of invasion at its primary site it is an extremely costly exercise to monitor its continued invasion (see Navaratnam and Catley, this volume). Very few cases of the latter are recorded in the scientific literature.

Most biogeographers concerned with the colonisation of land masses depend largely on inferences drawn from lists of species and the differences that are found between contiguous areas. Only a few studies (for instance, Simberloff 1969; Fredericksson 1975) give detailed accounts of individual species colonising new areas and these usually deal with the special cases of islands. One of the few scientific disciplines in which invading species are monitored precisely involves the release of biological control agents. In such instances the invader is released deliberately but in a controlled way and generally under controlled conditions that are known to suit the released invader. Hall and Ehler (1979) showed on a world-wide basis that success of establishment of insects involved in classical biological control programs was significantly greater in areas of climatic certainty. A favourable climate over the invasion period seems to be paramount to success, at least for insects.

CLIMATE

Climate and habitat are the two major physical obstacles an invader must overcome to become established and to spread. Climate is a major determinant of the vegetation of a region; in turn, plants exert an influence on climate, and particularly microclimate. Both climate and vegetation interact to profoundly affect soil fertility and soil development. In developing my theme, I shall discuss briefly a few of the more important climatic

[1]   South Australian Department of Agriculture, G.P.O. Box 1671, Adelaide, S.A. 5001

factors, before discussing the role of habitat as an obstacle to invasive success. Several case histories of invasions will then be presented to illustrate the interaction of climate with habitat in influencing the success of these invasions.

Temperature

When we consider the temperature range of thousands of degrees known to occur in the universe, biological life exists within only a very small part of this range — from about $-200°$ to about $+100°C$. Even this comparatively small range is far too vast for most species which live in an extremely narrow band of temperatures. Generally, the upper limits of temperature are more critical to life processes than lower limits, even though most organisms tend to function more efficiently toward their upper limit. Temperature can be the limiting factor that spells success or failure for an invader, even though its importance is often overstated because organisms are so sensitive to it and because it is so easy to measure, compared with the measurement of some other physical factors.

Moisture

Rainfall, humidity, evaporation rate and the amount of surface water available are important components of moisture as a factor influencing invasive success. Because water is a physiological necessity, its availability is one of the main limiting physical attributes of terrestrial environments. The total amount of moisture available is important; so too is the annual distribution of that moisture. At a site having a mean annual rainfall of 625mm, about five years out of ten may have a yearly total below 625mm (and often as low as 325mm), whilst the other five years may show rainfall in excess of the mean of 625mm. This variability will be compounded by whether the rain falls in a restricted time of the year or evenly throughout the entire 12 month period. In general, rainfall tends to be unevenly distributed over the year in the tropics and subtropics, with wet and dry seasons extremely well defined. In temperate climates, on the other hand, rainfall is more evenly distributed, although there are many exceptions in both regions. Soil moisture has played an important role in the invasion by *Trifolium* and *Bromus* species in southern Australia (Tiver and Crocker 1951).

Interaction of temperature and moisture

The interaction between temperature and moisture may be more important than either factor acting singly. As with most interactions, both the relative and absolute values of temperature and moisture will be important. Thus temperature exerts a greater influence on organisms when moisture is limiting than when moisture is abundant. Similarly, moisture plays a critical role at the extremes of temperature.

On a continental scale, classification of climates of areas based on temperature and moisture interactions correspond well with zones for crop plants and for native vegetation (Odum 1982). Hence the interaction of temperature and moisture may be critical to the success or failure of a biological invader if by chance it enters at an inappropriate season of the year. It may well find that not only are climatic conditions unsuitable but that as well there is no food supply. A classic example is the invasion by *Melaleuca quinquenervia* in Florida where Myers (1983) found that if sites were moist to saturated for several months over the time of the year with appropriate temperatures optimum conditions for establishment occurred. Extended periods of dry soil or flooding reduced site suitability for invasion.

Wind

Wind can be an important factor in the establishment and subsequent invasion of a species. Particularly in the case of plant and insect invaders, wind may be a critical factor, as they may never reach a suitable habitat, or else, in the dispersal phase of an invasion, they may be unable to spread against the prevailing winds. In Australia where the prevailing winds are predominantly from west to east and to which most species enter naturally from the east or northeast, wind could play a major role in the establishment and dispersal of those classes of invaders which may require wind assistance or which may be unable to fly against prevailing winds, as, for instance, in the case of some insects. Similarly high level winds (jet streams) can account for dispersal of seeds; however, these also only apply from west to east in Australia. Their effectiveness in moving propagules between countries (e.g. Australia and New Zealand) has been reported by a number of workers (e.g. Close *et al.* 1978).

Light

To the human eye visible light lies in the range 3900 to 7600 A. Organisms on the earth's surface are exposed to an environment consisting of solar radiation and the flux in long-wave thermal radiation from nearby surfaces. Both of these contribute to the climatic environment of an organism although much of the solar radiation is attenuated as it passes through the earth's atmosphere. Passage of short-wave ultraviolet radiation (below 0.3μ) is terminated abruptly by the ozone layer; visible light is reduced uniformly in the atmosphere. Passage of infra-red radiation is also reduced by absorption in the atmosphere, such that on a clear day the radiant energy reaching the earth's surface is about 10 per cent ultra-violet, 45 per cent visible and 45 per cent infra-red (Reifsnyder and Lull 1965). Photosynthesis can continue even on cloudy days because light required for it is restricted to the visible range and is least reduced as it passes through dense cloud or water in the atmosphere. Light, or more exactly the lack of it, can restrict invasions of closed swards or dense canopy situations. Wesson and Wareing (1969) showed light to be a major factor in the germination of some buried seeds.

Nutrients and soil

These two physical factors are generally linked, other than in aquatic environments. The most important macronutrients are phosphorus, nitrogen, potassium, calcium and magnesium, of which the first two are probably in greatest demand. Hutchinson (1957) claimed that of all the elements required by living organisms, phosphorus is likely to be the most important ecologically. A deficiency of phosphorus is more likely to limit the production of any region of the earth's surface than is a deficiency of any other material except water. One has only to look at Australia's low agricultural potential without the use of added phosphate fertiliser to realise how important a nutrient phosphorus can be. The micronutrients (iron, copper, zinc, manganese, boron, silicon, molybdenum, chlorine, vanadium and cobalt) are also necessary for living systems but are required only in minute traces. Often an abundance of any one of these will lead to acute toxicity and the eventual death of living matter.

Soil is not only a mixture of nutrients, however, but is formed as the net product of the action of climate and biota, especially vegetation, on the parent material of the earth's surface. It is not only the habitat and environment of organisms but it in turn is produced by them as well.

HABITAT

Having entered a new territory a biological invader must seek out a favourable habitat. I use the term here simply to mean a place to live, as distinct from the more specialised term 'ecological niche'. Invaders are faced usually with totally new habitats and they must adapt to these new circumstances if they are to succeed at all. Usually invaders occupy disturbed habitats more easily and most habitats are disturbed to some extent in Australia, if only by fire.

Depending on one's definition, the addition of even one species to an area could class it as 'disturbed'. In the example of the pea aphid (*Acyrthosiphon pisum*), newly introduced to Australia, which transmits an introduced virus, it could be said that the aphid sees a pea or lupin crop as a disturbed habitat, but it is conjectural as to what degree the crop represents a disturbed habitat to the virus which happens to be the offending invader.

Habitat can be viewed from two dimensions, viz. those of heterogeneity in time and heterogeneity in space. These dimensions form the axes of Southwood's reproductive matrix, as shown in Table 1 (Southwood 1977). The options available to an organism may be expressed in a two-by-two matrix (Table 1) with 'now' and 'later' on the time axis, and 'here' and 'elsewhere' on the space axis. Each of these sets of conditions may be considered to offer a level of favourableness for reproduction which is expressed in terms of 'r', the mean intrinsic rate of increase that could be obtained under each set of time-space conditions. This is tempered somewhat by the expectancy value 'E', which represents the chances of surviving dormancy or migration and being able to find a suitable habitat in which to breed. In simple terms, it puts a value on the chance of being present under different circumstances. The final factor is a measure of variation, 'V', which represents the variance of the propitious nature of a habitat. The combination of these three matrices (r, E, V) gives the reproductive success rating of which there will be two values for each particular strategy. The range between the two values is a measure of the uncertainty of each strategy. It would seem, using Southwood's concepts, that a biological invader could be linked to two strategies represented by the reproductive success matrix. Initially, it should disperse (migrate) and breed, then follow this closely with a strategy of staying-put and breeding. This is in fact what some highly successful invaders adopt with an almost military precision of regrouping prior to advancing, followed by a period of consolidation, as for instance in the invasion of South Australia by the spotted alfalfa aphid (Wilson, Swincer and Walden 1981).

It should also be understood that availability of a suitable habitat in an area open for colonisation need not necessarily guarantee a successful colonisation or subsequent invasion. Ayal and Safriel (1983) found that a cerithiid species of the Sinai coastal region was capable both of immigrating and finding a suitable habitat in the Red Sea but was not found to colonise there; these authors thought that physico-chemical factors were involved in its inability to colonise.

DISCUSSION

The interactions and effects of physical factors can be gauged only by closer examination of individual case histories. For example, the Portuguese millipede (*Ommatoiulus moreletii*) has invaded areas of southeastern Australia very successfully without regard to climate. Baker (1975) found that temperature and moisture extremes were of no consequence to the millipede as long as the shelter of grass tussocks could be found. The millipede does not like to be exposed for long periods and will not invade open or cleared ground. The only limiting factor to successful invasion by this millipede seems to be the lack of suitable shelter.

The invasion of Australia in 1978 by the blue green aphid (*Acyrthosiphon kondoi*) was strictly related to climate, however, and in particular to temperature. The host range of this aphid is wide and did not at any stage limit its invasion. The spread of the aphid within South Australia was monitored from the time of its arrival in

TABLE 1. *Matrix illustrating reproductive options in time and space available to an invading organism (from Southwood 1977). See text for explanation of symbols.*

		Time	
		Now	Later
Space	Here	Ea (ra ± Va)	Eb (rb ± Vb)
	Elsewhere	Ec (Rc ± Vc)	Ed (Rd ± Vd)

October 1977 until it had covered all agricultural areas of the State by June 1978. It was found initially in a field of lucerne (*Medicago sativa*) at Loxton, but after this initial recording in October 1977 it was not found anywhere else in South Australia until April 1978. With hindsight, this was because of the high temperatures over summer. However, from April 1978 the blue green aphid took only 12 weeks during the cooler autumn and winter months to cover the entire agricultural areas of South Australia (Figure 1) (Swincer, unpublished data).

So far in this section I have discussed examples where habitat or climate may be the primary influence on an invader's success. In most cases, however, it seems to be the interaction of these physical factors which explains success or failure. The rabbit (*Oryctolagus cuniculus*) is perhaps amongst the most successful invaders of Australia, but by no means has it been able to colonise the entire continent; the reason for this seems to lie in the interaction between climate and habitat. The northern limits of the general distribution of the rabbit in Australia correspond roughly to the Tropic of Capricorn (Cooke 1977), although isolated populations may be found well to the north of this latitude. Cooke postulated that the most likely reason for this limited distribution is simply that in the tropics rabbits encounter severe reproductive difficulties. Both male and female rabbits show adaptations to an autumn-spring breeding season in direct response to the availability of green feed. Fertility of male rabbits is also influenced by decreasing day length, so that they become fertile prior to the onset of the plant growing season. These basic adaptations for efficient reproduction are suited to rabbits living in the winter-rainfall areas of southern Australia, but not to those in northern Australia where pasture growth occurs in summer when day temperatures are high and days are longer.

Rabbits are not confined only to those regions where rains occur mainly in winter, however. In the inland regions of Australia, rainfall is distributed erratically and pasture plants are adapted to respond opportunistically to rainfall in any season. Consequently, even in areas having a peak in rainfall in summer, some pasture growth may occur at those times of the year when it is cool enough for rabbits to breed. The only major habitat which rabbits do not appear to have colonised is the area where reliable summer rains support a pasture which does not respond opportunistically to unseasonal rains but instead has a regular period of growth in summer. Extensions of the rabbit's range into this northern area of unsuitability are found, but are associated with specific microhabitats. For instance, some rabbit colonies occur in granite outcrops where the effectiveness of unseasonal rains is enhanced by run-off from the rocks. An instance where habitat alone can influence dispersal is seen by the absence of rabbits from the black soil plains of southern Queensland, where the soils are unsuitable for burrowing; in this instance, climate (especially summer rainfall) plays no role.

Another recent invader that has probably been studied more intensively than most other in Australia is the spotted alfalfa aphid (*Therioaphis trifolii* fm. *maculata*). The spotted alfalfa aphid is indigenous to the Mediterranean region of Europe and Africa. It has invaded Mexico, United States of America, Canada and more recently, Australia and South Africa (Wilson, Swincer and Walden 1981).

Lucerne, or alfalfa (*Medicago sativa*) is the principal host of spotted alfalfa aphid, but the aphid is also known to infest other *Medicago* species, as well as species of the legume genera *Trifolium, Trigonella, Melilotus, Ononus, Astragalus, Onobrychis* and *Vicia* (Peters and Painter 1957; Bishop and Crockett 1961; Hille Ris Lambers and van den Bosch 1964; Carver 1978).

A large program was established by the South Australian Government to monitor the invasion of spotted alfalfa aphid over the State. The invasion of this aphid was potentially of immense economic importance to South Australia which was 700 000 ha of lucerne and a further 4.6×10^6 ha of lucerne-mixed pasture. Spotted alfalfa aphid can attack its host by causing defoliation, stunting, poor seed set and eventually plant death. Excess sugars excreted by the aphids as honeydew provides a medium for mould growth which facilitates secondary attack by pathogens.

The first record of the spotted alfalfa aphid in Australia was on 29 March 1977 at Gatton in Queensland. In the following month it was discovered in Victoria and New South Wales and on 10 May 1977 at Salisbury in South Australia (Wilson, Swincer and Walden 1981).

No information is available of the spread of this aphid in other countries or in other States of Australia. Information on the first sightings of spotted alfalfa aphid in South Australia was obtained from the following sources:

1. Sweep-net and stem samples taken at weekly intervals from 15 selected sites within a 200 km radius of Adelaide. Similar samples were also taken from a further 12 sites at distances greater than 200 km from Adelaide. Sweep-net samples were taken by walking through a lucerne paddock and taking 100 sweeps with an insect net 34 cm in diameter. Stem samples were taken by dividing the paddock up into ten equal bays and selecting randomly the stems from each bay. All samples were returned to the laboratory for examination.

2. Samples were also collected by 22 District Agronomists stationed in all the main agricultural areas of South Australia.

3. Samples were also sent in by farmers for identification (most farmers were aware of the imminent arrival of the aphid).

In this way approximately 200 samples per week were examined between May and November 1977. The number of samples was thereafter reduced to approximately 60 per week until May 1978, by which time all known susceptible *Medicago* stands were infested by spotted alfalfa aphids. The monitoring program was thus highly intensive and the exact spread and movement of spotted alfalfa aphid within South Australia's agricultural areas is known with considerable precision.

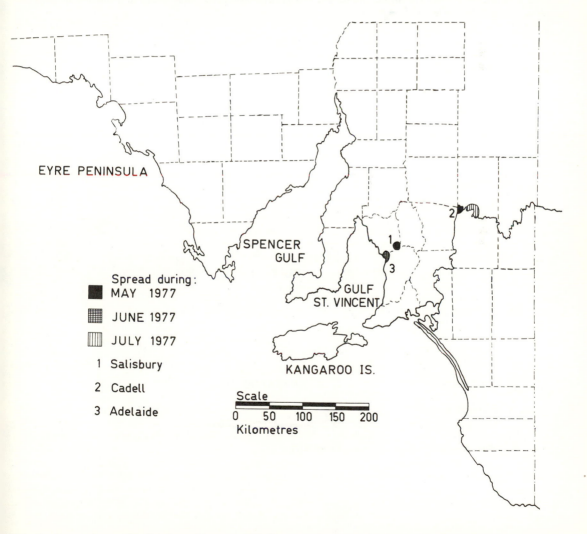

Fig. 1. Approximate distribution of lucerne (*Medicago sativa*) and susceptible annual *Medicago* spp. in the agricultural areas of South Australia. The shaded area was susceptible to invasion by the blue green aphid (*Acyrthosiphon kondoi*) between April and June 1978.

Results of this study show it to be a classical example of the interaction of temperature and micro-habitat in influencing the spread of a biological invader. Spotted alfalfa aphid was first discovered in South Australia on May 10 1977 in a small patch of irrigated lucerne on the Adelaide Plains (Figure 2). In the same month an infestation was discovered at Cadell on the River Murray in irrigated lucerne about 120 km north-east of Adelaide. Over the next 6 months the aphid spread. It always invaded irrigated lucerne in different areas of South Australia from the full length of the River Murray to the Adelaide Plains and to the southeastern region (Figures 2 and 3).

Two aspects stand out in this pattern of spread of spotted alfalfa aphid:

1. it spread over the cool months, even though the aphid prefers high temperatures;
2. no infestations were found other than in irrigated lucerne.

It seems that spotted alfalfa aphid was utilising a suitable microhabitat in irrigated lucerne at the time of otherwise unsuitable weather conditions to increase in numbers and continue its invasion. Irrigated lucerne stands are dense, relatively tall plant communities which offer substantial protection from external weather conditions, in stark contrast to dryland pastures which are short, sparse and exposed to extremes of weather and offer little or no protection to an insect.

Spotted alfalfa aphid expanded its territory subsequently until by April 1978 it had occupied all areas of South Australia containing susceptible host plants (Figures 4 and 5). Over this period, which includes the hot summer months, spotted alfalfa aphid had been able to invade all types of pastures, including lucerne on deep sands in southeastern South Australia where lucerne is often the only plant found and usually at very low densities (2 plants/m² or less).

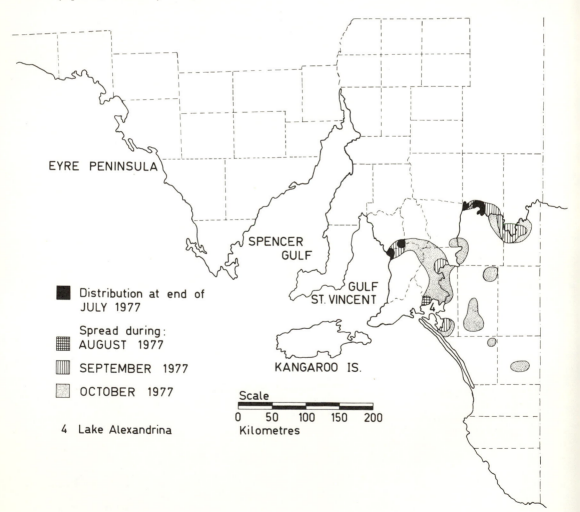

Fig. 2. Spread of spotted alfalfa aphid (*Therioaphis trifolii* fm. *maculata*) in the agricultural areas of South Australia from May to July 1977.

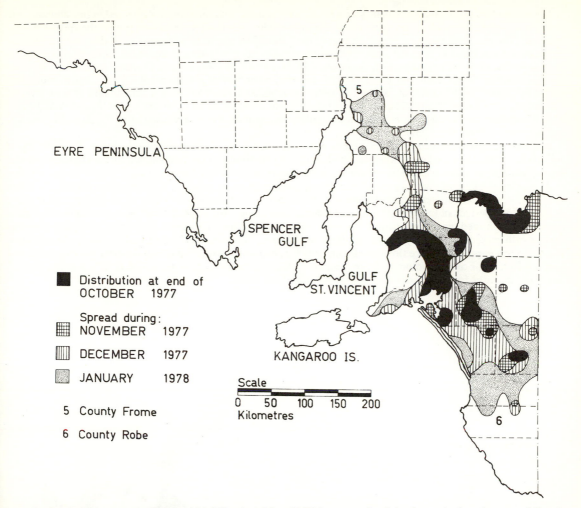

Fig. 3. Spread of spotted alfalfa aphid (*Therioaphis trifolii* fm. *maculata*) in the agricultural areas of South Australia from July to October 1977.

Spotted alfalfa aphid thus was an extremely successful invader not only of South Australia but of southeastern Australia generally. Perhaps the hallmark of such a successful invader was its ability to exploit a particular habitat to enable the aphid to survive unfavourable conditions and yet to still thrive and continue to invade new territory.

There are occasions where humans change habitats which then allow a successful biological invasion to occur. In southeastern South Australia, near Kalangadoo, very little plant life grew other than magnificant trees of red gum (*Eucalyptus camaldulensis*). A winter rainfall pattern coupled with a high water table made it too wet for grasses or annual herbs to grow successfully. In addition, low levels of soil fertility contributed to the lack of plant life. However, in the early part of this century, subterranean clover (*Trifolium subterraneum*) was introduced to the region. This deliberate introduction had a two-fold effect: firstly, it lowered the water-table of the area during the wet winter months; and secondly, after some time, because of the plant's ability to fix nitrogen symbiotically, soil fertility began to improve. These changes led to one of the most spectacular biological 'invasions' of introduced grasses to the area (Tiver and Crocker 1951). This invasion by *Bromus* has led to a remarkable increase in the productivity and consequently the intensity of human usage of the area.

CONCLUSIONS

In this chapter we have seen how different species of plant and animal require their own specialised set of conditions to make invasions possible. In most cases, a favourable climate appears to be important to success. However, as in the case of the Portuguese millipede, it is not necessarily critical. We have also seen how a highly successful invader, viz. the spotted alfalfa aphid, can ameliorate its own climate by making use of a micro-environment that will buffer it against unsuitable external conditions.

If we were to dissect each case history of a biological invasion, including those discussed in this chapter, one feature in common may be the importance of climatic certainty. Three examples (the rabbit, the spotted alfalfa aphid and the blue green aphid) show that, even though modifications to habitat were available (such as granite outcrops for the rabbit or irrigated lucerne stands for the spotted alfalfa aphid), the basic climatic criteria had to be met for the invasion to be possible. As previously mentioned, biological control agents are among the most studied of all invaders. Hall and Ehler (1979) reviewed examples of insects involved in classical biological control programs and found that, at least in terms of establishment, there was a statistically greater level of establishment in areas of climatic certainty. Establishment does not mean invasion, however, and in biological control programs very often the criterion for establishment simply means presence after the most climatically unfavourable period of the year.

Another common characteristic that stands out from considering these three case histories is the ability of successful biological invaders to tolerate a wide range of variability in climate and habitat. Extremes may not be optimal but the mid-range allows continued gain of territory with few losses.

The coastal fringe of southeastern Australia represents an ideal invasion site for many species. It has a relatively mild Mediterranean-type climate with no temperature extremes. Very few areas are covered in snow or ice for long periods of the year. From an invader's point of view the coastal fringe of Australia is like a giant bowl of growth medium maintained at relatively even temperatures. European settlement has contributed to that growth medium by supplying the nutrients in the form of agricultural crops and plantings. In addition, Australia has gaps in its native flora and fauna, which may allow invaders to penetrate these gaps and succeed (but see Fox and Fox, this volume). Even from an agricultural point of view we do not as yet have the range of pests and diseases found in other comparable regions of the world.

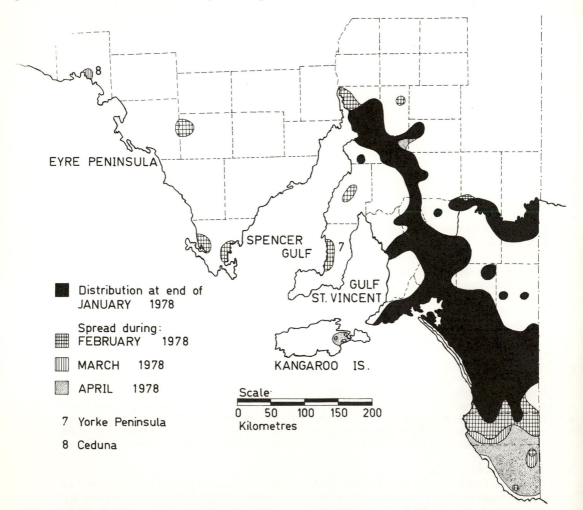

Fig. 4. Spread of spotted alfalfa aphid (*Therioaphis trifolii* fm. *maculata*) in the agricultural areas of South Australia from October to January 1978.

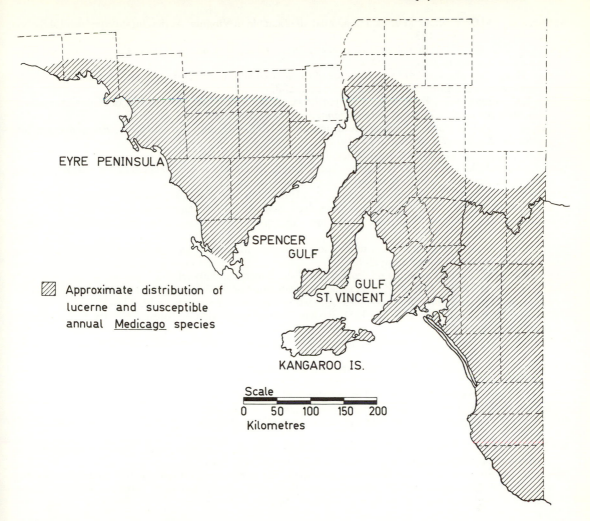

EYRE PENINSULA

SPENCER
GULF

☒ Approximate distribution of
   lucerne and susceptible
   annual <u>Medicago</u> species

GULF
ST. VINCENT

KANGAROO IS.

Scale
0   50   100   150   200
Kilometres

Fig. 5. Spread of spotted alfalfa aphid (*Therioaphis trifolii* fm. *maculata*) in the agricultural areas of South Australia from January to April 1978.

There is some evidence (Weir 1977) that natural systems are more highly adapted to cope with a biological invader. Browning (1977) claimed that it is unlikely that introduced species will invade unmodified areas of native rainforest, sclerophyll forest or shrubland. Browning says that no special effort need be expended to conserve the integrity of those native ecosystems against invasion by introduced species, except by preventing their modification by humans.

From the viewpoint of the invader there is some evidence to suggest that those species which on arrival in a system are found to have an array of options or strategies to adapt to that system, will succeed. This is the argument of a generalist versus a specialist, and it seems from the viewpoint of physical factors presented in this chapter that generalists are indeed superior invaders.

Physical factors such as have been discussed in this chapter may separately or interactively impede or prohibit the invasion of an species, but their importance is greatly reduced in the mild climatic zone of coastal southeastern Australia. Given that we can broadly group successful invaders as generalists, which are capable of tolerating broad ranges of physical factors, then it seems to me that Australia can only look forward to more 'successful' invasions by introduced species.

REFERENCES

Ayal, Y., and Safriel, U. (1983). Does a suitable habitat guarantee successful colonisation? *Journal of Biogeography 10*, 37–46.

Baker, G.H. (1975). The ecology and life history of the introduced millipede *Ommatoiulus moreletii* (Lucas, 1860) in South Australia. Ph.D. thesis, University of Adelaide.

Bishop, J.L., and Crockett, D. (1961). The spotted alfalfa aphid in Virginia. Agricultural Experimental Station Technical Bulletin No. 153.

Browning, T.O. (1977). Establishment and success of exotic animals in South Australia. *Proceedings of the Ecological Society of Australia 10*, 27–38.

Carver, M. (1978). The scientific nomenclature of the spotted alfalfa aphid (Homoptera : Aphididae). *Journal of the Australian Entomological Society 17*, 287–288.

Close, R.C., Moar, N.T., Tomlinson, A.I., and Lowe, A.D. (1978). Aerial dispersal of biological material from Australia to New Zealand. *International Journal of Biometeorology 22*, 2–19.

Cooke, B.D. (1977). Factors limiting the distribution of the wild rabbit in Australia. *Proceedings of the Ecological Society of Australia 10*, 113–120.

Fredricksson, S. (1975). *Surtsey*, John Wiley, New York.

Hall, R.W., and Ehler, L.E. (1979). Rate of establishment of natural enemies in classical biological control of arthropods. *Bulletin of the Entomological Society of America 25*, 280–282.

Hille Ris Lambers, D., and van den Bosch, R. (1964). On the genus *Therioaphis* Walker 1870, with descriptions of new species (Homoptera : Aphidae). *Zoologische Verhandelingen Leiden 68*, 1–47.

Hutchinson, G.E. (1957). *A Treatise in Limnology, Geography, Physics and Chemistry,* Vol. 1, John Wiley, New York.

Myers, R.L. (1983). Site susceptibility to invasion by the tree *Melaleuca quinquenervia* in southern Florida. *Journal of Applied Ecology 20*, 645–658.

Odum, E.P. (1982). *Fundamentals of Ecology*, 3rd Edn, Saunders, Philadelphia.

Peters, D.C., and Painter, R.H. (1957). A general classification of available small seeded legumes as hosts for three aphids of the yellow clover complex. *Journal of Economic Entomology 50*, 231–235.

Reifsnyder, W.E., and Lull, H.W. (1965). Radiant energy in relation to forests. USDA Forest Service Technical Bulletin No. 1344.

Simberloff, D.S. (1969). Experimental zoogeography of islands. A model for insular colonisation. *Ecology 50*, 296.

Southwood, T.R.E. (1977). Habitat, the template for ecological strategies. *Journal of Animal Ecology 46*, 337–365.

Tiver, N.S., and Crocker, R.L. (1951). The grasslands of southeast South Australia in relation to climate, soils and developmental history. *Journal of the British Grassland Society 6*, 29–80.

Weir, J.S. (1977). Exotics: past, present and future. *Proceedings of the Ecological Society of Australia 10*, 4–14.

Weeson, G., and Wareing, P.F. (1969). The role of light in the germination of naturally occurring populations of buried weed seeds. *Journal of Experimental Botany 20*, 402–413.

Wilson, C.G., Swincer, D.E., and Walden, K.J. (1981). The origins, distribution and host range of the spotted alfalfa aphid, *Therioaphis trifolii* (Monell) f. *maculata*, with a description of its spread in South Australia. *Journal of the Entomological Society of Southern Africa 44*, 331–341.

MANAGEMENT OF INVASIONS

With the increasing level of exchanges between Australia and other countries and an increased level of ecosystem disturbance within Australia, the rate of increase in the number of invading species may be increasing with time. Certainly, the number is not decreasing. Costs of some of these invasive species to the Australian community are high, whether they are expressed directly or indirectly. The economics of controlling some unintentional invasions may not always be beneficial but in a few documented instances the benefit/cost ratios are high, as with the control of serrated tussock described in the subsequent chapter. The benefit/cost ratios of some intentional planned invasions have also been high and very much to Australia's agricultural advantage, as for example the planned and deliberate manipulation of pastures in southern Australia to favour growth of the accidentally introduced Mediterranean annual *Trifolium subterraneum*. The second chapter in this section cautions us, however, about some of the long-term ecological consequences of a research program in northern Australia which nevertheless may have obvious short-term economic benefits.

If invasions are inevitable, how can we better manage them? Perhaps the most effective management of invasions is to exclude the propagule, as the Australian Quarantine Service attempts to do with full legislative authority. Once an organism is in the country and increases its population it then becomes the task of the land or water manager to so control the numbers of its propagules that the species no longer represents a substantial cost to the community. One of the cheapest ways to manage invasions is by the planned use of fire, as a further chapter in this section outlines for southwest Western Australia. Other forms of management of invasive species such as chemical control or the introduction of natural enemies have also limited populations of invading species in Australia, and usually cost-effectively. Much research remains to be done, however, to provide effective alternatives for the manager of biological invasions. Despite some successes, there is no place for complacency among the research community, either nationally or internationally, as several chapters make clear.

IMPACT ASSESSMENT OF BIOLOGICAL INVASIONS

B.A. Auld[1] and C.A. Tisdell[2]

Primary invasion of an area by an organism may occur at one or more sites or foci; we use the term 'invasion' to define this process and 'spread' to describe subsequent occupation of new areas. Invasion as we define it generally has little impact, but attempts by quarantine to prevent invasion of introduced organisms represent a major cost to society.

Many species of plants and animals which are now regarded as pests in Australia were introduced deliberately: grasses such as carpet grass (*Axonopus affinis*), Johnson grass (*Sorghum halepense*) and weeping love grass (*Eragrostis curvula*) were all introduced as fodder species; bitou bush (*Chrysanthemoides monilifera*) was introduced for dune stabilisation; and many other plants now regarded as weeds were introduced as ornamentals. The rabbit and the progenitors of the feral pig were also introduced deliberately. Even when they became naturalised many of these species were not regarded at first as being troublesome or potentially so. Usually only some time after initial introduction, when an organism has begun to increase its population markedly, spread and cause damage, is it regarded as an invader.

In this chapter we discuss the problems of impact assessment of weeds and feral animals as biological invaders to Australia, with particular emphasis on the grass serrated tussock (*Nassella trichotoma*) and the feral pig (*Sus scrofa*).

SPREAD OF ORGANISMS AND EXTERNALITIES

An externality occurs when action (or lack of it) by an individual in one place affects individuals elsewhere and the action is not subject to compensatory payment or agreement between the parties. A farmer introducing a plant to his property, which is capable of spreading to other properties where it is regarded as a weed, is creating an unfavourable externality if he or she fails to compensate the other property owners for their losses.

On this basis, a species which is spreading, or is capable of spreading, poses a threat to uninfested areas and as such represents a cost to the occupiers of those areas. Occupiers of uninfested areas may be involved in such practices as regular searching, modification of fencing, growing resistant varieties, restricting movement of stock or other farm produce. Thus the spread of harmful organisms or their potential spread, across boundaries between farms or any other private lands or between public and private land, takes the problem from the domain of the individual into the public arena. In economic terms, this is an externality effect or spillover as defined above. The faster the rate of spread and/or damage caused, the greater the rationale for governmental involvement.

The rate of plant spread can be influenced by the pattern of spread. Other things being equal, plants which spread as scattered colonies will have a faster spread rate than those that spread as an advancing annulus or front (Auld, Menz and Monaghan 1979). The tendency to spread as an advancing front or scattered colonies can be summarised by the frequency distribution of new infestations of a species in relation to distance from

---

[1] Agricultural Research and Veterinary Centre, N.S.W. Department of Agriculture, Orange, N.S.W. 2800
[2] Department of Economics, University of Newcastle, Newcastle, N.S.W. 2308

previous infestations. This is analogous to the method used to describe the progress of plant diseases (Gregory 1968). Distributions of this kind can be described by the family of exponential curves:

$$n = ke^{-sf(d)} \dots \dots \dots (1)$$

where 'n' is the number of new infestations,

'e' the exponential constant,

'f(d)' some function of distance, 'd', and

'k' and 's' are constants.

The double log form provides a convenient method of comparing curves:

$$\log n = c - s \log d \dots \dots \dots (2)$$

where 'c' is a constant.

The regression coefficient 's' which can be thought of as a 'spread gradient' (Auld, Hosking and McFadyen 1983) is a single measure which is a useful indicator of spread pattern. The lower the value of 's' the greater the tendency to spread as isolated colonies rather than as an advancing front. Values of 's' will also tend to be lower the longer the period of spread considered, as there is increasing opportunity for secondary spread.

Parthenium weed (*Parthenium hysterophorus*) has spread rapidly in Queensland over the last 12 years. The 's' value for parthenium weed over the period 1975–79 is 0.31, which is very low for such a short period, and its subsequent rate of spread has continued to increase (Figure 1). In contrast, tiger pear (*Opuntia aurantiaca*)

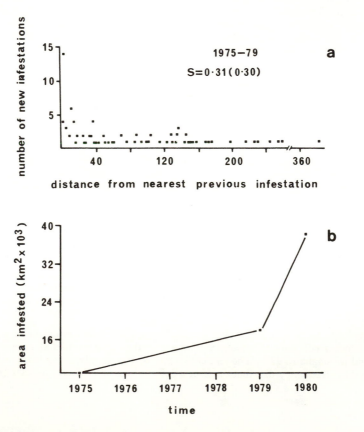

Fig. 1. Spread of *Parthenium hysterophorus* in Queensland. (a) Frequency distribution of new infestations during 1975–9 in relation to distance from infestations existing prior to 1975; 's' value (± s.e.) see eqn. (2). (b) Cumulative area infested (after Auld, Hosking and McFadyen 1983).

has spread at a decreasing rate in New South Wales in recent years (Figure 2). Its 's' value over the 20 year period 1938–58 is 0.56. In the period 1958–78, the 's' value increased to 0.85 so that a decreasing rate of spread can be anticipated (see Auld, Hosking and McFadyen (1983) for a fuller discussion of these examples).

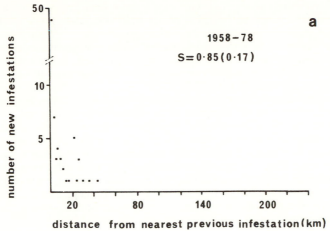

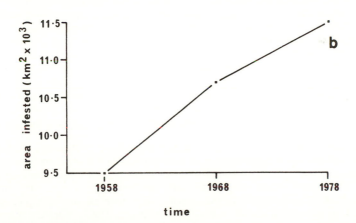

Fig. 2. Spread of *Opuntia aurantiaca* in New South Wales. (a) Frequency distribution of new infestations during 1958–78 in relation to distance from infestations existing prior to 1958; 's' value ($\pm$ s.e.) — see eqn. (2). (b) Cumulative area infested (after Auld, Hosking and McFadyen 1983).

The scatter of new infestations (Figures 1a and 2a) may affect the logistics of control or containment programs. Menz, Coote and Auld (1980) showed how both rate and pattern of spread could influence optimal control strategy. Furthermore, effective restriction of spread requires co-ordination of control tactics. It follows that a major cost of the impact of spreading organisms is, in many cases, in the provision of governmental bodies to control and restrict spread of organisms. The cost of maintaining a campaign to eradicate a single species, skeleton weed (*Chondrilla juncea*), in Western Australia, for instance, is currently estimated as greater than $0.4 m per year (F.D. Panetta, personal communication). Government response to spreading organisms is found in many ways — e.g. in noxious plant and animal legislation, in certification schemes, in direct intervention in the control of organisms, in grants and loans and in research and advisory work. For organisms with very high rates of spread (e.g. rusts), prevention of spread is usually impractical and apart from quarantine, other long-term approaches such as the breeding of resistant hosts must be adopted.

APPROACHES TO IMPACT ASSESSMENT

Assessment of the impact of many species is difficult because they may be useful in some areas or to some people and troublesome to others and moreover, as we have noted already, the status of species is not static with time. This applies particularly to plants, but as illustrated later may also be true for animals. For example, paspalum (*Paspalum dilatatum*) is a valuable pasture grass but also an important weed of citrus. Many orchardists spend up to $85/ha/yr over and above other weed control practices to control this species.

Difficulties can arise in identification of some organisms because of the lack of trained staff and visual aids, especially when a species is spreading unexpectedly into a new area. It may also be difficult to distinguish between density fluctuation of a population and actual spread of species. Moveover, many vertebrate pests conceal themselves and their presence is often surmised only from damage caused.

Even a species which is regarded universally as undesirable can present problems in assessing its impact, if it is widespread. Rarely can the entire area occupied be surveyed accurately for a species or the damage it causes.

Mail questionnaire surveys are sometimes used to provide a rather subjective assessment of the incidence and effect of spreading organisms. Questionnaires are usually sent either to local government bodies, or to special interest groups or to a random sample of the population. The response between a true random sample and interest groups may differ significantly (Auld 1971).

Tisdell (1982) surveyed by mail special interest groups (e.g. Pastures Protection Boards) and 'experts' in the field (such as district foresters and wildlife rangers) to obtain general information about the population levels of feral pigs and damage caused by them in Australia. This information was supplemented by reported results from limited surveys undertaken by others and other data to enable the costs of damage to be estimated. This approach had the advantage that a general picture was obtained quickly at a relatively low cost. It had the disadvantage that some strategic bias may have been introduced (e.g. by farming groups surveyed who wanted stronger governmental action against feral pigs) and the fact that some respondents may have had a faulty view of the number of feral pigs present and the damage caused by them. Feral pigs tend to be wary of humans and become more so if they are hunted. Unlike weeds they tend to avoid humans — they may, for example, seek shelter by day and adopt nocturnal habits.

Many introduced and native animals tend to avoid human contact and this makes it difficult to count their populations and monitor their movements. Indirect methods such as dung counts and inferences from harvest rates may have to be used in the field to improve population estimates. Aerial stock-taking of animals in relatively open country is used in inland Australia for instance to estimate populations of the red kangaroo (*Macropus rufus*) (Frith and Calaby 1969; Caughley and Grigg 1981, 1982). No doubt in inland parts of Australia aerial surveys could also be used to give relatively accurate counts of feral animals such as donkeys (*Equus asinus*) and brumbies (*E. caballus*). It needs to be remembered, however, that from the economic point of view it is only rational to improve our knowledge about the impact of an introduced pest up to the point where the expected extra benefit from the additional knowledge equals the extra cost of obtaining it (Tisdell 1983, 1984). Depending upon the circumstances, this utilitarian attitude may justify wide variation in the degree of accuracy of scientific information — near enough may not only be good enough, it may be best from this point of view!

Physical surveys are time consuming and costly. Usually some form of stratified sampling must be used unless the survey itself is to become a major project. It is important, however, to undertake physical surveys (and/or supplement these by experimental evidence) when the knowledge of respondents is likely to be poor or their answers biased. For example, whilst much of the damage done by feral pigs is obvious to landholders, damage caused by feral goats (*Capra hircus*) is less obvious, since their environmental effects cannot always be easily distinguished from those of domestic sheep (cf. Breckwoldt 1983). Farmers therefore may tend to underestimate the amount of damage done by feral goats relative to that caused by feral pigs. In the light of this it is probably not surprising that only one state, namely Western Australia, has declared the feral goat a noxious animal. In New South Wales, even though feral goats roam from national parks just as frequently as feral pigs and have similar estimated populations in many areas, the relative frequency of complaints about feral goats straying from national parks is much less than that for feral pigs (Tisdell 1982).

Inspectors with specific responsibilities for noxious plants or animals over limited areas are a fairly reliable source of information for proclaimed 'noxious' species. Their local knowledge can be incorporated into large-scale surveys (Auld 1969).

Given that one can obtain some primary data on extent of a spreading organism, subsequent impact assessment remains a formidable task.

ASSESSING THE IMPACT OF WEEDS

The vast majority of weeds in Australia are introduced. Robert Brown noted that by 1804, only 16 years after European settlement, many introduced plants had already begun to spread (Swarbrick 1984). In the broadest sense they became 'weeds' as soon as they were growing in situations where they were not wanted.

Weeds occur in both agricultural and non-agricultural areas such as national parks and urban bushland. Although a certain degree of 'contamination' may be tolerated in the latter situations, any introduced plant is usually regarded as a weed and many conventional weed control techniques are inappropriate. Use of herbicides is often impossible because of the range of susceptible plants in the native flora. Moreover, any technique which removes a weed without replacement with a desired species will almost certainly need to be repeated regularly because of reinvasion of the same or another weed. Thus the impact of weeds in these situations is either a continuing cost of removal of weeds into perpetuity or the cost of removal and replacement over a shorter period. This ignores the aesthetic cost of the presence of the weeds which is difficult to estimate since the invaded areas themselves are not marketed or priced.

Weeds of agriculture can be divided into weeds of crops and weeds of pasture or rangeland, although some species are a problem in both situations. If we regard agriculture as a money-making enterprise, we should tighten our definition of a weed in this context, to a plant whose presence results in a reduced economic output.

The major effect of weeds of crops is by direct competition for water, nutrients and light, resulting in reduced crop yield. There are several crop loss functions relating weed density to crop yield loss; the usual response is depicted in Figure 3. Commercial firms marketing herbicides and agricultural advisors commonly describe economic thresholds of weed density below which it is uneconomic to control a weed species. Yet there is no 'threshold' in the sense of a definite step in crop loss response but rather a steep, smooth curve which makes assessing critical densities very difficult, especially as the shape of the curve is affected by crop sowing time, crop density and other agronomic factors. Additionally, whilst say 95% control of a weed species in a crop might be regarded as a successful result, the species needs only a modest reproductive capacity to reinfest to the original density in the following year from the 5% residual population (without allowing for buried dormant seeds). Thus the cost of 'control' becomes a continuing non-decreasing cost.

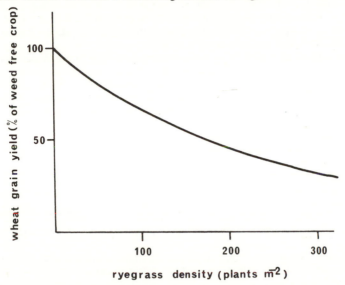

Fig. 3. Typical crop loss/weed density relationship. Example: the weed annual ryegrass (*Lolium rigidum*), and the crop, wheat (after Medd, Auld and Kemp 1981).

Weeds of pasture may cause economic loss through direct effects on grazing animals or farm produce and, more commonly, through competition with pasture plants. Thus the assessment of the economic effect of weeds involves a calculation of the monetary value of pasture. Pasture value varies rather more than crop value, as its value changes with its supply (a function of day-by-day growth rate) and the demand for it (i.e. grazing animal numbers, their size and condition) (Auld, Menz and Medd 1979). A unit of pasture in a prime lamb enterprise at Orange (Figure 4) has a higher value in winter than in spring. Thus effects of weed competition are more serious in winter than the same degree of competition in spring. Note also that the pattern of demand will change with a change in management strategies, e.g. changing lambing dates and/or sale dates. This in turn will affect pasture value and, consequently, the impact of weeds.

In addition to this kind of estimation some allowance should be made for any useful attributes of the species such as grazing value in droughts (e.g. *Chondrilla juncea*), a source of honey (e.g. *Echium plantagineum*) or other food (e.g. *Rubus fruticosus*) or for soil erosion control (e.g. *Eragrostis curvula*).

In the case of a weed of perennial pasture with no useful attributes, an analysis of its effects is more tractable. An extensive study of the control and economics of control has been made of one weed of perennial pastures, viz. serrated tussock (*Nassella trichotoma*) (Campbell 1977, 1982; Vere and Campbell 1979). In the following section we examine the impact of this weed.

SERRATED TUSSOCK (*NASSELLA TRICHOTOMA*)

Invasion and spread

A native of South America, the species was first identified in Australia from specimens collected at Yass, New South Wales, in 1935, but it was apparently introduced much earlier (Campbell 1982). It was recorded subsequently in Victoria in 1954 and in Tasmania in 1956 (Parsons 1973).

The species is propagated mainly by wind-borne panicles of seeds in late summer. If unchecked it becomes dominant in temperate grassland on which sheep are grazed. In New South Wales a total of 680,000 ha were infested by 1975 (Campbell 1977) and the species has continued to spread in some areas of the Central and Southern Tablelands of that State. Although principally a weed of agriculture it also occurs in national parks.

Assessing the impact of serrated tussock on agricultural production in New South Wales

The area occupied by serrated tussock at three infestation levels was assessed from a mail survey questionnaire to local government weed inspectors and Department of Agriculture agronomists by Campbell (1977). There were 71,200 ha of dense infestation, 147,100 ha of moderate infestation and 461,700 ha of light infestation.

Unimproved pastures of native grasses in the Central and Southern Tablelands have a carrying capacity of about 2 dry sheep equivalents (d.s.e.) per hectare. Pastures which have been partially improved at some time by the application of superphosphate and sowing of subterranean clover (*Trifolium subterraneum*), the majority of the area, can support from 3 to 5 d.s.e./ha. If a totally improved pasture (including the perennial grass, phalaris, *Phalaris aquatica*) were sown in the infested areas the land would be capable of carrying 7 to 15 d.s.e./ha. Thus the impact of serrated tussock can be measured in terms of the potential production loss as well as its reduction of actual production.

Dense infestations of serrated tussock have a carrying capacity of 0.25 to 0.5 d.s.e./ha whilst moderate infestations reduce carrying capacity by about 1 d.s.e./ha. Light infestations do not have a measurable effect on carrying capacity (M.H. Campbell, personal communication).

The total actual loss in production caused by serrated tussock in New South Wales is, conservatively, of the order of 260,000 d.s.e./yr [(2 − 0.375) × 71,200) + 147,100]. If we assume that the net value per d.s.e. in wool is 5 kg/yr and the price for wool is \$3.50/kg, the total monetary loss to the New South Wales grazing industry caused by serrated tussock is about \$4.5 million/yr. Note that in addition to this cost is the cost of local government programs on tussock control and research and advisory programs of the Department of Agriculture.

The presence of serrated tussock requires greater expenditure on herbicide (+ \$10–15/ha) than if the same improved pasture were established on native/naturalised pasture. Once established, an improved pasture which includes a perennial grass (e.g. *Phalaris aquatica*) is relatively immune from reinvasion.

Vere and Campbell (1979) estimated the annual potential loss in production caused by serrated tussock (compared with improved pasture) as \$11.8 million. The benefit:cost ratio for controlling the weed over a 20 year period was 1.7:1 and the internal rate of return was about 25%.

Auld, Vere and Coote (1982) simulated control policy options for government in a limited specific area (36 km × 28 km) in the Central Tablelands of New South Wales where serrated tussock is still spreading. The options included:

1. to annually control light infestations only, by spraying herbicide — a 'containment' approach;
2. to control moderate and heavy infestations by pasture improvement over a 10 year period;
3. the combination of options 1 and 2.

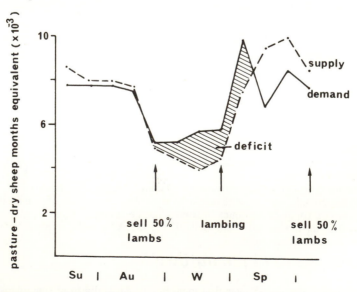

Fig. 4. Pasture supply and demand for a prime lamb enterprise at Orange, New South Wales (after Auld, Menz and Medd 1979).

They compared the outcome of adopting each of these policies projected into perpetuity in terms of cost and returns. Untreated areas of the weed were allowed to continue to spread, using a model of plant spread (Auld and Coote 1980) and assessment was by discounted cash flow analysis (Table 1).

TABLE 1. *Investment criteria for three policies to control* Nassella trichotoma *in one study area (After Auld, Vere and Coote 1982).*

Policy (see text)	1	2	3
Cost ($ $\times$ 10^6) (10% discount)	3.19	0.91	0.85
Net Returns ($ $\times$ 10^6) (10% discount)	-3.19	$+0.66$	$+0.61$
First year expenditure ($ $\times$ 10^3)	27	141	167
Benefit/Cost	—	1.73:1	1.72:1
Internal Rates of Return (%)	—	19.3	19.2

The results of this study showed that although the containment approach appeared attractive because of its low annual cost, it was the most expensive option in the long term. This was because no returns accrue from treating light infestations, reinvasion from heavy infestations continues indefinitely and the opportunity costs of existing heavy infestations remain. There was little difference in the other two options in terms of benefit:cost ratio and internal rates of return on invested funds. Hence the importance of treating the heavy and medium infestations was emphasised.

THE FERAL PIG (*SUS SCROFA*)

Invasion and spread

Feral pigs became established in Australia not long after the first Europeans settled in 1788. Domestic pigs came with the First Fleet and with subsequent shipping arrivals. The practice of allowing domestic pigs to roam soon resulted in the establishment of feral colonies. By 1795, pigs were a problem in Sydney Cove and orders were issued that they could be shot if they trespassed on private property (Pullar 1953).

The introduction of the feral pig to Australia was not deliberate. It was an incidental product of the introduction of domestic pigs and the initial spread of the feral pig was also a by-product. However, in recent years, there have been incidences of the deliberate introduction or reintroduction of feral pigs, in particular localities, mainly by amateur hunters (Tisdell 1982). Sometimes amateur hunters release domestic boars in an attempt to upgrade feral stock, or release pigs in new areas to have a stock of feral pigs close to hand. On rare occasions individual farmers have introduced feral pigs to a new locality in the hope of benefiting commercially, e.g. by the sale of hunting rights and holiday accommodation (Tisdell 1982).

It might be noted that the European wild boar was not introduced to Australia for hunting purposes but several species of deer were brought in during the last century, for example, by acclimatisation societies such as the Victorian Acclimatisation Society (Frith, 1973, Chapter 3).

Feral pigs occur widely in Australia and populations in some regions are obviously separated by natural barriers from those in other regions. The feral pig population of Kangaroo Island off the coast of South Australia has no contact, for example, with that on the mainland because of the sea barrier, and the feral pig population in southwest Western Australia has no contact with that in New South Wales because of the arid land barrier imposed by the Nullabor Plain. Feral pigs in Australia may live in a number of separated enclaves, the borders of which may alter with weather variations. Nevertheless, it would seem likely that some enclaves, for example, those in the Murray-Darling catchment area, are very large. To date, however, there appear to be no scientific data about such enclaves and there are few scientific data for Australia on the movements of feral pigs, and especially on their movement from one region to another.

There is likely to be some variation in the composition of feral pig stock in different enclaves. The domestic stock from which feral pigs are derived may be slightly different in different areas. In the Northern Territory, for example, a substantial number of pigs were imported from Timor in 1827 and these formed the nucleus of feral pig stock there. Once again, in-depth scientific evidence is lacking on the genetic homogeneity (or its lack) of feral pig stocks in Australia.

Whilst the feral pig is capable of colonising new areas without human aid and probably has spread to some regions of Australia on its own accord, Europeans have been the prime agent in its initial establishment and spread.

Assessing the impact of the feral pig

The impact of the feral pig in Australia is varied. It has impacts on agriculture, forests, native wildlife and natural ecosystems. These effects are adverse on the whole, but the feral pig has benefits for recreational hunting and for a limited amount of commercial use. The costs and benefits of the feral pig in Australia have been considered in detail elsewhere (Tisdell 1982).

The feral pig causes considerable damage to grain crops in Australia, especially wheat. The sheep and cattle industries, but particularly the former, register substantial losses on account of its presence, for example, because of lamb predation, spreading of diseases, competition for food, damage to watering points. Damage occurs also in some other agricultural industries, for instance, in sugar cane. Losses of around $70 m per year to the agricultural sector seem probable. In assessing the impact of the feral pig there is also a need to take into account its possible role in the spread of any introduced disease.

The impact of the feral pig on Australian forests is more uncertain. In some instances the feral pig may have a beneficial effect in providing improved seed beds for a few tree species of value but, except in the subtropical wet areas of northern Queensland, most foresters believe that its presence is adverse but of little consequence for forestry. In northern Queensland the feral pig is reputed to spread and facilitate attacks on trees of fungal dieback caused by *Phytophthora cinnamomi*, to add to erosion problems, to 'undermine' trees, thereby causing them to fall in wet weather, and also to have an adverse impact on native flora and fauna. It is believed to cause significant commercial loss to the forest industry in this area. More scientific evidence is required about the impact of the feral pig on Australian forestry systems.

Whilst feral pigs damage native flora and fauna and destroy habitats their effects have not been studied systematically and quantified. Some intensive ecological study of the subject is warranted. However, even if these effects are quantified, it is not a straightforward matter to express them in dollars and cents. The services of wildlife, unlike agricultural and forest products, are not marketed and priced (or sufficiently so) for us to easily impute monetary values to their loss. Furthermore, public attitudes to the value of particular forms of wildlife sometimes alter over time (consider here changing attitudes to the dingo) and this adds to the valuation problem.

A further complication in a cost-benefit analysis of the feral pig in Australia is that its presence is beneficial to some groups. It is an important resource for amateur hunting. Indeed, it is the most important game animal in Australia and a total annual value of $30–35 m (see Tisdell, 1982, Chapter 3) can reasonably by imputed to it for this purpose. Whilst this benefit does not offset the $70-m-plus annual loss to agriculture, forestry and native wildlife, it needs to be taken into account.

The feral pig is now also harvested commercially in Queensland for export as game meat. The industry is small as yet but an economic allowance needs to be made for the benefit of the feral pig as an input to this industry (Tisdell 1982, Chapter 5). On a limited scale, some farmers also obtain benefits from the sale of rights for hunting wild pigs.

Feral pigs may also provide a useful genetic reserve for the development of domestic pigs in the future. Thus, whilst it seems that the feral pig is a liability on balance at average population levels prevailing in Australia, this does not mean that it is economic or desirable to eliminate it (cf. Tisdell 1979). However, in some cases it is undoubtedly economic to control its population although this is complicated by its mobility.

Mobility of the feral pig and consequences for its control

The mobility of a species is not only important ecologically for its survival (Andrewartha and Birch 1954) but also from an economic standpoint. The greater the mobility of a pest species the less economic it is for an individual landholder to control its population. The mobility of the feral pig reduces the willingness of individual farmers to control its population because of spillovers — other farmers may in large measure benefit from the control effort by an individual farmer and pigs destroyed on a property may soon be replaced by pigs moving from elsewhere. Individual farmers may appropriate only a small fraction of the benefits from their control of feral pigs.

Daily movements by feral pigs from bedding grounds to food, such as grain, of up to 10 km (one way) have been widely reported but there has been little mapping of the movements of feral pigs in Australia. The Australian Standing Committee on Agriculture reported that under normal conditions, adult male feral pigs have a home range of 10–50 km^2, dry sows a range of 5–20 km^2 and lactating sows a range of 5 km^2. Thus these ranges may encompass several properties, and the ranges of different pigs may overlap.

The home range of the feral pig is not fixed, however, in its location. Under stress, pigs migrate and disperse considerable distances. Giles (undated) has reported that feral pigs have been known to migrate 20 km in 48 hours when suffering from food shortages. Migrations by feral pigs of 100–200 km/yr are widely reported overseas (Sludskii 1956; Heptner, Nasimovic and Bannikov 1966; Barrett 1978) and regular seasonal migrations (100–150 km one way) are common. Hence, under suitable conditions, feral pigs can easily extend their range by 50 km per year and a 100 km extension per year is quite possible. In Australia, the feral pig has colonised most areas that are environmentally suitable for it — the main problem is no longer the extension of its range but its recolonisation or reinvasion of areas after its numbers have been controlled in them.

Movement patterns of feral pigs reinforce the need for co-operative action by landholders in controlling feral pigs (Hone, O'Grady and Pedersen 1980; Tisdell, 1982, p.372). Depending upon patterns of movement, different control procedures may be called for. In order to improve control procedures much more work is needed in Australia to map patterns of movement of feral pigs, to determine more precisely factors influencing such movements, and to specify any natural limits or barriers to such movements.

As in the case of the feral pig, movement patterns of other introduced vertebrate pests in Australian agriculture such as the rabbit (*Oryctolagus cuniculus*), the fox (*Vulpes vulpes*) and the feral goat (*Capra hircus*) complicate the assessment of their impact. But it is important to study such movements in order to improve control measures. Studies of the territoriality and social behaviour of the rabbit (factors which influence its movement) have proven to be very useful in this regard, for example in suggesting appropriate seasons and locations in which rabbit control measures (such as poisoning and the ripping of warrens) are likely to be most effective (Saunders and Kennedy 1981; Breckwoldt 1983). No in-depth study has been completed of similar factors influencing movements of feral pigs and goats in Australia.

CONCLUDING REMARKS

The feral pig and many vertebrate pests differ from serrated tussock and other weeds in their ability to make independent and rational movement and to spread in and out of areas over relatively short periods. Thus the assessment of impact of such pests is extremely difficult. Moreover, even if the feral pig were eliminated from Australia there is a high probability of its 'reinvasion' as a result of the escape of domestic pigs. This is also true for many other feral animals such as goats, horses, donkeys and cattle. In contrast, many weeds pose particular problems because of long-lived propagules, particularly dormant seeds, in soil.

The presence of the feral pig makes it easier for other introduced biota to spread in Australia (e.g. foot-and-mouth disease). In this respect some weeds are similar in that they are hosts for parasites and pathogens of useful plants. Given the uncertainties of the likely introduction of biota, this further adds to the difficulty of impact assessment.

The complex ramification of effects of introduced organisms are difficult to cost accurately. Fischer (1968), Power and Harris (1973), Feder and Regev (1975) and Bradbury and Loasby (1977) all discuss further issues which we have not covered. However, the estimates of the effect of the two examples discussed here indicate the overall magnitude of the economic costs of introduced pests in Australia.

A common complication in impact assessment is, as we noted early in this chapter, that the status of species is static neither in space nor time. The status of species especially changes when the species begin to spread to areas where they are not wanted.

The economic impact of spreading organisms is closely linked with their population changes, their rates and patterns of spread, and the consequent externality or spillover effects. It is also this dynamic behaviour which, in itself, makes impact assessment difficult.

REFERENCES

Andrewartha, H., and Birch, L.C. (1954). *The Distribution and Abundance of Animals*, University of Chicago Press, Chicago.

Auld, B.A. (1969). The distribution of *Eupatorium adenophorum* Spreng. on the far north coast of New South Wales. *Journal and Proceedings of the Royal Society of New South Wales 102*, 159–161.

Auld, B.A. (1971). Survey of weed problems on the far north coast of New South Wales. *Tropical Grasslands 5*, 27–30.

Auld, B.A., and Coote, B.G. (1980). A model of a spreading plant population. *Oikos 34*, 287–292.

Auld, B.A., Hosking, J., and McFadyen, R.E. (1983). An analysis of the spread of tiger pear and parthenium weed in Australia. *Australian Weeds 2*, 56–60.

Auld, B.A., Menz, K.M., and Medd, R.W. (1979). A bioeconomic model of weeds in pastures. *Agro-Ecosystems 5*, 69–84.

Auld, B.A., Menz, K.M., and Monaghan, N.M. (1979). Dynamics of weed spread: implications for policies of public control. *Protection Ecology 1*, 141–148.

Auld, B.A., Vere, D.T., and Coote, B.G. (1982). Evaluation of control policies for the grassland weed, *Nassella trichotoma*, in south-east Australia. *Protection Ecology 4*, 331–338.

Barrett, R.H. (1978). The feral hog on the Dye Creek Ranch, California. *Hilgardia 46*, 283–335.

Bradbury, F.R., and Loasby, B.J. (1977). Cost benefit analysis and investment appraisals in relation to pest control measures. *Pesticide Science 8*, 366–376.

Breckwoldt, R. (1983). *Wildlife in the Home Paddock: Nature Conservation for Australian Farmers*, Angus and Robertson, Sydney.

Campbell, M.H. (1977). Assessing the area and distribution of serrated tussock (*Nassella trichotoma*), St. John's wort (*Hypericum perforatum* var. *angustifolium*) and sifton bush (*Cassinia arcuata*) in New South Wales. New South Wales Department of Agriculture Technical Bulletin No. 18.

Campbell, M.H. (1982). The biology of Australian weeds. 9. *Nassella trichotoma* (Nees) Arech. *Journal of the Australian Institute of Agricultural Science 48*, 76–84.

Caughley, G., and Grigg, G. (1981). Surveys of the distribution and density of kangaroos in the pastoral zones of South Australia, and the feasibility of aerial survey in large and remote areas. *Australian Wildlife Research 8*, 1–11.

Caughley, G., and Grigg, G. (1982). Numbers and distribution of kangaroos in the Queensland pastoral zone. *Australian Wildlife Research 9*, 365–372.

Feder, C., and Regev, V. (1975). Biological interactions and environmental effects in the economics of pest control. *Journal of Environmental Economics and Management 2*, 75–91.

Fischer, L.A. (1968). Some economic aspects of pest control in agriculture. *Canadian Journal of Agricultural Economics 16*, 90–99.

Frith, H.J. (1973). *Wildlife Conservation*, Angus and Robertson, Sydney.

Frith, H.J., and Calaby, J.H. (1969). *Kangaroos*, Cheshire, Melbourne.

Giles, J.R. (undated). 'The ecology of the feral pig in New South Wales. II. The dynamics of a colony in the Macquarie Marshes, 1971–75'. Noxious and Feral Animal Research Centre, New South Wales Department of Agriculture, Glenfield, (roneoed).

Gregory, P.H. (1968). Interpreting plant disease dispersal gradients. *Annual Review of Phytopathology 6*, 189–212.

Heptner, V.G., Nasimovic, A.A., and Bannikov, A.G. (1966). *Die Saugetiere der Sowjetunion*, Vol. I, Gustav Fischer, Jena.

Hone, J., O'Grady, J., and Pedersen, H. (1980). *Decisions on the Control of Feral Pig Damage*, Agriculture Bulletin No. 5, New South Wales Department of Agriculture, Sydney.

Medd, R.W., Auld, B.A., and Kemp, D.R. (1981). Competitive interactions between wheat and ryegrass. *Proceedings of the 6th Australian Weeds Conference, Broadbeach 1*, 39–43.

Menz, K.M., Coote, B.G., and Auld, B.A. (1980). Spatial aspects of weed control. *Agricultural Systems 6*, 67–75.

Parsons, W.T. (1973). *Noxious Weeds of Victoria*, Inkata Press, Melbourne.

Power, A.P., and Harris, S.A. (1973). A cost benefit evaluation of alternative control policies for foot and mouth disease in Great Britain. *Journal of Agricultural Economics 24*, 573–600.

Pullar, E.M. (1953). The wild (feral) pigs of Australia: their origin, distribution and economic importance. *Memoirs of the National Museum, Victoria 18*, 7–23.

Saunders, G., and Kennedy, D. (1981). Rabbit control on small holdings. *Agricultural Gazette of New South Wales 92*, 30–32.

Sludskii, A.A. (1956). *The Wild Boar: Its Ecology and Economic Importance*, Izadatel, Alma-Ata. (Translation by P. Aukland, CSIRO, Melbourne, 1974).

Swarbrick, J.T. (1984). Weeds of Sydney Town, 1802–04. *Australian Weeds 3*, 42.

Tisdell, C.A. (1979). Wildlife: a national asset or pest to be managed?. In *Environmental Economics*, pp. 79–87, Department of Science and Environment, Australian Government Publishing Service, Canberra.

Tisdell, C.A. (1982). *Wild Pigs: Environmental Pest or Economic Resource?* Pergamon Press, Sydney.

Tisdell, C.A. (1983). Application of cost-benefit analysis with particular reference to biological resources. In *Economic and Environment Policy: The Role of Cost-Benefit Analysis*, pp. 65–70, Department of Home Affairs and Environment, Australian Government Publishing Service, Canberra.

Tisdell, C.A. (1984). Cost-benefit analysis, the environment and information constraints in LDCs. *Information Economics and Policy*, in press.

Vere, D.T., and Campbell, M.H. (1979). Estimating the economic impact of serrated tussock (*Nassella trichotoma*) in New South Wales. *Journal of the Australian Institute of Agricultural Science 45*, 35–43.

PLANNED INVASIONS OF AUSTRALIAN TROPICAL SAVANNAS

J.J. Mott[1]

Most of the ecological literature concerned with the invasion of introduced plants into natural communities has assumed that the invading species would be 'weedy' and be deleterious to either the stability or the productivity of the existing ecosystem (e.g. Baker 1974). Because of this assumption, much of the ecological information available is oriented towards either restricting the introduction of new material or minimising its effect on the natural vegetation. However, this philosophy ignores the important subject of pastoral utilisation. Many pastures of temperate regions are subclimax systems, dominated either by invasive native or introduced species, e.g. the perennial ryegrass pastures of Europe, the pastures of exotic annuals in California, and the introduced grass/clover pastures of southern Australia (Davies 1960; Baker 1978). Indeed, in many cases the attributes outlined as being necessary for a desirable pasture species parallel those put forward by Baker (1974) as being ideal characteristics for a weed.

With an acceptance that introduced plant material could yield potentially valuable pastures, the history of planned introductions to northern Australia has been a long one. Active introduction of material appears to have begun in the 1880s. Eyles and Cameron (1985) cite information showing that by 1915 some 117,000 ha of artificially sown pastures existed in Queensland. Many of these pastures were in the wetter areas and based on introduced grasses, but accidental introductions of the legume Townsville stylo (*Stylosanthes humilis*) and buffel grass (*Cenchrus ciliaris*) were reported as being well established in northern regions. Sporadic introduction of new material continued until the early 1950s. Following this period, a major effort was put into all aspects of the agronomy of introduced pastures, with emphasis not only on the development of newly introduced species by plant introduction and breeding, but also on determining their establishment and management requirements.

In this chapter I do not propose to review the extensive experimental literature on number and type of plant introductions into northern Australia, nor to evaluate the large amount of experimental work on management techniques used to introduce and establish the material into native savanna pastures of northern Australia. Rather the chapter addresses both the philosophy behind these planned introductions of invasive material and attempts to evaluate the constraints operating both on the introduced material and the animal production systems incorporating both introduced species and the native grasslands.

GRAZING IN NATIVE SAVANNA LANDS

The main vegetation communities I shall consider are the Monsoon, Tropical and Subtropical Tallgrass lands (Mott *et al*. 1985) (Figure 1). These lands form an arc across northern Australia, and extend down the east coast to the Queensland border. The three communities are broadly confined to a region with more than 650 mm annual rainfall, which falls predominantly in the warm summer period. These subhumid savannas have a dense ground stratum of graminoids with a variable overstorey of trees usually dominated by eucalypts. In the eastern tropics and subtropics, black speargrass (*Heteropogon contortus*) is dominant in the dense disclimax sward, whilst in the northern zone kangaroo grass (*Themeda australis*) dominates pastures.

Forage production in these savanna regions is distinctly seasonal (Figure 2). When the protein content of the forage falls below 7%, cattle are increasingly unable to select a diet which is above metabolic maintenance level and they lose weight (Milford and Haydock 1965). Thus animal production on these pastures of low quality requires low stocking rates to enable selective grazing of the most nutritional forage. With this constraint, stocking rates vary from one animal to 5 hectares in better quality pastures of southeastern

---

[1] CSIRO, Division of Tropical Crops and Pastures, Cunningham Laboratory, St. Lucia, Qld 4067

Queensland to one animal to 35 hectares in the northern tropics (Mott, Tothill and Weston 1981). This limitation in food quality for animal production means there is a considerable quantity of surplus unused forage of low quality, which is burnt off in most years.

Given the above limitations to animal production, the general pattern of the pastoral industry is one of an extensive nature with grazing on properties of fixed area. These areas are large, and range from 5000 hectares

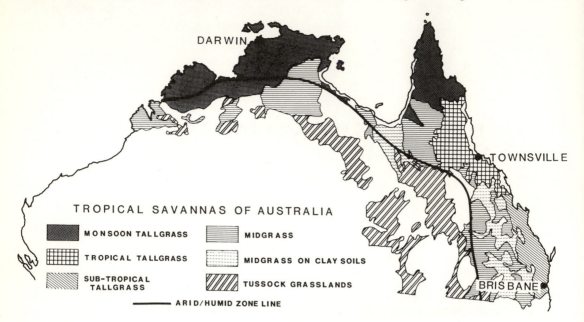

Fig. 1. Major pasture lands of the tropical savannas of Australia (from Mott *et al.* 1985).

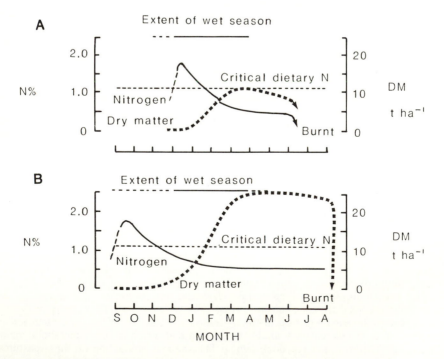

Fig. 2. Pasture yield (tonnes D.M./ha) and nitrogen (N) content in (a) Monsoon Tallgrass woodlands, and (b) Subtropical Tallgrass woodlands (Norman 1963; Tothill, unpublished). The horizontal dashed line in (a) and (b) represents the level of dietary nitrogen required to maintain cattle growth (Milford and Haydock 1965). Approximately 90% of the herbage is burnt annually (from Mott and Tothill 1984).

in the southeast to more than 250,000 hectares in the northern tropics. The high labour costs in Australia require labour input to be optimised, and this is met by substituting labour-saving devices based on fossil fuel (e.g. fencing materials, etc). By this means some stations are reported to carry over 1000 cattle per labour unit (Holmes 1985). As well as making more efficient use of manpower by technology, the possibility of increasing both productivity and reliability of the existing forage by establishing introduced species has gained considerable impetus over the past 20 years. Thus although over 80% of animal production is still from native pastures, economic pressures will increasingly lead to an exploration of all possibilities which in turn may lead to an increased efficiency of production.

The essential part that improved animal nutrition plays in any increase of production from these lands was emphasised by McCosker, Emerson and Garrard (1982). They addressed the problem of improving animal production from a large beef property in northern Australia, and produced a series of improvement steps. In this analysis the key factor was identified as a need to improve animal nutrition before any improvement in herd management, and thus achieve an increase in economic return.

INTRODUCTION OF SPECIES

With the strong economic pressures to improve animal nutrition in the northern savannas, several options are open to the pastoral industry. These options include the introduction of better adapted animals, use of mineral supplementation and the introduction of forage species of higher quality and higher digestibility (e.g. Jones 1984; Mott and Tothill 1984; Winks 1984; Winter *et al*. 1985). This chapter deals specifically with only the implications and results of the planned introduction of new genetic material.

As was stated previously, there has been a long history of planned plant introduction into northern Australia. At the present time more than 16,000 separate accessions of forage plants are held by CSIRO Division of Tropical Crops and Pastures, with some 70 cultivars of grasses and forage legumes having been released commercially by the Queensland Department of Primary Industries and by CSIRO (Eyles and Cameron 1985). The review by Eyles and Cameron highlights the magnitude of the efforts involved in devising animal production systems incorporating this introduced plant material. As noted in several reviews, the management of introduced plants has been carried out at several levels of input (Gillard and Winter 1984; Mott and Tothill 1984; Eyles and Cameron 1985). At the lowest level, legumes have been sown into native pastures without fertiliser, whilst at higher levels of management input, the original pastures have been replaced completely with either introduced grass or grass/legume pastures.

As a result of a series of experimental trials since the 1960s, there has been considerable improvement in animal production in response to introducing legumes into the pasture system over a wide range of environments in northern Australia. Much of this experimental information has been summarised by Gillard and Winter (1984) and Tothill *et al*. (1985) and is shown in Figure 3. These positive results prompted optimistic statements on the potential impact of sown pastures on animal productivity in the pastoral industry. Begg (1972) calculated that as much as 40 million hectares of northern Australia could potentially be sown to Townsville stylo, whilst Winter (1978) estimated that there was a six-fold potential to increase animal production by improved animal husbandry and introduction of legumes into native pastures. Although a study of the total areas sown with introduced pasture species showed a sharp increase from 1960–76, to *c*. 3.5 million hectares, there has been little increase since then (Figure 4). The period of rapid growth reflected the combined effects of optimistic attitudes, advances in pasture technology and favourable balance of income from pastoral production relative to the costs of pasture improvement.

The drop in rate of increase of sown pastures was for two reasons, namely the drastic drop in beef prices in the mid 1970s and a continuing poor economic return from improvement, both of which acted strongly to reduce this initial rapid increase (e.g. Myers and Henzell 1985). Significant sowings of new pasture lands have continued, however, with 180,000 hectares being sown in Queensland in both the 1981–82 and 1982–83 seasons (Eyles and Cameron 1985). Considerable areas of previously sown pasture land have been found subsequently to be unproductive, however, because of biological and management constraints.

INSTABILITY OF INTRODUCED SPECIES

The first signs of instability of pastures of introduced species managed intensively were reported in the Monsoon Tallgrass savannas of the Northern Territory in the late 1960s. Although pastures predominantly of *Stylosanthes humilis* were found to be continuously productive in the Subtropical Tallgrass region (Shaw 1978), dense pastures of this species were unstable in the northern areas, with legume productivity dropping after an initial highly productive phase (Torssell 1973). This rapid decline in legume yield was because of invasion and competition from nitrophilous annual grasses, consequent on an increase in soil fertility in the system (Torssell 1973).

The planned release of perennating legumes such as *Stylosanthes hamata* cv. Verano and *S. scabra* cv. Seca in the early 1970s provided genetic material which was able to form stable legume swards in the northern Monsoon Tallgrass regions and thereby give high legume yields in experimental areas (Winter, Mott and McLean 1979). Some land holders also reported satisfactory animal production from these pastures (e.g. Edye and Gillard 1985). However, in the 1970s another major biological problem was found to limit animal

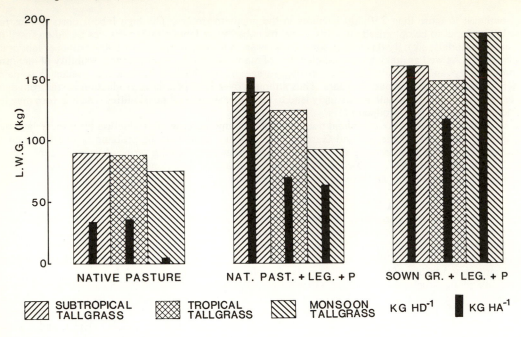

Fig. 3. Summarised animal production data obtained from experimental grazing trials in the savannas of northern Australia (adapted from Tothill *et al.* 1985).

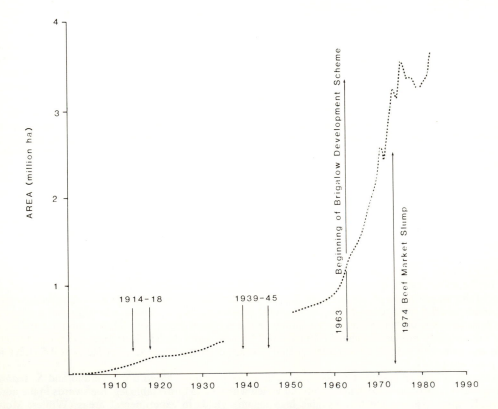

Fig. 4. Area of effective sown pasture in Queensland over the period 1905 to 1983 (from Eyles and Cameron 1985).

productivity from many pastures based on *Stylosanthes* spp., viz. the invasion of the fungal pathogen anthracnose (*Colletotrichum gloeosporioides*) (Irwin, Cameron and Lenne 1984). This pathogen is native to South America and spread rapidly through the tropics and the subtropics of Australia after its initial outbreak in the early 1970s. It damaged or destroyed large areas of the widespread naturalised *S. humilis* as well as sown areas of other *Stylosanthes* species, apart from the tolerant *S. hamata* cv. Verano and resistant *S. scabra* cv. Seca. The impact of this pathogen (Figure 5) was such that in one region of northern Queensland the area of productive *Stylosanthes* pasture dropped by over 50% 12 months after the first appearance of the pathogen in epidemic proportions.

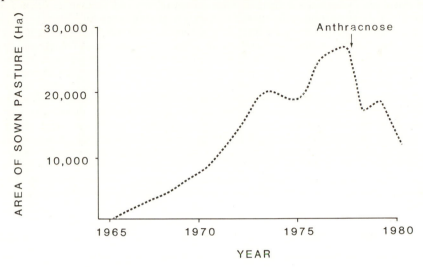

Fig. 5. Reduction in area of productive *Stylosanthes* pastures in Dalrymple Shire, northern Queensland following outbreak of anthracnose (*Colletotrichum gloeosporioides*) in 1977 (from P. Lloyd, unpublished data).

Productivity of sown pastures has also decreased as a result of inappropriate management. Although experimental pastures of Siratro (*Macroptilium atropurpureum*) can give good legume and animal productivity for a considerable period (Tothill and Jones 1977), there have been logistical problems in translating experimental results to large-scale farm pastures. In a survey of properties in the humid Subtropical Tallgrass zone, Anderson *et al.* (1983) found that in pastures previously sown to legume, only 34% still maintained a legume content which could be classed as giving a substantial increase in animal production over unimproved native pasture. Also, in sown grass pastures on heavy clay soils, only 30% still maintained the original productive pasture because of either reduced availability of nutrients (Catchpole 1982) or shrub invasion (Anderson *et al.* 1984).

These biological and managerial constraints on the success of the planned invasion of northern savannas are still the subject of active research. Results of recent studies have shown that leguminous shrubs such as *Leucaena leucocephala* may be more persistent than some of the herbaceous species, but other problems, such as establishment, may be important (Jones 1979; Foster and Blight 1983). Studies are under way which aim both to understand the reasons behind the instability of the introduced species and to evaluate new genetic material with potential for future utilisation. Other constraints have arisen within the ecosystem, however, to further reduce the ecological stability of these systems.

ECOSYSTEM STABILITY

Except for a complete replacement of the indigenous pasture base with sown species, all options to improve animal production result in an increased grazing pressure on the native species incorporated in the management system. The major impact of this increased pressure on the native grasses occurs during the summer period when they are actively growing. Under conditions which promote increased stocking pressure, there have been major differences in the stability of the native grass understorey across the savanna regions. The dense subclimax black speargrass is relatively stable; on the other hand, the kangaroo grass pastures of the north are proving to be very unstable under heavy grazing (Mott and Tothill 1984).

In the northern areas, native pastures dominated by kangaroo grass are extremely sensitive to defoliation during the early months of the wet season, a particularly important time for grazing animals which have survived on the low quality forage of the dry season. Under high grazing pressure, pastures have been found to break down quickly. Grass clumps die and the exposed soil surface then degrades to form scalded areas (Mott,

Bridge and Arndt 1979) and/or there is an increase in the less palatable grasses, such as *Chrysopogon latifolius* (McCosker and Emerson 1982). The addition of fertiliser has led to dramatic increases in weedy species such as *Sida* spp. and *Hyptis suaveolens* in some situations (Sturtz, Harrison and Falvey 1975). This degeneration of pastures has occurred where areas of native pasture have been oversown with legume and then grazed more intensively, but also by the use of feed supplements or blocks of improved pastures within open areas of native pasture (T.H. McCosker, personal communication).

Although as yet there are few results available to help elucidate the reasons behind this differential stability in the native grass systems, a similar inability of perennial native grasses to withstand heavy grazing has been noted in the nutrient-poor seasonal savannas of West Africa (Cissé and Breman 1980) and Venezuela (Z. Baruch, unpublished). An evaluation of the major constraints to growth in the Australian savannas showed that in contrast to the Subtropical Tallgrass pastures, the dominant factor controlling productivity in the Monsoon Tallgrass regions was nutrient availability (Mott *et al.* 1985). Comparison of the growth strategies of the dominant perennial species in each system show that *T. australis* falls into the nutrient-stressed category of Grime (1979), whilst *H. contortus* has the characteristics of a more nutrient-demanding invasive species (Table 1). Grime postulated that the low growth rates of stress-tolerant plants are associated with their particular vulnerability to physical damage; he listed a variety of factors which reduce herbivory in such stress-tolerant species. In the seasonal conditions of the savanna grasslands the intensity of grazing has been controlled naturally by the poor quality of the dry season forage and it is only with the removal of this control that heavy defoliation can take place during the growing season. Following Grime's postulate, it could be proposed that species adapted to enhance nutrient stress may have difficulty withstanding heavy defoliation.

TABLE 1. *Growth strategies and stability under heavy grazing pressure for dominant understorey communities of the Monsoon Tallgrass and Subtropical Tallgrass savannas (from Mott* et al. *1985).*

Savanna type	Establishment	Growth	Regeneration
GRAZING-INTOLERANT, NUTRIENT-STRESSED, CLIMAX COMMUNITY			
Monsoon Tallgrass	No long term seed dormancy	Long lived tussocks (> 9 yrs)	Poor
(*T. australis* dominated systems)	Little effect dry season fires	Low nutrient requirement	
		Slow growth rate	
	Low germination (4-8 m^{-2})	Short growing period	
		Upright growth form	
GRAZING-TOLERANT, SUBCLIMAX, INVASIVE COMMUNITY			
Subtropical Tallgrass	No long term seed dormancy	Short lived tussocks (≈ 5 yrs)	Good
(*H. contortus* dominated systems)	Promotive effect dry season fires	Median nutrient requirement	Invasive
		Rapid growth rate	
	High germination (300 m^{-2})	Long growth period	
		Prostrate growth form under grazing	

CONCLUSION

In spite of the long history of voluntary and accidental introduction of plants into Australia, there is still less than 6% of the potential land sown to these species (Eyles and Cameron 1985). Whilst the use of introduced genetic material has potential to remove the constraint of low quality feed in savanna pastures, the widespread adoption of this technology has been restricted both by economic and biological constraints.

The effect of these biological constraints has been to limit the major success of pasture improvement to the better soils and higher rainfall areas of the subtropical regions. These areas also have a pastoral industry which is managed much more intensively. The problems have been greatest in developing a technology appropriate to the extensive pastoralism practised in the Monsoon Tallgrass systems. For future improvement of animal production throughout the savanna zone, research must be aimed at understanding the implications of integrating both the sown and native pasture components of the animal production system, as well as the provision of species better adapted to specific constraints such as tolerance of pathogens. An example of a potential low cost management option for Monsoon Tallgrass systems may be the better managed use of fire to remove rank growth and enable cattle to fully utilise pastures, rather than the restriction of grazing to small patches with resultant rapid death of plants (Mott and Andrew 1985).

Whilst it is difficult to forecast future economic trends in the pastoral industry, the predictions for future improvements in the present low returns for extensive pastoralism have been pessimistic (e.g. Holmes 1985).

There will also be substantial costs associated with the need to achieve land control for the national campaign to eradicate tuberculosis and brucellosis. Holmes (1985) reported that in some areas of the northern cattle industry the most viable procedure appeared to be the destocking of the least productive cattle lands. He went on to state that the guaranteed market prices associated with the destocking program have provided an opportunity for underfinanced buyers to obtain very large cattle stations, recovering the purchase price by the sale of all cattle and leaving the station unstaffed and unstocked. The final outcome of the disease control measures is difficult to predict, but the need for good animal control will mean that the old 'cattle hunting' techniques are no longer practicable and that major changes will be needed in current management practices.

Given the additional constraints incurred by disease control the option of improving efficiency of production by introduced forage species could be a viable one, assuming a stable level of pasture production. It would seem that in the more extreme of the northern regions the principles highlighted by de Wit (1978) could be important in the grazing industry. De Wit discussed the philosophy that in low-yielding situations heterogeneity of the environment should be exploited, rather than aiming at the type of uniform utilisation which is optimal in high-yielding situations. If this philosophy were put into practice there could be an increasing change to concentrate pasture improvement on highly responsive areas with the consequent neglect or destocking of the non-responsive areas. Such a philosophy would agree with disease control requirements and also appears to provide the best chance to overcome the biological and management constraints involved with the use of introduced species. Efficiency of labour would be increased as well as the maintenance of production levels from fewer but more productive animals (e.g. Edye and Gillard 1985). The less productive areas of native pasture would remain ungrazed, or if utilised, the inherent 'autoprotection' of the dry season feed of low quality would limit grazing pressures to below critical levels.

REFERENCES

Anderson, E.R., Russell, F.J., Scanlan, J.C., and Fossett, G.W. (1983). Pastures under development in central Queensland. I. Mackay region. Queensland Department of Primary Industries, Brisbane.

Anderson, E.R., Scanlan, J.C., Fossett, G.W., and Russell, F.J. (1984). Pastures under development in central Queensland. II. Northern Brigalow region. Queensland Department of Primary Industries, Brisbane.

Baker, H.G. (1974). The evolution of weeds. *Annual Review of Ecology and Systematics* 5, 1–24.

Baker, H.G. (1978). Invasion and replacement in Californian and neotropical grasslands. In *Plant Relations in Pastures* (ed. J.R. Wilson) pp. 368–384, CSIRO, Melbourne.

Begg, J.E. (1972). Probable distribution of Townsville stylo as a naturalised legume in tropical Australia. *Journal of the Australian Institute of Agricultural Science* 38, 158–162.

Catchpole, V.R. (1982). Regeneration of grass pasture. In *CSIRO Tropical Crops and Pastures, Annual Report 1980–81*, p. 60, CSIRO, Melbourne.

Cissé, M.I., and Breman, H. (1980). Influence de l'exploitation sur an paturage à *Andropogon gayanus* Kunth von Fridentatus. *Revue d'élevage et de médecine vétérinaire des pays tropicaux 33*, 407–416.

Davies, W. (1960). *The Grass Crop — its Development, Use, and Maintenance*, Span, London.

Edye, L.A., and Gillard, P. (1985). Pasture improvement in semi-arid tropical savannas: a practical example in northern Queensland. In *Ecology and Management of the World's Savannas* (eds J.C. Tothill and J.J. Mott), pp. 303–309, Australian Academy of Science, Canberra.

Eyles, A.G., and Cameron, D.G. (1985). Contributions of pasture research in northern Australia. *Journal of the Australian Institute of Agricultural Science 51*, (in press).

Foster, A.J., and Blight, G.W. (1983). Use of *Leucaena leucocephala* to supplement yearling and two year old cattle grazing speargrass in south-east Queensland. *Tropical Grasslands 17*, 170–178.

Gillard, P., and Winter, W.H. (1984). Animal production from *Stylosanthes* based pastures in Australia. In *The Biology and Agronomy of* Stylosanthes (eds H.M. Stace and L.A. Edye), pp. 408–430, Academic Press, London.

Grime, J.P. (1979). *Plant Strategies and Vegetation Processes*, John Wiley, Chichester.

Holmes, J. H. (1985). Policy issues concerning rural settlement in Australia's pastoral zones. *Australian Geographical Studies 23*, (in press).

Irwin, J.A.G., Cameron, D.F., and Lenné, J.M. (1984). Responses of *Stylosanthes* to anthracnose. In *The Biology and Agronomy of* Stylosanthes (eds H.M. Stace and L.A. Edye), pp. 295–309, Academic Press, London.

Jones, R.J. (1979). The value of *Leucaena leucocephala* as a feed for ruminants in the tropics. In *World Animal Review*, Vol. 31, pp. 1–11, FAO, Rome.

Jones, R.J. (1984). Improving the nutrition of grazing animals using legumes, fertiliser and mineral supplements. In *Eastern Africa/ACIAR Consultation on Agricultural Research, Nairobi, Kenya, July 1983*, pp. 122–137, ACIAR, Canberra.

McCosker, T.H., and Emerson, C.A. (1982). The failure of legume pastures to improve animal production in the monsoonal dry tropics of Australia — a management review. *Proceedings of the Australian Society of Animal Production 14*, 337–340.

McCosker, T.H., Emerson, C.A., and Garrard, A.E. (1982). Extensive beef property development strategies for north Australia. *Proceedings of the Australian Society of Animal Production 14*, 333–336.

Milford, R., and Haydock, K.P. (1965). The nutritive value of protein in subtropical pasture species grown in south-east Queensland. *Australian Journal of Experimental Agriculture and Animal Husbandry 5*, 13–17.

Mott, J.J., and Tothill, J.C. (1984). Tropical and subtropical woodlands. In *Management of Australian Rangelands* (eds G.N. Harrington, A.D. Wilson and M. Young) pp. 255–270, CSIRO, Melbourne.

Mott, J.J., and Andrew, M.H. (1985). Effect of fire on the grass understorey of Australian savannas. In *Towards an Expert System for Fire Management in Kakadu National Park* (eds J. Walker, J.R. Davis and A.M. Gill), *CSIRO Division of Water and Land Resources Technical Memorandum* (in press).

Mott, J.J., Bridge, B.J., and Arndt, W. (1979). Soil seals in tropical tall grass pastures of northern Australia. *Australian Journal of Soil Research 30*, 483–494.

Mott, J.J., Tothill, J.C., and Weston, E. (1981). The native woodlands and grasslands of northern Australia as a grazing resource for low cost animal production. *Journal of the Australian Institute of Agricultural Science 47*, 132–141.

Mott, J.J., Williams, J., Andrew, M.H., and Gillison, A.N. (1985). Australian savanna ecosystems. In *Ecology and Management of the World's Savannas* (eds J.C. Tothill and J.J. Mott), pp. 56–82, Australian Academy of Science, Canberra.

Myers, R.J.K., and Henzell, E.F. (1985). Productivity and economics of legume-based vs. fertiliser-N-grass-based forage systems. In *Forage Legumes for Energy-efficient Animal Production* (eds R.F. Barnes, P.R. Ball, R.W. Brougham, G.C. Martin and D.J. Minson) in press, USDA, Washington and CSIRO, Melbourne.

Norman, M.J.T. (1963). The pattern of dry matter and nutrient content changes of native pastures at Katherine, N.T. *Australian Journal of Experimental Agriculture and Animal Husbandry 3*, 119–124.

Norman, M.J.T. (1965). Seasonal performance of beef cattle on native pasture at Katherine, N.T. *Australian Journal of Experimental Agriculture and Animal Husbandry 5*, 227–231.

Shaw, N.H. (1978). Superphosphate and stocking rate effects on a native pasture oversown with *Stylosanthes humilis* in central coastal Queensland. *Australian Journal of Experimental Agriculture and Animal Husbandry 18*, 800–807.

Sturtz, J.D., Harrison, P.G., and Falvey, L. (1975). Regional pasture development and associated problems. II. Northern Territory. *Tropical Grasslands 9*, 83–91.

Torssell, B.W.R. (1973). Patterns and processes in the Townsville stylo — annual grass pasture ecosystem. *Journal of Applied Ecology 10*, 463–478.

Tothill, J.C., and Jones, R.M. (1977). Stability in sown and oversown Siratro pastures. *Tropical Grasslands 11*, 55–65.

Tothill, J.C., and Mott, J.J. (1985). Effect of defoliation on Australian savannas. In *Ecology of Wet-Dry Tropics*, in press, Ecological Society of Australia, Canberra.

Tothill, J.C., Nix, H.A., Stanton, J.P., and Russell, M.J. (1985). Land use and productive potentials of Australian savanna lands. In *Ecology and Management of the World's Savannas* (eds J.C. Tothill and J.J. Mott), pp. 125–141, Australian Academy of Science, Canberra.

Winks, L.W. (1984). Cattle growth in the dry tropics of Australia. Australian Meat Research Council Review No. 45.

Winter, W.H. (1978). The potential for animal production in tropical Australia. *Proceedings of the Australian Society of Animal Production 12*, 86–93.

Winter, W.H., McCosker, T.H., Pratchett, D., and Austin, J.D.A. (1985). Intensification of beef production. In *Agro-Research for the Semi-arid Tropics of North-west Australia*, in press, CSIRO, Melbourne.

Winter, W.H., Mott, J.J., and McLean, R.W. (1979). Pasture systems study — Menbulloo. In *CSIRO Tropical Crops and Pastures, Annual Report 1978–79*, pp. 30–31, CSIRO, Melbourne.

Wit, C.T. de (1978). Summative address. In *Plant Relations in Pastures* (ed. J.R. Wilson) pp. 405–410, CSIRO, Melbourne.

FIRE: AN OLD TOOL WITH A NEW USE

P.E. Christensen[1] and N.D. Burrows[1]

Climate, vegetation and fire have a long association on the Australian continent and one which pre-dates the arrival of humans by many millions of years (Kemp 1981). Fossil records indicate that in the warm and humid conditions of the Eocene, much of southern and eastern Australia was covered by rainforest and fires were probably infrequent. The middle of the Miocene saw a climatic change and the onset of aridity in northern and central Australia. Over many thousands of years grasslands and open woodlands became established and fires were probably more frequent. The modern sclerophyllous forests which cover much of Australia and which are fire-prone, probably had their origins some 13 million years ago in the early Pliocene (Kemp 1981). Thus, the general trend through time from rainforest to a sclerophyllous forest has been interpreted as a direct result of climatic changes towards increasing aridity. The frequency of natural fires (caused by lightning) probably increased with increasing aridity. These conditions would have favoured the spread of sclerophyllous woodlands and the development of pyrophytic communities at the expense of fire-sensitive rainforests. Changes in floristics, structure and life forms of the Australian flora occurred over many millions of years and there is little evidence to suggest anything cataclysmic prior to the arrival of humans. Within this 'closed' system, fauna and flora, tempered by climate and fire, achieved something of an 'oscillating equilibrium' through a process of gradual change.

These gradual processes of displacement and replacement of plant communities and individuals within a closed system and without human interference, may be considered evolutionary. By contrast, the comparatively rapid introduction of an organism from outside the system (usually by humans) and the subsequent establishment of the organism often at the expense of indigenous individuals or communities, can be described as a biological invasion. This description conjures up events of cataclysmic proportions. The arrival of the first Aborigines about 40,000 years ago may not qualify as a biological invasion, but their use of fire and the introduction of a new fire regime across the continent probably caused dramatic changes in the environment.

FIRE AND HUMANS

Stewart (1956) believed fire to be as important to early humans as speech and tools. He believed that the importance of widespread burning as a cultural technology and as a modifier of the environment had received inadequate ethnographic attention. Fire was an essential tool in the life of Australian Aborigines, who used it for a variety of purposes. Fire was deliberately and skilfully used to flush game, improve access, fashion hunting weapons and in many other ways (Hallam 1974; Nicholson 1981). The Aborigines no doubt first obtained fire from natural sources and carried slow-burning torches around with them. At some stage, they learnt to make fire from the heat generated by the friction of two pieces of wood rubbed briskly together. Perhaps sparks from striking flint were also an ignition source, but this was not in widespread use (Nicholson 1981). The Aborigines' ability to make fire freed them from the burdens of sustaining slow-burning torches and must be regarded as a major technological innovation. They had acquired a tool which they could use at will and with which they could shape their environment and promote their quality of life. The frequency of fires increased dramatically as Aborigines populated the continent.

Studies by Singh, Kershaw and Clark (1981) of sediments from various lakes around Australia have revealed changes in vegetation with changes in climate and fire frequency. Lynch's Crater, in northeastern Queensland, was surrounded by rainforest from about 100,000 years ago to about 70,000 years ago, but as the climate became drier, the area of rainforest diminished and was replaced by the fire-prone sclerophyll forest. Charcoal levels in the lake sediment suggests an increased fire frequency accompanying this change, especially

[1] Forests Department of Western Australia, Manjimup Research Station, Manjimup, W. Aust. 6258

about 40,000 years ago. The arrival of Aborigines about this time probably accounts for the increased fire frequency which helped in the transition of vegetation from rainforest to sclerophyll forest (Singh, Kershaw and Clark 1981). Similar observations were made at Lake George, southern New South Wales, and Singh concluded that humans may have been one of the greatest factors in the expansion of fire-prone vegetation, such as the sclerophyllous types, at the expense of rainforest species.

There is further evidence that frequent firing by Aborigines over thousands of years have contributed to the development of much of Australia's grasslands and sclerophyll forests. Helleger, in 1827, first saw large open grasslands in northwestern Tasmania extending south-wards to areas of rainforest; he claimed that they were the resorts and hunting grounds of Aborigines who regularly burnt the grass. By 1835, no longer were there any Aborigines, but the plains were filled with unpalatable grass and light scrub (Nicholson 1981). Examples are known where frequent fires in the past have maintained a grassy understorey in woodlands and sclerophyll forests and there is ample evidence to suggest that frequent firing by Aborigines converted large areas of forest into grassland plains and savanna woodlands (Leigh and Noble 1981; Tindale 1981). Similar transformations have been observed in Africa, where a large portion of the extensive grasslands owe their origins and maintenance to regular firing over thousands of years (Rose-Innes 1972). Large parts of the North American grasslands are now being usurped by woody shrubs, largely because of the decreased fire frequency in recent years (Cooper 1961).

With such a long association with fire, many Australian plants have evolved traits which enable them to survive and reproduce in fire-prone environments. The most common adaptations which enhance the survival of plants in fire-prone environments include: bud protection by bark or soil; sprouting (from stem buds or subterranean lignotubers); fire-induced and synchronised flowering; storage of seeds on the plant and their dispersal stimulated and synchronised by fire; and fire-stimulated germination (Gill 1977). It is incorrect to say that these mechanisms enable plants to survive fire. Specifically, plants and plant communities have evolved to survive a fire regime, which is described as the interaction between fire frequency, fire intensity, season of the fire and fuel and soil characteristics (McArthur and Cheney 1966). The fire regimes experienced on the Australian continent have, as discussed earlier, changed over millions of years. Changing climate and the arrival of the Aborigines and their use of fire were the most significant factors affecting fire regimes. Consequently, it is likely that Australian vegetation types have adapted to survive different and variable fire regimes. The most likely fire frequency best suited to a vegetation type can be estimated by factors such as climate, fuel accumulation rate, and the fire dependence expressed by plants in the community (Mount 1979). Mutch (1970) hypothesised that vegetation which has developed in a fire environment and adapted to fire had inherited characteristics that make it flammable. There is considerable evidence of the validity of this hypothesis for Australian vegetation types.

Over the 40,000 years of Aboriginal occupation and an accompanying higher frequency of fire, the Australian vegetation again shifted to a position of 'oscillating equilibria' with this most 'recent' fire regime. Given this time period, it is not unreasonable to assume that the Australian continent was in a pristine condition prior to the arrival of Europeans, even though humans have occupied the continent for the last 40,000 years. It is on this assumption that the following discussion is based. Prior to European settlement and in what could be described as a closed system, plants and animals evolved and adapted into some form of order and equilibrium. The factors affecting environmental change and the genetic base of life forms participating, have been well established over the millennia. However, with the arrival of Europeans some 200 years ago, the barriers were removed and hitherto unknown environmental disturbances were experienced. A completely foreign, untested and vigorous array of life forms launched themselves into the arena, displacing those which had existed before that time. This was the true advent of biological invasions.

BIOLOGICAL INVASIONS AND FIRE: THE LAST 200 YEARS

Since the arrival of Europeans, fire regimes across the continent have altered considerably (Gill 1975). Unprecedented disturbances, such as the clearing of forests, roading, logging and the introduction of plants and animals destroyed much of what had existed. The early settlers lacked the empirical understanding of fire in the Australian environment, an understanding built up over 40,000 years by the Aborigines. To the early settlers, fire was a tool which aided in the clearing of the bush for crop and pasture establishment. To the early users of forests, fire was a destructive agent which damaged trees and threatened the lives of those who lived and worked in them. The settlers burnt their windrows at the driest time of year for maximal removal of debris, but too often these fires escaped into nearby bushland. The fires, usually of high intensity, damaged or killed many commercial tree species.

In parts of northern Australia, grasslands and woodlands experienced a different seasonality of fire as graziers attempted to maximise meat and wool production. Suijdendorp (1981) reported that fires lit in winter by graziers have resulted in different vegetation associations and consequently, different levels of feed available for indigenous and introduced animals in northwest Western Australia. Winter fires encourage the germination of herbs which take the place of the more palatable and nutritious grasses. The pre-European regime of summer fires also controlled invasions of native shrubs such as those of *Acacia translucens*. Smith (1960) found that the production of biomass and the nutritional value of perennial pasture and woodlands near Katherine,

Northern Territory, were decreased by burning in the wet season and that the pasture composition changed. Through most of northern Australia, the objectives of burning in recent years has been much the same, viz. to destroy the coarse, unpalatable material of low nutritive value in the hope of producing fresh growth of more nutritious green feed (Perry 1960). The frequency of fires has increased. Arndt and Norman (1959) commented that "Nothing definite is yet known of the long term effects of burning upon botanical composition. It is likely that frequent fires have been a feature of the environment for a long period, and the present association may well represent a fire sub-climax in relative equilibrium". This comment has not stood the test of time in some areas. For instance, Tothill (1969) reported an increasing dominance of *Heteropogon contortus* (black spear grass) as a result of regularly burning native pastures in eastern Queensland. He found that the removal of ground cover by frequent burning significantly increased the temperature of the soil surface and favoured the germination of *H. contortus* seed buried there.

The combined practice of burning and grazing of spinifex country (*Triodia* spp.) in the Northern Territory and Western Australia has, in some cases, caused an expansion of spinifex across the plains at the expense of other species, such as the Mitchell grasses (*Astrebla* spp.) (Perry 1960). In other parts of northern Australia, heavy grazing has altered the fire regime. Less palatable, woody shrubs have invaded these areas to the detriment of grasses. Such changes decreased the fire frequency and increased the intensity of fires. The opposite effect has also been observed where grazing has resulted in the invasion of less palatable, but flammable grasses and fires are more frequent (Stocker and Mott 1981).

The introduction of cattle and sheep onto the grasslands and savanna woodlands of northern Australia has resulted in a changed fire regime, one which is aimed at increasing fodder production. Whilst the composition of these vegetation types does not include introduced species, there have been changes in the abundance and distribution of native species which has often created imbalances in native herbivore populations. Expansion of spinifex and the location of permanent watering holes for stock have caused an increase in the distribution and abundance of the euro (*Macropus robustus*), a rock wallaby (Ealey and Suijdendorp 1959). In the Tanami Desert, the fire regime has changed from non-specific, patch burning by Aborigines to more frequent and widespread fire when Aborigines left the land earlier in this century. Bolton and Latz (1978) have attributed the decline in numbers of the western hare wallaby (*Largorchestes hirsutus*) to this comparatively recent change in the fire regime.

Since the early days of settlement when fire was used to clear the land, its role in agriculture has declined. There are, however, instances where fire is used to control weeds in pasture. This is mostly achieved by: preventing seeding; killing the seed on the plant; killing established plants; or by assisting with other methods of control such as cultivation and herbicide application (Johnson and Purdie 1981). The effectiveness of fire in controlling weeds, either alone or synergistically, depends largely on the physiology and life form of the invading organism. Many weed species are successful invaders because they possess physiological attributes which enable then to survive, regenerate and compete favourably under harsh environmental conditions (see Newsome and Noble, this volume). Often these traits equip the organism to survive disturbances such as fire. A typical example of a successful invading organism is skeleton weed (*Chondrilla juncea*), a noxious weed in agricultural districts of eastern Australia. This plant readily establishes from seed on recently disturbed sites and rapidly develops a deep vertical tap root which is very efficient at obtaining moisture and nutrients. It can regenerate from the parent rootstock and from adventitious roots (Groves and Cullen 1981). These traits enable the plant to survive most fire regimes. In some situations of high fire frequency, the plant probably has a competitive advantage over species less able to take advantage of frequent fire. Many other problem weeds behave similarly, so that fire has only a limited role; in fact, exclusion of fire, or a long interval between fires, may be desirable to limit the level of invasion. Application of selective herbicides have largely replaced fire in pasture management. The role of fire in controlling pests and disease in agriculture has also been of limited use. There are reports of fires of high intensity reducing the populations of the red-legged earth mite (*Halotydeus destructor*) in annual pastures (Wallace 1961) and in destroying cattle ticks in northern Australia (Leigh and Noble 1981). Doubts exist about the long-term effectiveness of this practice, however.

FIRE, BIOLOGICAL INVASIONS AND NATIVE PLANT COMMUNITIES

Since European settlement, hundreds of plant and animal species have been introduced from other continents. Many have been deliberately introduced for food, fodder, ornamentals, or sport, whilst others have probably arrived by accident. Attention has mostly centered around those organisms which have caused economic loss, particularly in agriculture. Less effort has been directed towards studying the impact of invading organisms on native bushland and little is known of the role that fire plays on the type, rate and severity of invasion.

From the most cursory of observations, it is obvious that the edge of forests and bushlands are most often invaded by introduced plant species. Having achieved a foothold on the nearby disturbed landscape these organisms move in on a front from the forest edge. The type, extent, seriousness and rate of invasions varies considerably. Bridgewater and Kaeshagen (1979) concluded that not all invading organisms cause the destruction of native plant communities. Many invaders are able to exploit niches unused by native flora and do not pose a threat to the bushland ecology. There are many instances, however, where introduced plants seriously threaten the stability of native communities. Small reserves which experience a high level of human disturbance such as roads, walking trails and burning, are most prone. Bridgewater and Kaeshagen (1979) studied such a reserve near Melbourne and reported a severe decline in the number of native species owing to invasion by introduced plants. They also noted that 50% of the invaders displayed life forms similar to those of the native species.

The role of fire in either enhancing or minimising biological invasions in native communities will depend on the physiological properties of both the native community and the invading organisms and the fire regime. Fire effects must be evaluated in terms of frequency, intensity, seasonality and stage of vegetation development. Generally, frequent burning favours resprouting perennials over non-resprouting species, disadvantages species which rely solely on on-site storage of seed, promotes herbaceous over woody plants, promotes grasses and forbs over dicotyledons, creates pure stands and reduces subsequent fire intensity (Vogl 1977). Frequent firing also favours aggressive introduced species. Frequent disturbance to the native plant community allows the wind-blown seeds of grasses and thistles to germinate and establish. Many other invaders are able to resprout from rootstocks or bulbs, and thereby survive a wide range of fire regimes. Once established, the invading organisms are able to pre-empt, to some extent, the subsequent fire regime, usually to their advantage. For example, the establishment of introduced grasses beneath a native woodland will probably result in an increased fire frequency and a reduction in fire intensity. This fire regime will favour the grasses. Baird (1977) reported the spread of South African veld grass (*Ehrharta calycina*) in a woodland park near Perth, Western Australia. She attributed this to frequent burning and to the construction of fire breaks. Frequent firing (every year or two) led to the deterioration of native understorey species with shrubs, such as species of *Hovea*, *Pimelea*, *Phyllanthus* and others, slowly dying out. Veld grass quickly overran the area. In one quadrat unburnt for 15 years, Baird reported a gradual decrease in the number of veld grass clumps from 115 to 6. Whilst veld grass was the most serious invader, introduced bulbs, such as species of *Gladiolus* and *Homeria* (Cape tulip), have also spread in the wake of frequent burning, mowing or disturbance to the top soil.

Jarrah dieback and forest management

Most biological invasions of native plant communities are generally the result of an introduced species taking advantage of recently disturbed sites. Fire, then, is a disturbance factor and its absence, or a prolonged interval

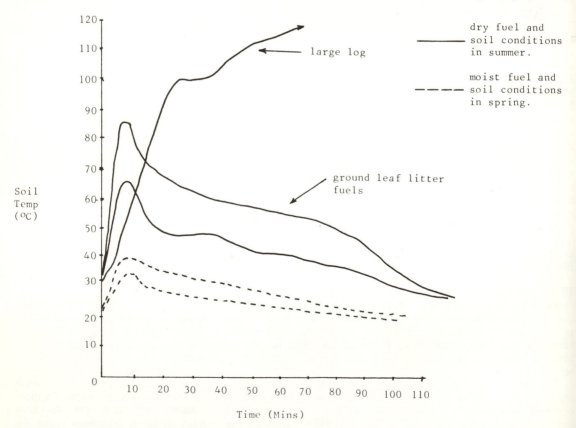

Fig. 1. Soil temperatures at a depth of 20 mm during spring and summer fires in jarrah forest, southwest Western Australia.

between fires, will help to maintain the stability of native communities. There is a direct interaction between fire, invading organisms and native species. However, a more indirect and esoteric interaction exists between fire, the native plant community and the introduced soil-borne pathogen *Phytophthora cinnamomi*. This

Fig. 2. Invasion of jarrah-*Banksia* woodland by the introduced plants wild oats (*Avena fatua*) and South African veld grass (*Ehrharta calycina*) on sandy soils near Perth, Western Australia.

fungus has been identified as causing dieback disease in forests of jarrah (*Eucalyptus marginata*) in southwest Western Australia (Podger, Doepel and Zentmyer 1965).

Considerable areas of commercial forest are affected by the disease. The degree of susceptibility of plants in the jarrah forest varies markedly; proteaceous species such as *Banksia grandis* are highly susceptible. The intensity of the disease varies considerably between seasons and with such factors as soil type, soil moisture, soil temperature, slope, inoculum level and host abundance (Shea 1975). The death of highly susceptible species results from the total invasion of the root system and in some species, from the complete destruction of living tissue around the base of the stem. New infections of disease may occur through the transport of soil or plant material. Unaided by artificial means, the rate of disease extension depends on soil moisture and slope and the presence of host species.

Reducing the abundance and density of highly susceptible species, especially *B. grandis*, is seen to be a necessary first step in the control of the disease. Logging has probably contributed to the development of dense thickets of *B. grandis*, especially on sites where there has been little or no regeneration of jarrah or other tree species following logging. A regime of frequent (5 — 7 years) fires of low intensity (< 350 kW/m) for hazard reduction does not impede development of *B. grandis* thickets, but reduces the abundance of disease-resistant and desirable species such as *Acacia pulchella* (Shea 1975). This species and other non-lignotuberous, hard-seeded species are disadvantaged by cyclic spring burning as they rely upon seed stored in the soil to regenerate. Successful germination and establishment of these species is best achieved by fires of moderate intensity (about 500 kW/m) set under conditions of dry soil and dry fuel. Fires of low intensity in spring kill parent plants but do not heat the seeds stored in the soil which is necessary to prepare the seed for germination (Figure 3). A seed which germinates in spring is unlikely to survive the ensuing summer drought.

An alternative fire regime to hinder the development and ramification of the dieback disease by reducing the abundance of *B. grandis* and increasing the presence of desirable species such as *A. pulchella* is being examined. Intensive measures to reduce *B. grandis* such as mechanical treatment or by use of herbicides are impracticable on a large scale and are costly. Fire is being used economically and in a skilful manner to control the accumulation of flammable fuel in the forest and, given its long association with the forest, appears to be the ideal tool to manage this invading organism and to enhance forest health.

Peet and McCormick (1971) have demonstrated the prolific legume response (as fire 'weeds') to wildfires in the jarrah forest. Such a response is absent after spring fires of lower intensity. Results of studies by Burrows

Fig. 3. Tree and shrub deaths caused by the jarrah dieback disease (*Phytophthora cinnamomi*), an introduced organism in forests of southwest Western Australia.

(1985) have shown that most *B. grandis* plants can be killed to ground level by fire intensities in excess of 600 kW/m. The smaller and younger plants re-sprout from a lignotuber, but many of the older, larger plants have lost this ability and are killed outright. Follow-up treatment, such as frequent burning to maintain the re-sprouts below flowering age or herbicidal treatment of residuals may effectively reduce the abundance of *B. grandis*. Shea (personal communication) has simulated the changes in *B. grandis* population structure following a fire regime designed to reduce the abundance of the species.

Attempting to set fires in lighter fuels but under severe weather conditions to achieve the intensities required to kill *B. grandis*, may result in a very patchy kill (due to variability in fire intensity) and an uncontrolled fire (Burrows 1985). Fires of moderate intensity could be implemented safely under less severe weather conditions if fuels in the jarrah forest were allowed to accumulate to a level of 12–14 t/ha. Heavier fuels would also result in a more homogeneous fire treatment (Burrows 1985). The benefits obtained from allowing fuels to accumulate for control of *B. grandis*, and hence dieback control, must be weighed against the risks of wildfire and damage to crop trees in commercial forests.

Further research is needed to determine the abundance level of *B. grandis* best suited for disease control; and more information about the species' life cycle is needed before the appropriate fire regime, or combination of fire and other control methods, is tested. The side effects of such a regime must also be clearly identified.

Fully exploiting the natural factor, fire, as a land management tool can only be preceded by an effective fire protection system. Fuel reduction burning and effective detection and suppression techniques are the key to forest fire protection. When this is achieved, then forest fire management in the broadest sense, is a real option. Continued research and experimentation are essential to fully understand the fire environment and to effectively apply this knowledge to benefit society.

European fox and vegetation management

Our second example concerns the introduced European fox (*Vulpes vulpes*). The fox came to Western Australia in the early 1900s following close on the heels of the European rabbit (*Oryctolagus cuniculus*) migrating from the east. It was first recorded near Eucla in 1915 and by 1925 it had spread along the coast and through the inland farming areas to Geraldton (Long, undated).

The spread of the fox coincided with the disappearance of several species of medium sized marsupials (see Christensen 1980) and a marked reduction in the numbers of others. Christensen believes that the fox is a major and important predator of medium sized marsupials in the southwest of Western Australia and that it limits the number and distribution of some native species.

The problem posed by this introduced predator is compounded by the fragmentation of areas of native vegetation and forest by farmland. The interface between forest or shrubland and pasture is the main habitat of the rabbit, the fox's primary food item; foxes are concentrated in these areas. From them foxes make nightly excursions into the forested areas to prey on native animals.

One native species which is in danger of extinction, largely as a result of this situation, is the mainland population of the tammar wallaby (*Macropus eugenii*). Once widespread on the mainland of Western Australia the tammar wallaby is now restricted to pockets of suitable habitat in a few isolated localities. Its habitat consists of monospecific stands of *Casuarina, Melaleuca* or *Gastrolobium* which are open beneath a closed canopy. These thickets provide cover and escape from predators. The abundance of the wallaby in an area appears to depend on the availability of grassy feeding areas in the immediate vicinity of such thickets.

'Tammar' thickets depend on periodic infrequent fires if they are to remain suitable habitat for the wallaby. In the absence of fire the plants die, the thickets become too open, and no longer provide cover for the tammar. Prescribed burning under mild spring conditions at frequent intervals also causes degeneration of the thickets. In either case predation by the fox increases and ultimately leads to local extinction of the tammar.

To protect the tammar from excessive predation the thickets require a special burning regime of intense autumn or summer fires at intervals of 25 to 30 years or more. Summer or autumn fires, burning under dry conditions, lead to mass germination of the species forming the thickets (Christensen 1980). A program of cyclic burning in summer or autumn should maintain a range of different-aged thickets suitable for the tammar. A simple fire regime may be devised to achieve this aim. However, tammar thickets are usually too few and too limited in extent to provide reasonable sized areas for burning. This has resulted in major practical problems. Firstly, it has proved extremely expensive and difficult to burn relatively small areas with high fuel loads under dry conditions immediately adjacent to other areas of high fuel weights, i.e. thickets of 25 years of age or more. Secondly, plants regenerating after small fires have proved to be extremely vulnerable to grazing by kangaroos (*Macropus fuliginosus*) and tammars.

In addition to problems related to size there are other difficulties. If the fire is not intense enough the thicket species may fail to regenerate successfully and the associated grasses will predominate. It is a delicate operation to achieve the correct balance between the thicket species and the grasses. Other problems include the invasion of weeds, and thistles in particular, following the fire. This problem may be particularly acute in areas adjacent to pasture. In other instances areas of thickets may fail to re-establish themselves following an apparently suitable fire.

In summary, it is considered possible to use fire to influence the level of predation of an introduced predator, the fox, on the tammar wallaby, and thereby save the species from ultimate extinction on the mainland. To achieve this, fire is used indirectly, i.e. to manage the tammar habitat, rather than the introduced predator itself. Success depends on a high level of skill in managing fire behaviour and a knowledge of tammar biology and the ecology of the tammar thickets. These problems have yet to be fully solved.

CONCLUDING DISCUSSION

Most introduced plants establish themselves following disturbance and fire causes regular and widespread disturbance in most Australian ecosystems. In many it now occurs with increased frequency following the advent of Europeans. Fires are started deliberately in many areas for fuel reduction, to encourage grasses on rangelands and for many other purposes. Mostly these fires are controlled, but a proportion of them get out of hand to become wildfires, sometimes of devastating proportions. All of these fires, as well as those started by natural causes, encourage the distribution and spread of introduced species. The range of species which are being spread by these means is immense and includes representatives of most groups of animals and plants. Some groups of plants, e.g. the hard-seeded leguminous species, species with wind-blown seeds and bulbous and corm-producing plants, are particularly favoured by fire.

Ecosystems created by Europeans, such as farmlands and introduced pastures, harbour a vast reserve of introduced species, a proportion of which are capable of invading native communities following disturbance by fire. In addition, human activities such as the construction of roads and railways, walking trails (Bridgewater and Kaeshagen 1979) and other such activities assist the establishment of foci of introduced species which will spread further given the right conditions. It seems likely that we are still witnessing the beginning of vast changes to many Australian ecosystems.

Fire inevitably is destined to play a major role in the distribution and spread of many species of introduced species. Many of these changes may be irreversible; in some cases they may also be self-generating. The establishment and spread of veld grass (*Ehrharta calycina*) in King's Park, Perth, as documented by Baird (1977), provides a good example of the latter. Increasing abundance of the introduced grass in a woodland community following fire led to increased fire frequency, which in turn led to an accelerated rate of colonisation by veld grass.

It is our belief that not all the changes which are occurring now and in the future are inevitable or uncontrollable. For thousands of years humans have used fire to manipulate communities of plants and animals in many different parts of the world. A high proportion of the species which humans have attempted to manipulate in the past have been 'weed' species, i.e. plants or animals which occupy the early successional stages following fire. It has been possible, for example, to maintain grasslands for herbivores through the use of fire in East Africa (Skovlin 1972). Fire can be used to replace spruce and birch stands with pine in Finland (Siren 1973). The groundwork for using fire to manipulate plant and animal community composition has been laid. Like many of the ancient crafts, much knowledge has been lost in recent times because of our pre-occupation with new technologies. Perhaps the time has come to have a closer look at the old skills of using fire for our purposes.

Recently, the management of natural lands has received more attention. There is a widespread community desire to conserve and perpetuate natural communities. Fire is still the cheapest available tool to achieve these aims. Our knowledge of natural processes, including ecology and fire behaviour, is far in advance of what it was even half a century ago. What is lacking is initiative to tackle the task. Ample information is available to initiate projects such as those on *Phytophthora cinnamomi* and the tammar in relation to fire, as we have outlined.

REFERENCES

Arndt, W., and Norman, M.J.T. (1959). Characteristics of native pastures on Tippera clay loam at Katherine, Northern Territory. CSIRO Australia Division of Land Research and Regional Survey, Technical Report No. 3.

Baird, A.M. (1977). Regeneration after fire in King's Park, Perth, Western Australia. *Journal of the Royal Society of Western Australia 60*, 1–22.

Bolton, B.L., and Latz, P.K. (1978). The western hare-wallaby *Lagorchestes hirsutus* (Gould) in the Tanami Desert. *Australian Wildlife Research 5*, 285–293.

Bridgewater, P.B., and Kaeshagen, D. (1979). Changes induced by adventive species in Australian plant communities. In *Werden und Vergehen von Pflanzengesellschaften* (eds O. Wilmanns and R. Tuxen) pp. 561-579, J. Cramer, Vaduz.

Burrows, N.D. (1985). Reducing the abundance of *Banksia grandis* in the jarrah forest by the use of controlled fire. *Australian Forestry 48*, 63-70.

Christensen, P.E.S. (1980). A sad day for native fauna. *Western Australian Forests Department Forest Focus 23*, 3–12.

Cooper, C.F. (1961). The ecology of fire. *Scientific American 204*, 150–156.

Ealey, E.H.M., and Suijdendorp, H. (1959). Pasture management and the euro problem in the north-west. *Journal of the Western Australian Department of Agriculture, 3rd Series, 18*, 273–286.

Gill, A.M. (1975). Fire and the Australian flora : A review. *Australian Forestry 38*, 4–25.

Gill, A.M. (1977). Plant traits adaptive to fires in Mediterranean land ecosystems. In *Proceedings of the Symposium on the Environmental Consequences of Fire and Fuel Management in Mediterranean Ecosystems* (eds H.A. Mooney and C.E. Conrad) pp. 17–26, USDA Forest Service General Technical Report WO–3.

Groves, R.H., and Cullen, J.M. (1981). *Chondrilla juncea* : The ecological control of a weed. In *The Ecology of Pests. Some Australian Case Histories* (eds R.L. Kitching and R.E. Jones) pp. 7–18, CSIRO Australia, Melbourne.

Hallam, S.J. (1975). *Fire and Hearth : A Study of Aboriginal Usage and European Usurpation in South-western Australia*, Australian Institute of Aboriginal Studies, Canberra.

Johnson, R.W., and Purdie, R.W. (1981). The role of fire in the establishment and management of agricultural systems. In *Fire and the Australian Biota* (eds A.M. Gill, R.H. Groves and I.R. Noble) pp. 497–528, Australian Academy of Science, Canberra.

Kemp, E.M. (1981). Pre-Quaternary fire in Australia. In *Fire and the Australian Biota* (eds A.M. Gill, R.H. Groves and I.R. Noble) pp. 3–21, Australian Academy of Science, Canberra.

Leigh, J.H., and Noble, J.C. (1981). The role of fire in the management of rangelands in Australia. In *Fire and the Australian Biota* (eds A.M. Gill, R.H. Groves and I.R. Noble) pp. 471–495, Australian Academy of Science, Canberra.

Long, J.L. undated. Introduced birds and mammals in Western Australia. Agricultural Protection Board of Western Australia Technical Series No. 1.

McArthur, A.G., and Cheney, N.P. (1966). The characterisation of fires in relation to ecological studies. *Australian Forest Research 2*, 36–45.

Mount, A.B. (1979). Natural regeneration processes in Tasmanian forests. *Search 10*, 180–186.

Mutch, R.W. (1970). Wildland fires and ecosystems — a hypothesis. *Ecology 56*, 1046–10.

Nicholson, P.H. (1981). Fire and the Australian Aborigine — an enigma. In *Fire and the Australian Biota* (eds A.M. Gill, R.H. Groves and I.R. Noble) pp. 55–76, Australian Academy of Science, Canberra.

Peet, G.B., and McCormick, J. (1971). Short term responses from controlled burning and intense fires in the forests of Western Australia. Forests Department of Western Australia Bulletin No. 79.

Perry, R.A. (1960). Pasture lands of the Northern Territory. CSIRO Australia Land Research Series No. 5.

Rose-Innes, R. (1972). Fire in West African vegetation. *Proceedings of the Tall Timbers Fire Ecology Conference 11*, 147–173.

Podger, F.D., Doepel, R.F., and Zentmyer, G.A. (1965). Association of *Phytophthora cinnamomi* with a disease of *Eucalyptus marginata* forest in Western Australia. *Plant Disease Reporter 49*, 943–947.

Shea, S.R., (1975). Environmental factors of the northern jarrah forest in relation to pathogenicity and survival of *Phytophthora cinnamomi*. Forests Department of Western Australia Bulletin No. 85.

Singh, G., Kershaw, A.P., and Clark, R. (1981). Quaternary vegetation and fire history in Australia. In *Fire and the Australian Biota* (eds A.M. Gill, R.H. Groves and I.R. Noble) pp. 23–54, Australian Academy of Science, Canberra.

Siren, G. (1973). Some remarks on fire ecology in Finnish forestry. *Proceedings of the Tall Timbers Fire Ecology Conference 12*, 191–210.

Skovlin, J.M. (1972). The influence of fire on important range grasses of East Africa. *Proceedings of the Tall Timbers Fire Ecology Conference 11*, 201–217.

Smith, E.L. (1960). Effects of burning and clipping at various times during the wet season on tropical tall grass range in northern Australia. *Journal of Range Management 13*, 197–203.

Stewart, O.C. (1956). Fire as the first great force employed by man. In *Man's Role in Changing the Face of the Earth* (ed. W.C. Thomas) pp. 115–133, University of Chicago Press, Chicago.

Stocker, G.C., and Mott, J.J. (1981). Fire in the tropical forests and woodlands of northern Australia. In *Fire and the Australian Biota* (eds A.M. Gill, R.H. Groves and I.R. Noble) pp. 425–439, Australian Academy of Science, Canberra.

Suijdendorp, H. (1981). Response of the hummock grasslands of northwestern Australia to fire. In *Fire and the Australian Biota* (eds A.M. Gill, R.H. Groves and I.R. Noble) pp. 417–424, Australian Academy of Science, Canberra.

Tindale, N.B. (1981). Prehistory of the Aborigines : Some interesting considerations. In *Ecological Biogeography of Australia* (ed. A. Keast) pp. 1763–1797. Junk, The Hague.

Tothill, J.C. (1969). Soil temperatures and seed burial in relation to the performance of *Heteropogon contortus* and *Themeda australis* in burnt native woodland pastures in eastern Queensland. *Australian Journal of Botany* 17, 269–275.

Vogl, R.J. (1977). Fire frequency and site degradation. In *Symposium on the Environmental Consequences of Fire and Fuel Management in Mediterranean Ecosystems* (eds H.A. Mooney and C.E. Conrad) pp. 193–201, USDA Forest Service General Technical Report WO–3.

Wallace, M.M.H. (1961). Pasture burning and its effect on the aestivating eggs of *Halotydeus destructor* (Tuck). *Australian Journal of Experimental Agriculture and Animal Husbandry 1*, 109–111.

QUARANTINE MEASURES TO EXCLUDE PLANT PESTS

S.J. Navaratnam[1] and A. Catley[1]

The objective of the Australian Plant Quarantine Service is to prevent the entry and spread within Australia of serious pests and diseases affecting plants and plant products. Quarantine services have legislative authority to exclude or control the entry, treatment and destruction of goods and to provide deterrents for offenders. This same legislation provides authority to respond to incursions of introduced pests and diseases.

In operational terms the task of the Service is to regulate the entry into Australia of goods and plants through 37 sea and air ports and at secondary sites in the country such as wharves, container depots and mail exchanges. This is a daunting prospect when one considers that in 1982/83, for example, 2.3 million passengers, 329,000 shipping containers, 23 million tonnes of cargo and 163.6 million postal articles arrived in the country. Obviously it is impossible to inspect all these imported items to ensure they are free of pests and diseases. Therefore, it is necessary to make risk assessments based on the goods, their origin and the likelihood of any associated pests and diseases becoming established in Australia.

Risk assessments are probably the most conjectural aspect of quarantine operations. Attempts have been made to reduce them to mathematical formulae or to computer models. One would have a lot more confidence in these approaches if they were developed on broader information bases. All too often the risk assessment finally reduces to a very subjective one based on experience and known biological information about pests and diseases, tempered by an ultra-cautious concern of the dire consequences which might result from a wrong decision.

This chapter focusses attention on three aspects of quarantine which are considered to deserve special mention. These are: (1) the assessment of risk associated with imported items; (2) the importance of detecting introduced pests soon after their arrival; and (3) the formulation of eradication measures. For the purpose of this chapter the term 'pest' is used in an all-inclusive sense and covers invertebrate pests, pathogens and weeds.

RISK ASSESSMENT

Kahn (1979) has attempted to present diagrammatically the concept of pest risk analysis and the interaction among biological, political, social and economic considerations. A pest risk analysis is necessary to determine the entry status of all items moved by humans from one region to another. Pest risk is based on an evaluation of its known biological components or variables. These may include:
1. availability and effectiveness of inspection methodology;
2. operation of many independent safeguards;
3. existence of diseases or disorders in the country of origin for which the causal agent is unknown;
4. knowledge of the life cycle of organisms of quarantine significance;
5. availability of technical backup in the importing country should any hazardous organism be introduced.

The pest risk curve (Figure 1) can be used effectively to communicate quarantine policies to importers.

It is now generally accepted that controls on imports must indicate the pests which the restrictions are intended to exclude. Restrictions of a general nature are unsound scientifically and cannot be justified, given today's knowledge of agricultural pests. This philosophy has led to amendments to the International Plant Protection Convention which now includes the term 'quarantine pest' which is defined as a pest of potential national economic importance to the country endangered thereby and not yet present there or present but not widely distributed and being actively controlled (Anonymous 1979). Trade in agricultural products often depends on phytosanitary certification under the terms of the Convention.

[1]   Plant Quarantine Branch, Department of Primary Industry, Canberra, A.C.T. 2600

In completing phytosanitary certificates, countries should make themselves aware of the importing country's quarantine pests and be able to confidently certify consignments as being free of them. Consignments must be substantially free of other pests but it is implied that their detection at low levels should not be grounds for any severe quarantine action. For instance, it would be unjustified to condemn a consignment because it was found infected or infested with a cosmopolitan pest.

Most countries restrict the entry of plants of economic importance because of the risk of introducing one or more serious pests, but few actually list the pests of quarantine significance. It appears, however, that publication of national lists of quarantine pests may now become necessary with the introduction of a revised international phytosanitary certificate. Baker and Bailey (1979) assessed the threat to British crops and remarked that no country has yet published full details of the assessment procedures by which species listed in national regulations were selected. Kingsolver, Melching and Bromfield (1983) stated that at present a rational basis to predict the establishment of a foreign pest in a new geographic area does not exist. Although pest distribution is provided by maps, it is not accompanied by host distribution and, more crucially, there is no information available on ecological requirements for establishment and the development of epidemics. In 1973 a USDA Import Inspection Task Force attempted to define and quantify the risks from entry of agricultural pests (Kingsolver, Melching and Bromfield 1983). The available records for nearly 2,000 foreign pathogens were examined and 551 were chosen as potential risks. A ranking system was developed according to the equation:

$$EEI = P \times E \quad\text{..} (1)$$

where 'EEI' is the expected economic impact,

'P', the probability of the pest becoming established,

and 'E', the economic impact.

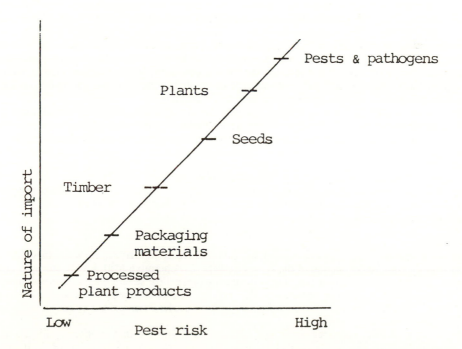

Fig. 1. A simplified pest risk curve to illustrate the quarantine risk with plants and plant products.

Of all the organisations which have given serious thought to establishing quarantine on a scientific basis special mention should be made of the European and Mediterranean Plant Protection Organisation (EPPO). The EPPO policy (Smith 1979) includes the following:

1. phytosanitary regulations should relate to specified pests and not to whole categories of plants or plant products, without any specification of the nature of the risk;
2. the aim with the specified pests should be a requirement for zero tolerance on importation into countries at risk;
3. regulations should make explicit requirements for each pest and on the procedures to be followed in the exporting country.

Pests selected were referred to collectively as List A of dangerous quarantine organisms. This list could be divided into List A_1 of pests absent from all EPPO countries and List A_2 of those present in some but not all countries.

Pests were selected for List A on the following criteria:

1. They cause major damage to economically important crop plants;
2. They are not liable to spread to EPPO countries by natural means;
3. There is a real possibility of spread by current and anticipated international trade;
4. They are capable of surviving in the open or under glass in the EPPO region.

Countries in EPPO may wish to include other organisms in their regulations, but with less stringent requirements. Contamination by these organisms regarded collectively as B organisms could be allowed a certain tolerance below which consignments would not be refused. Such organisms should not be regarded as posing a serious threat because they are either already very widespread or poorly adapted to local conditions and therefore unlikely to establish themselves or because they are very easy to control.

Whilst it is true that the Plant Quarantine branch in Australia pays particular attention to specific serious pests, our policy is to prevent the entry of all pests irrespective of their importance; this would include widely distributed indigenous pests as well as introduced species. This is because of our traditional philosophy to ensure that material released from quarantine is free of obvious pests. This philosophy has been necessary because of a lack of readily available identification services, the concern that a minor pest overseas could prove serious in the Australian environment and that new races of established pests could gain entry.

EARLY AWARENESS OF INTRODUCED PESTS

It is a common practice in quarantine to claim that pests not on the national pest list are absent from the country. These claims may be questionable because many lists were prepared many years previously and have not been revised regularly. This becomes obvious for diseases when Commonwealth Mycological Institute distribution maps are studied. According to these maps many serious diseases occur only in developed countries but not in developing countries. This applies in particular to virus diseases where qualified personnel and sophisticated equipment are lacking in many developing countries. In this manner, many countries which maintain effective identification services may be subject to quarantine prohibitions and restrictions whilst others which do not have these services may gain an unfair advantage.

Early detection is important if pest spread is to be minimised and eradication is to be attempted. Failure to maintain a surveillance system can lead to an erroneous understanding of the actual pest situation in the country. Some examples of new pest detections in Australia are described below (Morschel 1983).

Sirex wood wasp

The Sirex wood wasp (*Sirex noctilio*) was first detected in Australia near Hobart in 1952 where it had a devastating effect on a mature plantation of *Pinus radiata*. It was identified on the Australian mainland in Victoria in 1961 but it is thought to have been present since 1946, when it is believed to have been introduced on infested logs from New Zealand.

Warehouse beetle

The warehouse beetle (*Trogoderma variabile*) was first discovered at Griffith, New South Wales, in March 1977 in the vitamin enrichment section of the Rice Growers' Co-operative Mill. Paddy storages on the same premises were also infested, indicating that it may have been present for several years. A subsequent survey in May 1977 revealed that warehouse beetle was also present in the rice mills at Leeton, Coleambally and Deniliquin, the Coprice Mill and the Murrumbidgee Irrigation District Farmers' Co-operative at Leeton and on two farms at Griffith and one near Yanco.

The infestation at Griffith appeared to be well established. Evidence that supported this claim was that larvae collected at the Rice Mill had been held for over a year before being identified in 1977. It was common practice in the mill to collect samples of insects present and hold them in culture for quality control tests. Without close examination it could easily have been mistaken for carpet beetles which are common in rice mills.

Drywood termite

Cryptotermes brevis was found at Maryborough on the central Queensland coast in 1966. Between 1968 and 1977, 44 infested houses were fumigated. In 1977 it was found in 20 buildings in the Brisbane city area. It is suspected that the drywood termite arrived along the east coast of Australia during the latter half of World War II when there was considerable shipping activity between various Pacific Islands and the Queensland coast.

Boil smut of maize

Boil smut of maize caused by *Ustilago maydis* was first detected in Australia in the Bathurst area of New South Wales in 1911. Through the maintenance of an effective quarantine, the disease was prevented from spreading and finally eradicated. In March 1982 boil smut was again detected on one property on the north coast of New South Wales. Surveys undertaken soon after showed the disease to occur on at least 50 properties in northern New South Wales and southeastern Queensland (Allen and Jones 1982). Despite the spectacular nature of the symptoms, which are distinct from those of head smut caused by *Sphacelotheca reiliana*, the disease appears to have gone unnoticed. It is now believed to have been present in the north coast area for at least a few years before detection in 1982.

Black sigatoka

This disease of banana (caused by *Mycosphaerella fijiensis* var. *difformis*) was first detected in Bamaga on the northern tip of Cape York Peninsula and Australian islands in the Torres Strait in 1981. A careful study of the distribution of black Sigatoka indicates that it could have been present for some time before detection. The natural barrier of native vegetation between the settlements in the far north of Cape York Peninsula and the major banana growing areas in the south may have prevented its spread southwards.

Surveys for introduced pests

It is important to actively survey or monitor for introduced pests for several reasons:
1. to abide by a nation's international obligations under the FAO Plant Protection Convention which states that countries must maintain an effective surveillance system for pests and must notify FAO of any new occurrences and outbreaks of established serious pests;
2. to ensure early detection for eradication purposes;
3. to advise farmers on control measures.
   Procedures need to be developed to survey the more serious pests, using the following guidelines:
1. extension staff should be made aware of the characteristics of introduced pests;
2. pest identification skills should be improved;
3. reference material (e.g. antisera, stock cultures, herbarium specimens) should be maintained to enable pests to be identified more readily;
4. sampling techniques should be developed so that areas can be surveyed on a statistically meaningful basis.

There are very few countries which maintain a service solely to monitor for introduced pests and most depend on extension staff to report any unusual occurrence. In England and Wales there is surveillance for major diseases, records of which go back to 1917. The Agricultural Development and Advisory Service (ADAS) established in 1976 the National Plant Diseases Intelligence Service, which collates information for England and Wales and issues weekly bulletins. However, this is mainly for cereal diseases and potato blight (Jenkins 1978).

The US Disease Survey was initiated in the 1930s and continued throughout the 1940s. It represented a co-operative effort of the US Department of Agriculture and various States. In 1976 the Animal and Plant Health Inspection Service (APHIS) initiated a pilot monthly program in ten States for early detection of new pests, but this program has now been terminated (Kingsolver, Melching and Bromfield 1983). Recently, APHIS has taken the initiative to establish a co-operative pest survey and detection program. This will involve a pest identification system and a data collection, storage and retrieval network. Emphasis will be on the national co-ordination of programs formulated and carried out in the States.

In Australia, surveillance of crops is undertaken by extension services in each State Department of Agriculture. This, together with the information from farmers and pesticide firms, enables the Department of Agriculture to monitor the pest situation in each State. New South Wales publishes an annual plant disease survey which carries information on the incidence of plant diseases on crops as well as new disease occurrences. There is no monitoring of pests in Australia at a national level, the exception being new outbreaks of serious pests which are reported to the Commonwealth Department of Primary Industry.

It seems that the absence of a Commonwealth plant protection organisation to co-ordinate activities and monitor pest outbreaks and control measures is a serious deficiency. For instance, there is no central organisation in Australia which can deal with overseas organisations, including the Food and Agriculture Organisation of the UN on plant protection matters. Plant Quarantine relies heavily on States to eradicate or contain new pests, with its own involvement being limited to convening consultative meetings and some provision of finance.

MEASURES TO ERADICATE INTRODUCED PESTS

No plant quarantine service is anxious to admit that at some time there may be a need to undertake eradication measures against an insect, plant disease or weed that has escaped the vigilance of quarantine and has become established in the country. It is far more realistic to acknowledge this rather unpalatable possibility and prepare some preliminary plans rather than be confronted with a crisis without any plan of attack. Some well known examples of successful eradication of serious introduced pests include those of citrus canker (*Xanthomonas campestris* pv. *citri*) from a number of countries (Stall and Seymour 1983), giant African snail (*Achatina fulica*) from the USA (Rohwer 1979) and Australia (Morschel 1983), and coffee rust (*Hemileia vastatrix*) from Papua New Guinea (Shaw 1968). Because of the economic consequences of infestation and the availability of effective means of eliminating a new infestation, outbreaks of fruit flies have been eradicated successfully on a number of occasions in different countries.

The principles underlying eradication have been ably discussed by Lelliott and Aitkenhead (1979). It is interesting to note their comment that a successful plant health service must use all the scientific knowledge and expertise available to it but it must also rely on experience, intuition and imagination in planning and conducting its eradication campaigns.

Few countries in the world have taken seriously the need to plan in advance and establish the procedures to undertake an eradication campaign. In the USA, the Animal and Plant Health Inspection Service of the U.S. Department of Agriculture has developed action plans which provide guidelines for the eradication of a number of serious introduced pests (Anonymous 1981).

In Australia, although the Veterinary Consultative Committee, as set up in 1941, had drawn up comprehensive plans for a selected number of animal diseases, they are not necessarily applicable to the plant pest situation. There are several differing factors including the difficulty in predicting the reaction of the large number of introduced pests in the Australian environment and a lack of data on the costs and the benefits of eradicating particular pests. Acknowledging these difficulties, the Standing Committee on Agriculture established a Consultative Committee on Exotic Insect Pests, Weeds and Diseases early in 1977 (Anonymous 1980a). This Committee, whose membership varies individually according to the particular case, does not meet until the actual need and case arises. However, with all prior authorisation it is believed a competent and responsible group can be convened within 24 hours of the first report to clarify the particular situation and make a specific recommendation on eradication.

The experience gained in 1976 with a suspected 'Oriental' fruit fly exercise in northern Australia proved valuable in developing procedures on a more formal and permanent basis. Subsequently, in 1977, the agreed procedures were used effectively in the case of warehouse beetle and the giant African snail (see earlier).

Eradication may be defined as the total elimination of a pest from an area with a certainty that it does not continue to exist at levels within Australia which allow it to spread by natural means when suitable conditions arise. A sum of $20,000 (1976 base) is available to meet the costs of initiating any urgent action which may be required. Use of these funds are subject to approval by the appropriate Federal Minister. Eradication measures are subject to approval by Standing Committee on Agriculture. Where eradication is approved it is proposed that costs should be borne equally by the Commonwealth and the States. The allocation of each State's share would be assessed on the size in each State of the particular industry at risk.

The proposal envisages use of the Federal *Quarantine Act*. A limited number of introduced pests has been proclaimed as quarantinable pests. Authorities have prepared guidelines for the eradication programs in respect of these proclaimed quarantinable pests. It must be stressed, however, that the Consultative Committee is just as likely to be convened to arrive at decisions in respect of a pest not previously proclaimed as a quarantinable pest. If such an emergency did arise, no foreseeable difficulties are visualised in having an urgent proclamation gazetted.

No provision has been made for compensation but it is acknowledged that occasions could occur where significant real hardships arise unpredictably and this could make it necessary to eliminate totally or in part a person's source of livelihood.

Since the establishment of Consultative Committees in 1977, meetings have been convened for the following:

Trogoderma variabile — Warehouse beetle 1977
Achatina fulica — Giant African snail 1977
Mycosphaerella fijiensis var. *difformis* — Black Sigatoka 1981
Helix aperta — Green snail 1981
Ustilago maydis — Boil smut of maize 1982
Potato spindle tuber viroid — Spindle tuber 1982
Xanthomonas campestris pv. *citri* — Citrus canker 1984

Of the above listed new occurrences, timely action resulted in eradication of the giant African snail (Morschel 1983) and attempts to eradicate potato spindle tuber are also likely to be successful (Schwinghamer and Conroy 1983; Cartwright 1984). Black Sigatoka has not been eradicated from the Cape York and Torres Strait region, but its spread further south has been prevented. Five citrus trees found with citrus canker on

Thursday Island in the Torres Strait in 1984 were quickly destroyed and the disease has certainly been eliminated.

The effect of some of these diseases on local production costs becomes apparent when a few examples are chosen for study.

Black sigatoka of bananas

The total area of bananas in Queensland and New South Wales is approximately 7,550 hectares made up of 2,550 hectares in Queensland and 5,000 hectares in New South Wales. Not all bananas in Queensland and New South Wales are sprayed to control common Sigatoka (caused by *Mycosphaerella musicola*) and speckle (caused by *M. musae*). In northern Queensland spraying is necessary all the year round, with shortened intervals of 10–14 days during the wet summer months and less frequently during the drier months (Anonymous 1982). In southern Queensland and New South Wales spraying is required only during the wet summer months of December to March. Only 20% of all bananas are sprayed in New South Wales (Allen 1982).

In 1981 black Sigatoka (caused by the fungus *Mycosphaerella fijiensis* var. *difformis*) was detected in the Cape York and Torres Strait region (Jones and Alcorn 1982). Black Sigatoka, as with common Sigatoka, infects the leaves causing leaf spots and in epidemic form it can lead to the rapid killing of the lower and middle leaves. Black Sigatoka is more virulent than common Sigatoka and has a shorter life cycle (Stover 1980). Soon after its detection in Cape York and the Torres Strait, legislation was passed to ban the movement of plants and fruit from the infected area to the south. Until now the disease has not appeared in the major areas of production in Queensland and New South Wales. Because of climatic factors, black Sigatoka is not likely to pose a serious problem in southern Queensland and New South Wales except during the summer months. In northern Queensland, however, the disease could be a major factor limiting banana production.

Maize boil smut

Approximately 60,000 hectares are sown to maize and sweet corn in the eastern States of Australia. Of all the many diseases of maize and sweet corn not present in Australia, downy mildews (caused by various species of *Pernosclerospora*), bacterial wilt (caused by *Erwinia stewartii*) and boil smut (caused by *Ustilago maydis*) are considered to be the most serious. Strict measures apply to new introductions of maize with approved importers being permitted to establish in quarantine no more than 2,500 plants in any one year.

In March 1982 boil smut was detected on the north coast of New South Wales and southern Queensland (Allen and Jones 1982). Surveys undertaken soon after revealed that the disease was present on at least 50 properties. It was concluded that the disease had been present at least since 1981 and had possibly been confused with head smut (*Sphacelotheca reiliana*). Because of the widespread occurrence of the disease and the difficulty in controlling the movement of produce out of this area, it was decided by the Commonwealth not to legislate either to eradicate or contain the disease. However, State quarantines have been imposed to prevent the spread of the disease to new areas and to other States.

Losses from boil smut seldom exceed 2 percent in individual maize crops in the USA but in Europe losses of as much as 40 percent have been reported. However, with use of resistant varieties, losses can be minimised (Anonymous 1980b). The important lesson learnt from this occurrence of boil smut in Australia was that the present surveillance for introduced diseases is inadequate; early detection may have allowed eradication.

CONCLUSION

Despite the acknowledgment that scientific methods should prevail, many decisions taken in quarantine are subjective. The few scientific methods proposed for pest risk analysis are theoretical and not convincing enough for general acceptance. Assessment is essentially a question of the economic status of the pest and the commercial value of the crop. Whilst it is important to take a practical view, there is also the need to use simple criteria to determine the pest risk. Too little attention has been paid to monitoring for introduced pests and measures for their eradication. The existing systems have often proved to be ineffective and detections have occurred long after arrival of a pest thereby making attempts at eradication difficult. There is a need to develop a system to undertake regular surveys for introduced pests and to institute immediate action to eradicate them in the event of new detections.

REFERENCES

Anonymous (1979). Report of 20th F.A.O. Conference, Rome, November 1979.
Anonymous (1980a). *Guidelines for the Eradication of Some Exotic Plant Pests and Diseases*, Department of Health, Canberra.
Anonymous (1980b). *Corn Diseases*, The American Phytopathological Society, St Paul, Minnesota.
Anonymous (1981). *Emergency programs*, Plant Protection and Quarantine, United States Department of Agriculture, Washington, D.C.
Anonymous (1982). *A Handbook of Plant Diseases in Colour. Vol. 1. Fruit and Vegetables*, Queensland Department of Primary Industries, Brisbane.

Allen, R.N. (1982). *Leaf Spot of Bananas*, Agfacts, New South Wales Department of Agriculture, Sydney.

Allen, R.N., and Jones, D.R. (1982). New South Wales Department of Agriculture, Biology Branch, Plant Disease Survey, 1981-82.

Baker, C.R.B., and Bailey, A.G. (1979). Assessing the threat to British crops from alien diseases and pests. In *Plant Health, the Scientific Basis for Administrative Control of Plant Diseases and Pests* (eds D.L. Ebbels and J.W. King) pp. 43–54, Blackwell Scientific Publications, Oxford.

Cartwright, D.N. (1984). Potato spindle tuber viroid survey — South Australia. *Australasian Plant Pathology 13*, 4–5.

Jenkins, J.E.E. (1978). Monitoring disease in crops. In *Plant Disease Epidemiology* (eds P.R. Scott and A. Bainbridge) pp. 45–54, Blackwell Scientific Publications, Oxford.

Jones, D.R., and Alcorn, J.L. (1982). Freckle and black Sigatoka diseases of bananas in far north Queensland. *Australasian Plant Pathology 11*, 7–9.

Kahn, R.P. (1979). A concept of pest risk analysis. *European and Mediterranean Plant Protection Organisation Bulletin 9(1)*, 119–130.

Kingsolver, C.H., Melching, J.S., and Bromfield, K.R. (1983). The threat of exotic plant pathogens to agriculture in the United States. *Plant Disease 67*, 595–600.

Lelliot, R.A., and Aitkenhead, P. (1979). The eradication of diseases and pests from the United Kingdom: its practice and management. In *Plant Health, the Scientific Basis for Administrative Control of Plant Diseases and Pests* (eds D.L. Ebbels and J.E. King) pp. 185–197, Blackwell Scientific Publications, Oxford.

Morschel, J.R. (1983). *The Australian Plant Quarantine Service*, Commonwealth Department of Health, Australian Government Publishing Service, Canberra.

Rohwer, G.G. (1979). Plant quarantine philosophy in the United States. In *Plant Health, the Scientific Basis for Administrative Control of Plant Diseases and Pests* (eds D.L. Ebbels and J.E. King) pp. 23–34, Blackwell Scientific Publications, Oxford.

Schwinghamer, M.W., and Conroy, R.J. (1983). A viroid similar to potato spindle tuber viroid in the New South Wales potato breeders' collection. *Australasian Plant Pathology 12*, 4–6.

Shaw, D.E. (1968). Coffee rust outbreaks in Papua from 1892 to 1965 and the 1965 eradication campaign. Department of Agriculture, Stock & Fisheries, Port Moresby, Research Bulletin No. 2, Plant Pathology Services, pp. 20–52.

Smith, I.M. (1979). EPPO: the work of a regional plant protection organisation, with particular reference to phytosanitary regulations. In *Plant Health, the Scientific Basis for Administrative Control of Plant Diseases and Pests* (eds D.L. Ebbels and J.E. King) pp. 13–22, Blackwell Scientific Publications, Oxford.

Stall, R.E., and Seymour, P. (1983). Canker, a threat to citrus in the gulf-coast states. *Plant Disease 67*, 581–585

Stover, R.G. (1980). Sigatoka leaf spots of banana and plantains. *Plant Disease 64*, 750–756.

OVERVIEWS

The following three chapters attempt to bring together some of the main themes to emerge from the preceding reviews. As well, the reviewers bring an overall and sometimes different perspective to the invasion of Australia by micro-organisms, vertebrates and plants. Micro-organisms have certainly 'invaded' Australia and their effects have often been dramatic in terms of animal, plant or human health. Some vertebrates when introduced to Australia have flourished, such as the rabbit, until its numbers were reduced by the deliberate introduction of the myxoma virus; other groups of vertebrates, such as the deer, have never really become numerous in this country. Ecologically, it is interesting that the reverse pattern applies to vertebrate groups introduced to the United States. The final chapter reviews the situation for plants. A point is made that whilst there has been a large and continuing two-way exchange of plants between Australia and the rest of the world, the number of plant invaders to Australia in the 200 years of its European settlement is still relatively few. And perhaps the majority of these plants have been introduced deliberately for horticulture.

The width of the topic — the ecology of biological invasions in Australia — is attested to by the range of contributed research outlines; they include ostracods in rice fields, apple trees on roadsides, cane toads in northern Australia and introduced dune plants in southeastern Australia. These contributions show that there is research in progress on both basic and applied aspects of the topic. An international focus on the ecology of biological invasions, such as the SCOPE project provides, does indeed appear timely and warranted and these Australian contributions to it provide many case histories of research on the ecology of these invasions and their successful management.

MICROBIAL INVASIONS

Adrian Gibbs[1]

To review microbial invasions of Australia is a very broad task, that is simplified a little by the lack of information concerning all invasions except those involving parasitic microbes that affect human beings and various domesticated organisms. Such microbes have had a great effect on many aspects of human history. For example, the introduction of smallpox virus into the Americas by explorers from Europe enabled them to dominate the indigenous population; Cortes with eleven companions, one infected with smallpox, 'conquered' the Aztec nation. Similarly, one might argue that but for *Phytophthora infestans*, the fungus that blights potatoes and caused the Irish famine of 1845, fewer Irish would have migrated to the U.S.A.

Microbes sometimes cause spectacular and catastrophic epidemics of disease when they invade new territory and infect susceptible hosts. Viruses and bacteria cause the most obvious diseases of animals, such as foot-and-mouth disease of cattle or human plague, whereas the most spectacular diseases of plants are often those caused by fungi, such as late blight of potato or rusts of cereals.

The study of microbial invasions is of particular importance for Australia (Gibbs and Meischke 1985) because its agricultural economy is based on animals and plants introduced from other lands. These species were mostly introduced by sea during the 18th and 19th centuries. During the long voyages to Australia diseased animals often died in transit, and plants were carried as seed. The long sea voyage thus imposed an inadvertent form of quarantine long before quarantine was formally practised. As a result many of the important parasites of the plants and animals introduced into Australia were excluded (see Navaratnam and Catley, this volume).

The study of the ecology of invasions of parasitic microbes is of great scientific importance as both the invading microbe and its environment, namely its host, may be studied and defined. Indeed, some of the smaller microbes, such as viruses, have been defined totally by gene sequencing. Furthermore, the ecology of the microbe-infected host may readily be compared experimentally with that of the uninfected host, so that the dynamic ecology of the microbe, the host and their genes may be fully analysed. Recently, there have been many exciting discoveries in this area of research and I will give examples of these in this review.

SOURCES OF INVADING MICROBES

Many fungi and bacteria produce spores that are dispersed in air currents, and microbes have undoubtedly spread around the world in this way. Close *et al.* (1978) discussed the possibility that this is the way that many different biological materials, such as spores of rust fungi, aphids and pollen, have moved from Australia to New Zealand. However, not all the fungi that one might expect to spread in this way from other parts of the world are found in Australia (Walker 1983).

Other microbes are 'hitch-hikers'. Some use specific vehicles collectively called vectors, and it is probable, for example, that viruses of plants that are persistently transmitted by aphids, such as barley yellow dwarf luteovirus, enter Australia in this way. Other microbes are less specific and are transported in a variety of ways, including on human migrants. The possibility of their arrival in Australia depends on the type, amount and source of trade and travellers entering the country (Wace 1985).

ESTABLISHMENT

The establishment of an immigrant parasitic microbe depends on the availability of conditions to maintain it at the site of colonisation. The minimum requirement for the many fungi and bacteria, and few viruses, that spread abiotically (e.g. by wind-borne spores, or by contact) is a suitable susceptible host. However, most

[1] Research School of Biological Sciences, Australian National University, G.P.O. Box 4, Canberra, A.C.T. 2601

organisms are resistant to most microbes, susceptibility is the exception, and most parasitic bacteria and fungi infect one species or only a few closely related ones; parasites are, in general, good taxonomists. The chances of establishment of some parasitic microbes are even more constrained because their ecological life cycle involves two different species, for example the different stages of many rust fungi infect different plant species, and similarly many viruses of animals and plants are obligately spread by a vector, usually an invertebrate.

Australia, the island continent, became isolated from Gondwanaland over 50 million years ago, and, as it slowly drifted north across the Southern Ocean, was separated by great distances from the other major land masses. During that time the biota of Australia became genetically distinct. Thus, recent migrants, like most of Australia's crop plants and domesticated animals, are more likely to be susceptible to parasitic microbes from their countries of origin than from endemic Australian organisms, and *vice versa*. Thus quarantine measures are of great importance for maintaining the health of imported animals and plants.

A great range of genetical and ecological factors determine the success of a microbial invasion, however; the presence of a transmission mechanism and a susceptible host are not sufficient to ensure the establishment of a migrant microbe. For example, tobacco mosaic tobamovirus (type or U1 strain) and paratobacco mosaic tobamovirus (U2 or U5 strain) are found, respectively, in tobacco crops (*Nicotiana tabacum*) and the tobacco bush (*Nicotiana glauca*) throughout the world, and clearly spread naturally, yet the many other *Nicotiana* species throughout the world that are susceptible to infection by these two viruses (Holmes 1951) are rarely found to be infected. It is probably not a coincidence that all such host/parasite combinations that have been adequately studied, have been found to involve gene-for-gene relationships (Flor 1946; Sidhu 1975); it is probable that lasting relationships will co-evolve only when there are compensatory checks and balances between genes for suceptibility (and resistance) of the host, and virulence (and avirulence) of the parasite.

One other form of genetically controlled host resistance that may affect the establishment of a virus in a new environment is that called cross-protection or superinfection immunity (McKinney 1929). This phenomenon is the specific resistance shown by a virus-infected cell when attempts are made to infect it a second time with the same or a closely related virus. Cross-protection may be one of the reasons why some viruses, especially togaviruses, have a restricted distribution. Sabin (1952) noted that yellow fever flavivirus has not spread from East Africa into India and Southeast Asia, where there is a closely related virus, dengue flavivirus, despite trade around the Indian Ocean that has presumably been active for centuries. Sabin showed that *Aedes aegypti* mosquitoes infected with dengue flavivirus resisted attempts to infect them with yellow fever flavivirus, and wrote "the introduction of yellow fever virus into dengue epidemic areas may find enough mosquitoes relatively refractory to the yellow fever virus to prevent the establishment of yellow fever into the same area" (Sabin 1952, p. 38).

Similar, but more conclusive, experiments by Davey, Mahon and Gibbs (1982; and unpublished work), showed that Murray Valley encephalitis and Kunjin flaviviruses, which are sympatrically distributed in Australia, did not cross-protect against one another in mosquitoes or their cultured cells; whereas both viruses cross-protected mosquitoes against Japanese B encephalitis and West Nile flaviviruses, which are parapatrically and allopatrically distributed with respect to the two Australian viruses. Thus the cross-protection behaviour of the four viruses correlates with the notion that such behaviour affects their geographical distribution.

ADAPTATION

Once established, the migrant microbe and its host may adapt genetically by means of mutation and selection just as for plants and animals (see Barrett and Richardson, this volume). The fast reproduction of most microbes, often with deleterious effects on their hosts, may speed the process. The best studies of the process of adaptation were those done after myxoma poxvirus had been introduced into Australia and Europe to control rabbits, *Oryctolagus cuniculus*, which, at least in Australia, had become a serious pest.

Myxoma poxvirus occurs naturally in the Americas, where it infects several species of leporids of the genus *Sylvilagus*. In *Sylvilagus* rabbits the virus causes small skin tumours and is transmitted by mosquitoes from these to uninfected rabbits. At the end of the nineteenth century laboratory colonies of European rabbits established in South America were severely affected by outbreaks of the disease myxomatosis caused by this pox virus. In 1919, Aragao suggested that myxoma virus might be used to control rabbits in Australia and after a series of unsuccessful attempts (Fenner 1983, 1985) it was established and dramatically decreased the rabbit population. Initially, the virus killed almost 100% of infected rabbits within 2 weeks of infection, but in both Australia and in Great Britain, variants that killed more slowly (Figure 1) soon became dominant, and have remained so. These variants were selected by the vectors of the virus (Mead-Briggs and Vaughan 1975; Figure 2), namely, mosquitoes in Australia and fleas in Great Britain. The rabbit population also changed in its response to myxoma virus, though more slowly. In places, such as the Mallee region of Australia, where epidemics of myxomatosis occur almost every year, genetically resistant rabbits have been selected, and, in turn, more virulent isolates of myxoma virus have appeared. So far, however, the *Oryctolagus* rabbits of Europe and Australia have not produced variants that react to myxoma virus in the way that *Sylvilagus* rabbits do, and myxoma virus continues to control rabbit populations.

Fig. 1. Head of an *Oryctolagus* rabbit infected with myxoma poxvirus. This isolate is one of those most commonly found as it is of virulence grade III (see Figure 2). Photograph kindly provided by Professor F. Fenner.

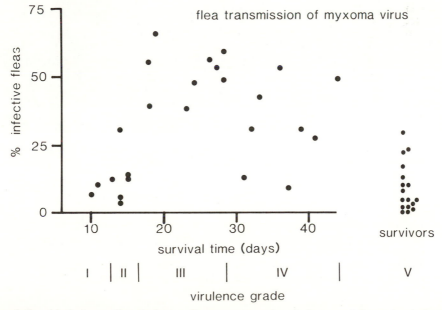

Fig. 2. The relationship between the virulence of myxoma poxvirus isolates and the transmission of virus by fleas from rabbits infected with those isolates; rabbits were infected with virus isolates of differing virulence and the time of their death recorded. Fleas were caged on the rabbit while they were alive and tested for their infectivity on healthy rabbits (modified from Mead-Briggs and Vaughan 1975).

At present nothing is known of the molecular changes involved in the adaptation of myxoma virus to *Oryctolagus* rabbits, compared with the better known molecular changes in influenza virus (Both *et al.* 1983).

Pests and parasites may adapt to a new location in various ways. It is usually found, however, that although a newly established parasite may cause much damage to its host, the degree of damage diminishes after some time. This may be the result of selection acting on either parasite or host, as discussed above, or the effect of hyperparasites. A clear example of the effect of hyperparasitism has been experienced recently by people in southeastern Australia, where a decade ago two species of rust invaded the region and caused premature defoliation of commercial and ornamental poplars. However, after 2-3 years of severe rust infections, the effect of the fungus diminished, and it was found that the rust, *Melampsora larici-populina*, was being parasitised by the fungus, *Cladosporium tenuissimum* (Figure 3) (Sharma and Heather 1978).

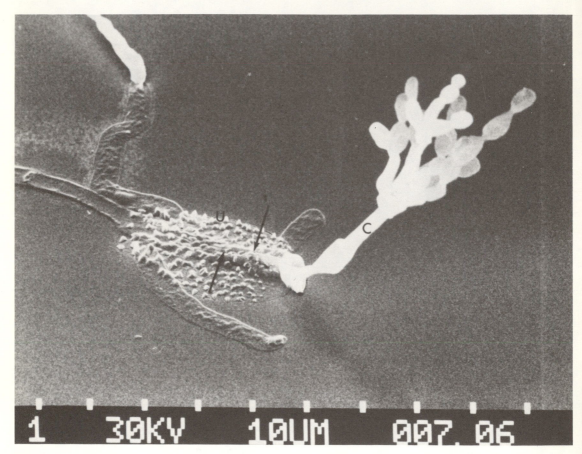

Fig. 3. Scanning electron micrograph showing fruiting mycelium of *Cladosporium tenuissimum* (C) on the lysed uredinospore (U) of *Melampsora larici-populina*. The outline of the internal parasitic hyphae is arrowed. Photograph kindly provided by Dr W.A. Heather.

CONCLUSIONS

The study of microbial invasions is important in that such invasions often greatly affect the newly colonised host, which may have great human value, directly or indirectly. Such studies are also of great interest to the scientist for the relative genetic simplicity of microbes enables the changes that occur during colonisation and adaptation to be directly studied and assessed. It is a pity that most of those studying the ecology of macro-organisms ignore the contribution of microbes to the processes they are investigating.

REFERENCES

Both, G.W., Sleigh, M.J., Cox, N.J., and Kendal, A.P. (1983). Antigenic drift in influenza virus H3 haemagglutinin from 1968 to 1980: multiple evolutionary pathways and sequential amino acid changes at key antigenic sites. *Journal of Virology 48*, 52–60.

Close, R.C., Moar, N.T., Tomlinson, A.I., and Lowe, A.D. (1978). Aerial dispersal of biological material from Australia to New Zealand. *International Journal of Biometeorology 22*, 1–19.

Davey, M., Mahon, R., and Gibbs, A. (1982). Superinfection immunity and the geographical distribution of togaviruses. In *Viral Diseases in South-East Asia and the Western Pacific*, (ed. J.S. Mackenzie) pp. 546–549, Academic Press Australia, Sydney.

Fenner, F. (1983). Biological control, as exemplified by smallpox eradication and myxomatosis. *Proceedings of the Royal Society of London B 218*, 259–285.

Fenner, F. (1985). Myxomatosis. In *Pests and Parasites as Migrants: An Australian Perspective* (eds A.J. Gibbs and H.R.C. Meischke) in press, Cambridge University Press, Cambridge.

Flor, H.H. (1946). Genetics of pathogenicity of *Melampsora lini. Journal of Agricultural Research 73*, 335–357.

Gibbs, A.J., and Meischke, H.R.C. (eds) (1985). *Pests and Parasites as Migrants: An Australian Perspective*, Cambridge University Press, Cambridge.

Holmes, F.O. (1951). Indications of a New-World origin of tobacco-mosaic virus. *Phtyopathology 41*, 341–349.

McKinney, H.H. (1929). Mosaic diseases in the Canary Islands, West Africa and Gibraltar. *Journal of Agricultural Research 39*, 557–578.

Mead-Briggs, A.R., and Vaughan, J.A. (1975). The differential transmissibility of myxoma virus strains of differing virulence grades by the rabbit flea *Spilopsyllus cuniculi* (Dale). *Journal of Hygiene Cambridge 75*, 237–247.

Sabin, A.B. (1952). Research on dengue during World War II. *American Journal of Tropical Medicine and Hygiene 1*, 30–50.

Sharma, J.K., and Heather, W.A. (1978). Parasitism of uredospores of *Melampsora larici-populina* Kleb. by *Cladosporium* sp. *European Journal of Forest Pathology 8*, 48–54.

Sidhu, G.S. (1975). Gene-for-gene relationship in plant parasitic systems. *Science Progress (London) 62*, 1265–1268.

Wace, N. (1985). Australia, the isolated continent. In *Pests and Parasites as Migrants: An Australian Perspective*. (eds A.J. Gibbs and H.R.C. Meischke) in press, Cambridge University Press, Cambridge.

Walker, J. (1983). Pacific mycogeography: deficiencies and irregularities in the distribution of plant parasitic fungi. *Australian Journal of Botany Supplementary Series 10*, 89–136.

INTRODUCED VERTEBRATES IN AUSTRALIA, WITH EMPHASIS ON THE MAMMALS

K. Myers[1]

Between 1860 and 1880 and to some extent in the decade or two preceding it, more than 60 species of vertebrates were released into the Australian environment. More were to follow later with the advent of a broader immigration policy and the development of aquaculture and aviculture as hobbies.

Many introductions were privately made, freely assisted by the British Government and ships' captains, who considered it their patriotic duty to turn Australia into another England. Others were stimulated by the world-wide movement in the nineteenth century to distribute the world's useful and beautiful animal species. Acclimatisation societies were formed at this time in many countries, including the Australian States of Victoria (1857), New South Wales (1861), Tasmania (1862), South Australia (1878) and Western Australia (1895).

Acclimatisation societies were not the only stimulus to importation of exotic vertebrates. Colonists required food and other resources. In earlier years commercial trading settlements were founded at Fort Dundas on Melville Island (1824) and at Fort Wellington in Raffles Bay (1827). These were followed by English military settlements at Port Essington in 1838; when they were finally abandoned in 1849, a legacy of feral animals was left which today continue to plague the north.

THE RABBIT (*ORYCTOLAGUS CUNICULUS*) —
AN EXAMPLE OF AN INTRODUCED VERTEBRATE

Rabbits were associated with the Australian colonies from the beginning. Five came out with the First Fleet to Sydney in 1788 and numerous rabbits were reported breeding around the houses there in 1825. During the following years they were present in all the States, and in the 1850s and 1860s their importation increased under the stimulus of the numerous acclimatisation societies set up to 'enrich the country and enhance its attractions'. In this activity the acclimatisation societies were aided by the governments of the day who not only subsidised their efforts but also imposed closed seasons for at least part of the year to protect rabbits from indiscriminate hunting.

Although many of the early importations were ungainly domestic breeds completely unfit for wild existence, wild-type rabbits are known to have been introduced into Australia more than 30 times, including places as widely distributed as Woody Island (Qld), Cooke River, Shoalhaven River, Barrier Ranges, and Menindee (N.S.W.), Glenelg (Vic.), Kapunda and Lake Alexandrina (S.A.) and Canning River (W.A.) (Stodart, in preparation). By 1875 the animal was well established in the Western District of Victoria and in South Australia at the southern end of the Flinders Ranges, as well as the earlier colony around Sydney. By 1879 the South Australian and Victorian infestations had amalgamated to cover one large area from Spencers Gulf to northeastern Victoria (Figure 1), and in 1881 farmers began abandoning their properties in the Mallee and the Wimmera regions of Victoria. The ensuing spread throughout the continent is now becoming well documented (Rolls 1969; Long 1972; Strong 1983; Stodart, in preparation).

Making use of the Murray-Darling River system in N.S.W., and the Diamantina and Georgina River systems in Queensland, rabbits moved at a rate of approximately 125 km/yr, to reach the Queensland border by 1866, and the Barkly Tableland and the Gulf of Carpentaria in northern Australia by 1910. Eastward, their progress slowed to about 15 km/yr, reaching the border ranges in 1905, Augathella in 1910 and the Winton district in 1922. In South Australia they reached Lake Eyre about 1886 and moved up the Finke and other rivers to invade the Musgrave, MacDonnell and other ranges and salt lake systems in central Australia. They

---

[1]   CSIRO, Division of Water and Land Resources, G.P.O. Box 1666, Canberra, A.C.T. 2601

surged northwards along drainage channels in the Simpson Desert, moving at a rate calculated at approximately 300 km/yr (Strong 1983). The Western Australian border was crossed in 1894 and the coast was reached near Geraldton in 1906, and at Port Hedland in 1912.

During the following years the rabbit continued to spread slowly, filling suitable environments along the coast and in the highlands, and is still progressing along the northern highlands inland from Cairns (Qld).

The spread of the rabbit was fastest across the dry southern savannas and along the arid watercourses, slowest in coastal woodlands and forests, and absent in the tropical north. Today the rabbit inhabits an area of some 4.5×10^6 km^2. It is common at latitudes higher than 25°S where environments are favourable, and becomes rare at latitudes less than 20°S. The greater proportion of its range was covered in 60 years. Despite modern studies which show the rabbit can move long distances (Parer 1982), by no figment of the imagination could this explosive emigration have resulted from the animal's own biological capabilities. It was carried around the country in large numbers by humans as a source of food. The main wave of colonisation and establishment was nevertheless a very real ecological phenomenon.

The rabbit in eastern Australia

Reasons for the success of the spread of the rabbit in the eastern States are to be found in historical records of those who witnessed and documented the event, and in the results of modern research programs.

The pastoral areas of eastern Australia were largely developed between 1830 and 1870. It took three years to get land ready for stocking, necessitating the building of long lengths of fencing and the digging of watering points in a generally waterless country. The descriptions tendered by more than 100 graziers, stock inspectors, and others to the Royal Commission on Western New South Wales (1901), from which the following excerpts are taken, stated that when development occurred the country was covered with a heavy growth of natural grasses, the ground was soft, spongy and absorbent and the country abounded in numerous edible shrubs and bushes. It was 'park-like, open forest country, with scattered pine-trees and currajongs' (referring to the region west of the Bogan River), 'beautiful open box country with large pines on it' (around Cobar), 'open box country with a waving mass of herbage' (around Nymagee).

About 1870 'the scrub grew to an enormous extent'. 'The country has deteriorated under sheep grazing transforming the land from its original soft absorbent nature to a hard, clayey, smooth surface . . . Rain runs off (the ridges) as fast as it falls, carrying with it the surface mould, seeds of all kinds . . . to enrich the lower-lying country and plant it with pine, box and other noxious scrubs.' 'Bush fires became less frequent.'

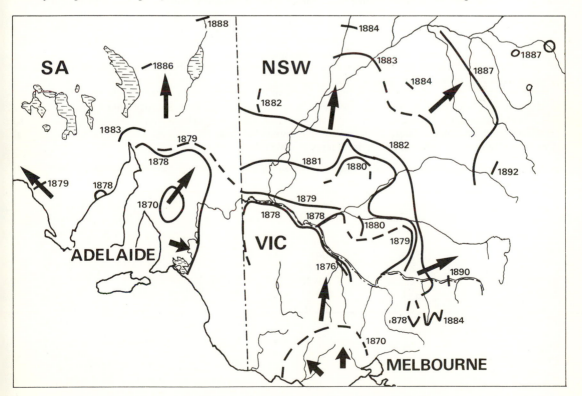

Fig. 1. Spread of the rabbit in southeastern Australia based on reports in newspapers and periodicals (after Stodart, in preparation).

The pastoralists who lived throughout that period recognised much more cogently than many of the present generation what was occurring. 'We all overestimated the capacity of the country (a pastoralist with 40 years experience).' 'Almost every holding west of the Wilcannia District had virgin country, and stock was carried for several years at a very high rate . . . as soon as the country was once eaten down everything began to fail.' 'Twenty-five years ago, a gradual storage of fodder was taking place every year on the bushes and smaller shrubs. The edible trees were . . . available to all stock. Since then conditions have changed. The grazing power of the land has now been reduced to what it will provide annually . . . there is no storage going on, and the rainfall becomes the regulating agent.' 'The edible shrubs and bushes have gone . . . now a six months' drought is more disastrous than a twelve months' one formerly was.' 'The people out west, instead of living on the interest of their capital, have been living on their capital.'

Evidence of this kind clearly indicates that throughout the drier parts of the eastern States large changes in environment had occurred *long before the rabbit came*. These changes were caused by domestic stock and included destruction of edible shrubs, permanent loss of top soil and nutrients, compaction of the soil, an increase in inedible shrubs and trees, a decrease in frequency of fire, and a rise in importance of annual plants. Primary production had been lowered and redirected to a large extent from shrubs and perennial herbs into woody plants and ephemerals (Harrington, Wilson and Young 1979).

Kangaroo numbers increased greatly with increase in watering points (Newsome 1975; Jarman and Johnson 1977) and bounties were placed on them in 1880. Scalp returns in Tamworth numbered 260,780 in 1884, long before the rabbit arrived (1909–1912). Kangaroos were shot out quickly, and attention was then focussed on wallabies (from 1885 onwards), rat kangaroos (from 1887 onwards) and possums, 40,210 of which were taken in the Corowa district of New South Wales in 1889. During this exercise several species were driven into rarity, or later became extinct. One of these species, viz. *Bettongia lesueur*, had already excavated an immense number of complex burrow systems across the southern half of Australia and these burrows would later come to be used by rabbits.

The predators did not fare any better. Aborigines and the dingo were reduced in numbers very early, and the tiger cat, native cat, and birds of prey were also mercilessly exterminated by poison, trap and gun from the beginning (Marshall 1966). The main destruction of its competitors and predators thus occurred before the rabbit began its colonisation of the continent.

Nor were these changes confined to the drier parts of Australia. In his history of the Monaro region of New South Wales, Hancock (1972) assembled evidence to describe in similar terms the adverse impact of livestock on the environment of the Southern Tablelands, and the enormous increase in indigenous wildlife consequent upon the destruction of their natural predators, viz. Aborigines and the dingo. Hancock also refers to the astonishing tallies of slaughter of wildlife in the annual reports of the Chief Inspector of Stock from the 1880s to the 1890s, a period of long-sustained and indiscriminate killing.

It is necessary to turn to the findings of modern research in order to understand the part played by the innate biological capability of the rabbit in its spread.

Rabbit populations in different geographical regions in eastern Australia show significant differences in almost every aspect of their biology, as evidenced in a simple tabulation of autopsy data (Table 1) (Myers 1971). These data show differences in body weights and body proportions, and variables pertaining to reproduction and physiology. There are no mysterious causes for these differences. They all have fundamental origins in the differences between the environments in which the animals live.

TABLE 1. *Regional differences in adult male rabbits in different regions of eastern Australia (older than 6 months).*

	Subtropical (n = 765)	Subalpine (n = 443)	Arid (n = 765)	Mediterranean (n = 423)	Significance of differences d.f. 3/2433
Weight (g)	1350	1304	1245	1304	0.001
Ear length (mm)	82.05	77.64	80.74	78.60	0.001
Foot length (mm)	92.01	89.38	90.76	89.65	0.001
Spleen (mg)	329	419	272	380	0.001
Pituitary (mg)	35.8	37.0	32.9	38.2	0.001
Adrenals (mg)	340	354	232	253	0.001
* Liver (g)	33	39	26	32	0.001
* Kidneys (g)	10.4	8.8	11.3	9.8	0.001
* Packed cell volume	38	35	30	37	0.01
* Serum protein (g/100ml)	5.6	5.4	5.2	5.4	0.01
Kidney fat index	1.26	1.61	1.93	1.40	0.001

* After Casperson (1968).

Rabbits in the Australian Alps are large-bodied, fast growing, healthy looking animals. They have shorter ears and legs, and the black band in the agouti pattern is longer than in other populations in Australia, making the pelage darker. Except when snow covers the ground they have access to a high protein diet. Rabbits at this altitude nevertheless have their problems. Because of the dampness of the environment, the early stages of the few internal parasites which managed to enter Australia with their host, face few environmental limits; the breeding female rabbit carries very heavy burdens of intestinal worms and the young rabbit runs a gauntlet of heavy coccideal infection. In addition to this, the lush grasses of spring are extremely low in sodium, a reflection of the heavy leaching of soils by snow. An examination of the large adrenal glands and blood discloses high levels of production of aldosterone, the salt-retaining hormone. The alpine rabbit is avid for sodium and will travel large distances to get it.

Rabbits in the arid zone are slow growing, small-bodied animals with long ears and legs, and the black band in the agouti pattern is shorter than in other populations, giving them a pale pelage. Because of the extreme dryness of their environment, internal parasites rarely worry them, but rabbits frequently thirst and starve. Except after rains their diet is low in protein, high in fibre and salty. Very small adrenal glands, low levels of circulating aldosterone and large kidneys with the power to concentrate urine, all illustrate the nature of their main environmental problem. Nor is this all that the arid zone rabbit has to contend with. Because of the extreme sandiness of the environment, foxes are able to dig down to the breeding chamber and consume up to 80 per cent of the young in a single breeding season.

Physiological and ecological differences of these kinds reflect the ability of a species to invade and colonise new environments. They affect rates of reproduction and survival, the final arbiters of ecological success.

In rabbits there are large differences in reproductive ability in different Australian environments. The reproductive histories of approximately 4000 female rabbits taken from populations in six diverse climatic regions in eastern Australia are summarised in Figures 2 and 3 and Table 2. Rabbits from the temperate mediterranean-type environment of Urana, N.S.W., exhibit a superior reproductive capacity in all ways, involving differences in rates of maturation and ovulation, and the occurrence of reproductive inadequacies (females exhibiting evidence of failure to implant or of resorption of embryonic young).

TABLE 2. *Reproduction in female rabbits older than 3 months from populations in six diverse climatic regions in eastern Australia.*

	Subtropical Qld	Subalpine N.S.W.	Semiarid N.S.W.	Temperate mediterranean N.S.W.	Coastal N.S.W.	Southern Tablelands N.S.W.
Pregnant (%)	32.1	24.1	24.8	43.4	26.6	33.9
Lactating only (%)	19.0	12.9	8.1	5.6	–	15.9
Litter size	4.80	4.52	4.49	5.65	5.23	5.01
Young per female/year	16.87	14.06	16.93	27.95	15.12	17.67
Reproductive inadequacies (%)	52.91	45.42	32.68	24.87	40.57	44.54
Number	548	636	937	412	301	889

There is a surprisingly constant pattern of seasonal production of young rabbits at all sites (Figure 4). Without exception more than 75 per cent of the young are born in the second half of the year with peaks of production between August and November, skewed towards the summer in the subalpine populations and towards winter in those in semiarid areas. The differences between the timing of production of the annual crop of young in each population can be represented by an average birth date at each site:

Subtropical	Queensland	Day 232 ± 86 days
Subalpine	N.S.W.	262 ± 99
Semiarid	N.S.W.	205 ± 75
Temperate mediterranean	N.S.W.	220 ± 69
Southern Tablelands	N.S.W.	247 ± 64
Coastal	N.S.W.	251 ± 78

There is also a clear annual pattern of inadequacies in reproduction. Most rabbit populations show low rates of losses in the spring and higher rates in summer and autumn. In Queensland high rates of loss occur in every month of the year. The population from the mediterranean-type region shows the lowest rates of loss (26.2 per cent) and the highest capacity for production (41.6 young per year). The Queensland population also shows a high capacity for production (35.8 young per year) but this is reduced to 17.0 by a reproductive loss of 52.9 per cent (Table 2). Irrespective of environment, rabbits always breed best in the spring, which is their ancestral pattern (Figure 5).

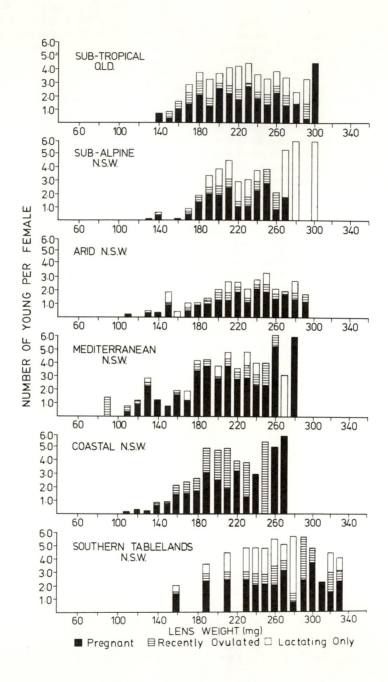

Fig. 2. Relationship between reproduction and age as indicated by the weight of the crystalline eye lens in 10mg intervals (Myers and Gilbert 1968) in six diverse climatic regions in eastern Australia. In the coastal data (after Dunsmore 1971), 'recent ovulations' and 'lactating only' are combined, and in the Southern Tabelands data (after Parer unpublished) the first three figures are means of rabbits aged 3–6, 6–9 and 9–12 months respectively; N as in Table 2.

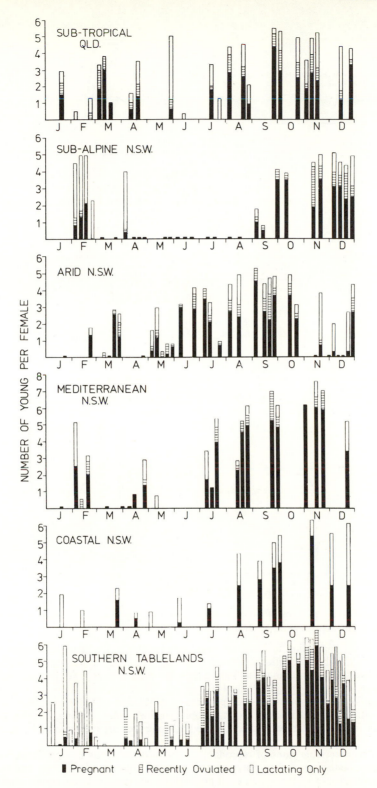

Fig. 3. The breeding season in female rabbits in six diverse climatic regions in eastern Australia; N as in Table 2.

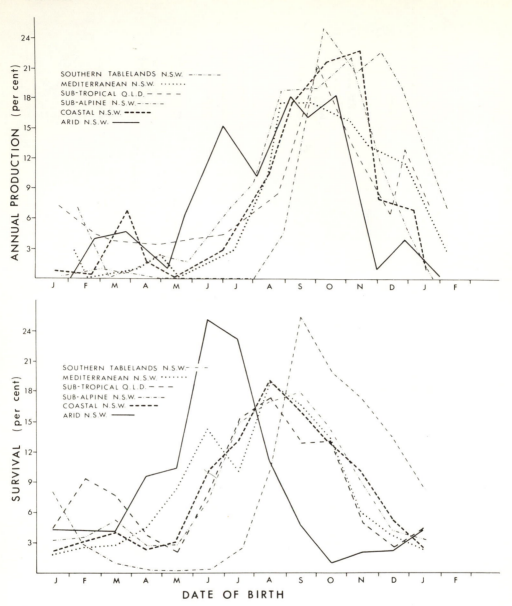

Fig. 4. The breeding season and rates of survival of rabbits during the first 12 months of life in populations in six different climatic regimes in eastern Australia.

The ability of a rabbit population to increase essentially resides in the rates of survival of the young. In experimental enclosures, with no significant predation, young born early in the season when food is plentiful and of the right kind, survive better than those born later, and young born at lower densities survive better than those born at higher densities (Myers and Poole 1963).

There are also significant differences between patterns of survival in different natural environments (Figure 4) as shown by plotting survival rates of young rabbits against dates of birth. In the subalpine climate favourable conditions for survival are very short. In the arid zone they are confined to the cooler months of the year.

The interplay between variable rates of reproduction and survival leads to significant differences in age-structure between the populations and to different capacities for increase. Such data can be manipulated to show the levels of mortality in young which each population can sustain as an annual loss and still remain extant. The population from the mediterranean-type environment possesses the highest rates of increase and can support an annual mortality of almost 90 per cent of its young (Table 3).

Modern studies of live rabbits are throwing more light onto the above statements but the central findings remain sound. The rabbit has succeeded as a coloniser of Australia for a number of reasons:

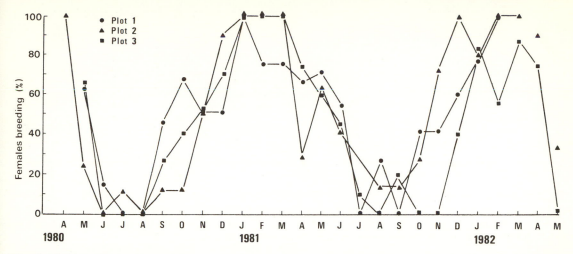

Fig. 5. The breeding season in three populations of rabbits in southern Spain. Plots 1 and 2 are experimental treatments irrigated to produce summer pastures, and plot 3 is a natural control (after Soriguer and Myers, in preparation).

1. It is perfectly preadapted physiologically to the climate of much of the southern half of the continent;
2. It carries a very depauperate parasite fauna when compared with rabbits in Spain, where it originated;
3. The alteration to the landscape by humans and domesticated stock which changed a predominantly perennial vegetation into one containing a large proportion of annuals presented the rabbit with a perfect and abundant food source;
4. Human persecution of native predators and grazing mammals left the rabbit almost completely free of predators and competitors during its primary irruption. Predators added later to the system (the fox, the cat and myxomatosis) came too late to be able to influence events;
5. Several of the native grazing mammals left behind them extensive burrow systems which were taken over by rabbits, thereby permitting rapid colonisation of arid environments;
6. The rabbit is an excellent ecological generalist, and has not had to call on special genetic selection for its survival.

These conclusions are not meant to intimate that the rabbit has not been able to penetrate environments without human assistance. It has, and on a large scale. But wherever this has been done it has been from a position of immense ecological strength derived almost completely from human activities.

I find it most useful to think of the rabbit in Australia in terms of Caughley's (1977) strategic model of plant-herbivore-predator relationships (Figure 6). European settlers set up the first trophic level by altering the environment and excluding predators, then added the herbivores and finally the predators to form second and third trophic levels.

TABLE 3. *Capacity for increase in five populations of rabbits in different climatic regions.*

		Number of litters per year	Finite rate of natural increase (Ro)	Capacity for increase (r_c)	Young mortality $= 0$ (%)
Average natality					
Subtropical	Qld	3.9	3.54	0.055	72.0
Subalpine	N.S.W.	2.9	1.04	0.002	3.0
Arid	N.S.W.	3.0	1.75	0.024	43.0
Mediterranean	N.S.W.	5.2	4.61	0.098	78.0
Coastal	N.S.W.	5.2	1.27	0.017	21.0
High natality					
Subtropical	Qld	4.0	4.43	0.065	77.0
Subalpine	N.S.W.	3.4	1.56	0.025	36.0
Arid	N.S.W.	4.0	2.92	0.047	66.0
Mediterranean	N.S.W.	6.0	6.29	0.118	84.0
Coastal	N.S.W.	4.8	2.17	0.055	54.0

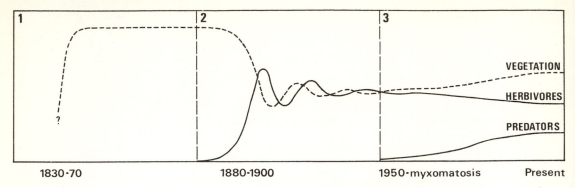

Fig. 6. General strategic model of Caughley (1977) depicting the relatively stable outcome when a herbivore is added to a system in which its food source (first trophic level) initially self-limiting, forms new equilibria (second and third trophic levels) due to herbivore-vegetation and prey-predator interactions. Caughley's example represents the well-known moose-wolf story on Isle Royale (Allen 1974).

OTHER MAMMALS

Approximately 47 mammals have been introduced into Australia (Table 4). Few of them have been studied in detail and those that have (*Mus musculus, Bubalus arnee bubalis* and *Sus scrofa*) have been examined only in relation to local pest situations. National overviews are still to come. Useful information is nevertheless to be found in their patterns of distribution within Australia (Strahan 1983) and what is known of their present status.

Herbivores

Deer. Approximately 16 species or subspecies of deer-like mammals were introduced into Australia. Records of their introductions are far from complete (Bentley 1978) and are unlikely ever to be fully accounted for. Due to historical precedents, the species came mainly from Europe and the Indo-Asian region.

Although concentrated in Victoria, deer releases were widely scattered throughout the settled parts of the continent and Tasmania, including the military settlements in Port Essington, and islands off the Queensland and Northern Territory coasts.

Several species, the specialists, failed from the start; some may never have been released. They included the rabbit-sized, primitive mouse deer (*Tragulus meminna*), which lives singly or in pairs in dense brush along the edges of the Himalayan forests in northern India; the small musk deer (*Moschus moschiferus*) from dense damp forests on steep mountain slopes in Asia; the solitary, aggressive forest-dwelling Chinese water deer (*Hydropotes inermis*); the European roe deer (*Capreolus capreolus*), a specialised browser which forms feeding herds in winter; and the barasingha (*Cervus duvauceli*), which requires swards of perennial grasses. The black buck (*Antilope cervicapra*), a migratory Indian gazelle, released fairly widely in southwest Western Australia, has managed to live on in one or two small herds under human protection.

Several species took advantage of the agricultural environment provided by humans and became strongly established. They were the fallow deer (*Dama dama*), red deer (*Cervus elaphus*), axis deer (*Axis axis*), and rusa (*Cervus timorensis*), sambar (*Cervus unicolor*), and hog deer (*Axis porcinus*). The first three species have strong herding behaviour, with a fixed seasonal rut, and although the red deer is also a browser, they all prefer agricultural lands. Like the rabbit, their populations erupted and brought them into competition with humans and their stock, especially in western Victoria where culling of the herds of fallow deer was carried out well before the turn of the century. Population growth came to an abrupt halt as closer settlement and persistent hunting fragmented the herds. Those that survive at the present time do so in general because humans permit it. Some populations, nevertheless, are essentially wild and self-perpetuating, e.g. the fallow deer in the Tasmanian lakelands and the red deer in the Grampians, and those at the headwaters of the Brisbane River in Queensland and in the southern highlands of New South Wales (Figure 7).

The sambar and hog deer live singly or in small groups and have no fixed seasonal rut. The sambar prefers openings in forests and the hog deer prefers thick brush adjoining swamplands. Sambar populations erupted during the early 1900s and by 1951 they were declared vermin in Victoria. This robust nocturnal grazing species capitalised on the opening up of bush by logging and fire and has gradually extended its range from southern Victoria to the A.C.T. highlands where it appears to be still spreading. The hog deer, confined to the Gippsland swamps and offshore islands of Victoria, maintains its numbers in the face of controlled hunting and predation by dogs, but is not capable of extending its range.

The rusa, a tropical species which forms feeding herds, failed to establish in the south, except for the herd in the Royal National Park, Sydney, but maintains good populations on the Cobourg Peninsula and on offshore islands nearby.

TABLE 4. *Mammals introduced into Australia.*

Common Name	Scientific Name	Reason for Introduction	Result	Origin
Eastern grey squirrel	*Sciurus carolinensis*	Aesthetics — public gardens Melbourne and Ballarat	Died out	North America
Three-striped palm squirrel	*Funambulus pennanti:*	Zoo release	Local populations in Sydney and Perth	India
Black rat	*Rattus rattus*	Commensal	Widespread	S.E. Asia
Brown rat	*Rattus norvegicus*	Commensal	Widespread	Asian Steppes
House mouse	*Mus musculus*	Commensal	Widespread	Central Asia
Ferret	*Mustela putorius furo*	Hunt rabbits	Died out	Mediterranean
Gold-spotted mongoose	*Herpestes javanicus aruopunctatus*	Control rabbits and rats	Died out	India, Java, Sumatra
Dingo	*Canis familiaris dingo*	Commensal	Widespread	Indonesia
Feral dog	*Canis familiaris*	Commensal	Widespread	—
Red fox	*Vulpes* vulpes	Hunt	Widespread	Europe
Domestic cat	*Felis catus*	Commensal	Widespread	Europe
European rabbit	*Oryctolagus cuniculus*	Hunt	Widespread	Western Mediterranean
European hare	*Lepus capensis*	*Hunt*	Widespread	Europe
Feral horse	*Equus caballus*	Draught, Transport	Widespread	Europe
Feral donkey	*Equus asinus*	Draught	Mostly arid north west monsoonal tropics	North Africa
Zebra	*Equus* sp.	?	Died out	Africa
Feral pig	*Sus scrofa*	Meat	Widespread	Eurasia
Arabian camel	*Camelus dromedarius*	Draught, Transport	Arid Central west	North Africa-Arabia
Llama	*Lama guanaco lama*	Draught	Died out	Mainly High Andes
Alpaca	*Lama guanaco pacos*	Wool	Died out	Mainly High Andes
Vicuna	*Lama vicugna*	Wool	Died out	High Andes
Indian spotted mouse deer	*Tragulus meminna*	Hunt	Died out	India
Musk deer	*Moschus moschiferus*	Hunt	Died out	Central and East Asia
Fallow deer	*Dama dama*	Hunt	Local herds	Mediterranean and Central Europe
Hog deer	*Axis porcinus*	Hunt	Large herds in Gippsland	India-Asia
Axis deer (Chital)	*Axis axis*	Hunt	Small local herds	India
Indian and Samatran sambar	*Cervus unicolor*	Hunt	Local populations, expanding range	India, Sumatra
Sunda sambar (Rusa)	*Cervus timorensis*	Hunt	Local herds	Borneo
Philippine sambar	*Cervus mariannus*	Hunt	?	Philippines
Barasingha	*Cervus duvauceli*	Hunt	Died out	India
Formosan and Japanese sika	*Cervus nippon*	Hunt	Died out	Japan
Red deer	*Cervus elaphus*	Hunt	Local herds	Europe
Wapiti	*Cervus elaphus canadensis*	Hunt	Died out	North America
Chinese water deer	*Hydropotes inermis*	Hunt	Died out	China
Roe deer	*Capreolus capreolus*	Hunt	Died out	Europe

TABLE 4. *Mammals introduced into Australia. (continued)*

Common Name	Scientific Name	Reason for Introduction	Result	Origin
Eland	*Taurotragus oryx*	?	Died out	Central and South Africa
Feral sheep	*Ovis ammon musimon*	Meat, Wool	Widespread	Mediterranean
Feral goat	*Capra hircus*	Meat, Milk	Widespread	Mediterranean
Indian black buck	*Antilope cervicapra*	Hunt	Local herd	India
Water buffalo	*Bubalus arnee bubalis*	Draught, Meat	Tropical north coast	Asia
African buffalo	*Syncerus caffer*	?	Died out	South-eastern Africa
Java banteng (Bali cattle)	*Bos javanicus*	Draught	Limited area, monsoonal tropics	Java
Feral cattle	*Bos taurus*	Meat	Widespread	Europe
Zebu	*Bos indicus*	Draught, Meat	Limited areas	India

(After Marshall 1966; Rolls 1969; Long 1972; Frith 1975; Bentley 1978).

The barasingha, and the remaining species all appear to have disappeared.

I have examined many of the Australian writings on deer. Of the 16 species listed, 4 were predominantly browsers, 12 were grazers, 11 were herding species, 8 had a fixed seasonal rut, 6 species were ecological specialists in a strict sense, and 4 were followers of agriculture. The 6 specialists failed, as did 3 of the 4 browsers (the red, which also grazes, survived). Three of the herd species (fallow, red and axis) still live on agricultural holdings or in reserves given some protection by humans.

Although meeting few problems in Australia in relation to climatic adaptation or predation, the deer as a group appear to have failed because Australian vegetation was not adequate as browse, and obligate herding species (those with a fixed seasonal rut) were direct competitors with stock.

The two most successful species, the sambar and hog deer, are non-herding grazers, with no fixed rut, living in habitats not used for grazing and which afford shelter from predators.

Other large herbivores. The many large mammals introduced into Australia for draught, transport, meat, milk and wool, show patterns of colonisation completely different from those of the deer (Figure 7), and completely different success rates as well.

The Camelidae (camels and llamas) exhibit extreme effects of environmental influence. The former species, *Camelus dromedarius*, is now extinct as a wild species in its North African and Arabian birth place, where it evolved in deserts, semi-deserts and grass steppes feeding on high fibre grass, herbs, fallen leaves and thin browse. It continues to be found in the driest centre of Australia where an adequate climate and food supply permit survival and reproduction. In these areas the species is now steadily increasing in numbers. The llamas, on the other hand, from dry cold grass steppes at 4000 m in the Andes, died out in the damp warm Australian environment, despite determined attempts, due to disease.

Almost all the large herbivores show the same kind of relationship to their original environment. The donkey (*Equus asinus*), a hybrid of three North African wild asses, like the camel, is an arid-adapted animal, with low water needs and the ability to digest food high in fibre. In Australia its centres of distribution are in the drier and hotter parts of central and northern areas. The wild horse (*Equus caballus*), with evolutionary roots in the Euro-Asian steppes, does best in dry grasslands of central and northern Australia where it has access to water.

Banteng cattle from swamp forests and woodlands with bamboo brush and grasslands in Bali and Java live successfully on the Cobourg Peninsula of northern Queensland. The water buffalo is strictly confined to areas in northern Australia where it has access to swamps during the hotter months. The wild pig, an unspecialised feeder on roots, herbs, grasses, fruit and animals, from swampy forests of Europe and Asia, likewise inhabits the same environments in Australia and eats the same foods. The wild goat is now almost extinct in Asia Minor and the Greek Islands, where it once inhabited forest and brush on mountains and slopes; it seeks out similar environments in Australia. Even the domestic sheep displays strong evolutionary relationships with its Mediterranean origin in Corsica and Sardinia.

The rodents

The rodents form an interesting group. The two squirrel species, food specialists from the North American softwoods, and Indian palm groves, failed to cope with the Australian environment. The eastern grey squirrel (Seebeck 1984) died out, and the palm squirrel remains isolated in Sydney and Melbourne where it depends on human handouts. The commensals, *Mus* and *Rattus*, however, have become widely established. *Mus* originated in central Asia, and because of its small size and unspecialised feeding habits it has been able to colonise the whole continent. *Rattus*, also Asian in origin, on the other hand, although successful and widespread, is strictly confined to environments with access to water. This is not only true for the modern *Rattus* species but also the seven species and subspecies of the ancient *Rattus* group which have now been on the continent for about one million years (Taylor and Horner 1973) and which remain clustered as far as density of species and subspecies is concerned, on the northeastern coast of Australia. Only one of the latter species, *R. villosissimus*, has managed to invade the arid interior, but results of recent studies clearly show that this species also remains closely controlled by the presence of water in its diet. For the rodents, the availability of a new environment is of little value unless accompanied by genetic plasticity.

The predators

Introduced mammalian predators show the same trends. The tropical mongoose and the ferret, both extreme specialists, died out. The mongoose was not widely released, but the ferret has escaped into the wild on

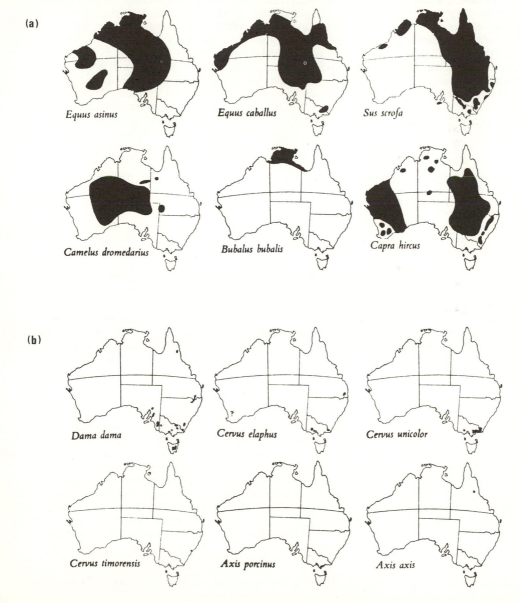

Fig. 7. Patterns of distribution of six large introduced herbivores which have thrived in environments where competition with stock has been minimal (a), in contrast to six species of deer (b), which have been heavy competitors with stock (Strahan 1983).

thousands of occasions and continues to do so. The Australian environment until now has not provided the ferret with buffer prey when its preferred diet, nestling rabbits, are absent; changing conditions in wildlife conservation may yet present it with an opportunity to become established in some of the larger new National Parks. The dingo, fox and cat, on the other hand, were very successful. The thylacine, present across the continent when the dingo was introduced some 3500 years ago, became extinct. The fox and cat, supreme generalists, followed the rabbit northwards and westwards about 20 years later.

Impact of the introduction of the human animal

All of these data emphasise the importance of humans as the most efficient conditioner of environment and the most competent of species to secure resources. Throughout history, wherever humans have colonised new areas, environmental change and changes in status of species has followed. Although remaining a contentious cultural issue, wherever there are good fossil records the above statement is well supported.

Olson and James (1982) examined thousands of fossil bird bones from the Hawaiian Islands collected since 1971 and showed that 39 species of birds became extinct prior to the entry of western people, due to predation on ground-dwelling species and clearing of lowland forest, primarily by fire, for agriculture. The record of human activities in New Zealand is equally as graphic. Within 500 years of the arrival of Polynesians approximately 12 species of the large wingless herbivorous birds, the Moas, became extinct. Before European settlement they had all gone, and extensive burning had destroyed up to 50 per cent of the podocarp forests which once covered the eastern half of the South Island, reducing them to grasslands and scrub. Europeans added to this pronounced ecological disturbance by introducing approximately 54 species of mammals and 138 species of birds, which then set about their own business of environmental alteration (Wodzicki 1959; Gibb and Flux 1973; Veblen and Stewart 1982). In Madagascar the evidence shows a rapid extinction of a great number of animal species and signs of heavy burning of forests within 500 years of human appearance.

The evidence of the effects of human colonisation of continents is more equivocal in that many of the changes registered occurred simultaneously with natural climatic changes of some magnitude. In North America some 40 species of large game mammals became extinct during the Pleistocene. There has been extensive argument as to causes, but it remains undisputed that more than 80 per cent of the species survived the first three glaciations and became extinct during the fourth, after Paleo-Indians arrived, and when the climate was improving and resources increasing. There was no terminal Pleistocene loss of small mammals, marine organisms or plants.

The extinction of the Australian megafauna also is still very open to question. Aborigines have lived in Australia for at least 35000 years. Tasmania separated from the continent some 12000 years ago due to a post-glacial rising of the sea. The dingo and new cultural influences from outside the continent appeared approximately 3500 years ago.

Faunal remains of a wide range of marsupials have been found in southwestern New South Wales in the same stratigraphic units as archeological material dated at about 26000 years BP. Although their primitive weapons and territorial behaviour may have limited the ability of early Australian Aborigines to overkill, they subjected their environment to massive and systematic burning. This is especially evident in western Tasmania where the large open grasslands caused by aboriginal use of fire have been slowly reverting to forest since the early 1800s. Modern Aborigines still carry on this practice in tribal lands. The early separation of Tasmania denied the dingo (and later the fox) access and the thylacine, driven to extinction in Australia, lived on in Tasmania until Europeans arrived.

The continued controversy as to whether humans, as colonisers of new environments, hunted large herbivorous mammals and birds into extinction seems to be based more on sociological than on ecological evidence. On islands they clearly did. On continents they may have, in conjunction with changing climates and habitat restriction. The evidence of wholesale use of fire by all cultures is nevertheless overwhelming. In new environments not previously exposed to this kind of fire regime the short-term ecological consequences are severe enough (Gill, Groves and Noble 1981), but completely unconsidered are the longer term changes. Burning results in direct loss of nutrients (especially C, N and S) from ecosystems, either by volatilisation or loss of ash due to the action of wind and water. Nitrogen is one of the major elements limiting the productivity of most Australian ecosystems and shows the greatest quantitative transfer to the atmosphere during fires (Walker, Raison and Khanna 1985); add the grazing animal, native or introduced, and drought, and it is difficult to envisage any system maintaining itself as such over a long period, especially those with low soil nutrient reserves which depend for their long-term stability on the retention and recycling processes in living biomass and litter.

Other vertebrates

Introductions of other vertebrates into Australia have exhibited much the same kinds of results as have the mammals.

Among the reptiles and amphibians three species have been introduced and established in Australia. Two small geckos, the house gecko (*Hemidactylus frenatus*) and an arboreal gecko (*Lepidodactylus lugubris*), introduced in ships' cargo from the Pacific Islands, exist essentially as commensals in human dwellings restricted to the northern and northeastern coasts, depending on insects attracted to house-lights as a source of food. A species of a different kind, the marine toad (*Bufo marinus*), originally from tropical South America, and introduced into northern Queensland in 1935 to control insect pests of cane, increased its range exponentially, facilitated by human transportation, at 8.1 percent per year for the next 40 years (Sabath, Boughton and Easteal 1981). The toad has recently crossed the Northern Territory border to the west and has entered northern New South Wales. Sabath, Boughton and Easteal have predicted on the basis of its known physiology that the species will colonise the whole of the more humid areas of Australia (Figure 8). Floyd and Easteal (this volume) estimate a final distribution somewhat more limited than this but both groups agree that climatic variables will be the ultimate barriers.

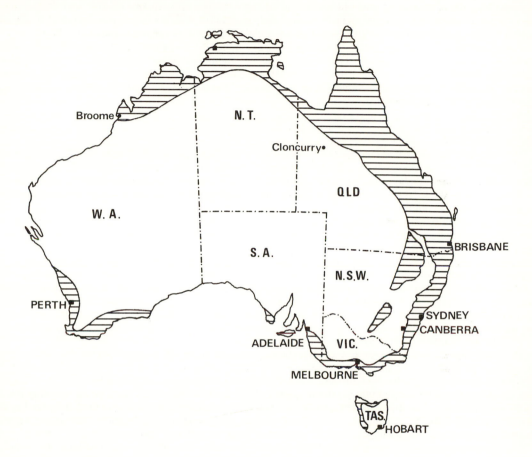

Fig. 8. Predicted expansion of the range of the introduced cane toad (*Bufo marinus*) in Australia (after Sabath, Boughton and Easteal 1981).

More than 20 species of fish have been introduced into Australia, of which 16 species have established self-maintaining populations (Arthington and Mitchell, this volume). The several food species brought in by early settlers from the cool sluggish waters of European rivers (roach *Rutilis rutilis*, tench *Tinca tinca* and redfin *Perca fluviatilis* and more recently, the European carp *Cyprinus carpio*) found favourable conditions in the cool waterways of southeastern Australia and Tasmania and prospered, especially where dams and other barriers slowed the natural rate of flow of streams. Two of the stenothermal sporting fish, the brown trout (*Salmo trutta*) and rainbow trout (*S. gairdnersi*), following massive human support, now maintain populations in the cooler waters of fast-running highland streams but the several salmon which require sea-runs continue to fail despite repeated reintroductions.

The mosquito fish (*Gambusia* sp.), introduced to control mosquitoes, has spread widely up and down the eastern coast of Australia and Tasmania, and numerous tropical aquarium species recently released into the warm waters of coastal Queensland are spreading. Almost without exception, as Arthington and Mitchell (this volume) show, like the reptiles and amphibia, the successful species of fish are those which have found resources in environments in climates similar to those from which they came.

Newsome and Noble (this volume) in dealing with the birds chose to consider translocation of 43 local species as well as 64 introduced species, and attempted to analyse life systems to explain success or failure.

The foreign species were introduced for a variety of reasons — for aesthetics (in parks and gardens), as game, as domestic pets and avicultural varieties, for the feather trade and in zoological gardens.

Fifty seven of the total 107 species became established. Significantly more foreign species failed than did local translocations. Foreign granivores were especially unsuccessful. The most successful foreign species became established in human-made environments. Native species were more successful in unaltered environments, although some natives (the galah *Cacatua roseicapilla* and crested pigeon *Ocyphaps lophotes*), like the kangaroo before them, expanded their range with agriculture. Foreign species adapted to other climatic regimes have been very unsuccessful — their success rate has been positively related to environmental change by humans.

The difficulty of measuring quantitative functional relationships between species and environment and the probability of successful establishment in a new location led Nix and Wapshere (this volume) to develop a model based on bioclimatic matching — the quantitative comparison of original climate and climate at site of introduction related to success of establishment. In showing that 80–90 percent of the variance in frequency of successful establishment is accounted for by simple linear exponential or square root transforms of bioclimatic distance for animals as varied as birds and invertebrates, Nix and Wapshere illustrate excellently what this chapter has been emphasising — namely, that evolutionary origins are extremely important in understanding colonisation of new environments.

CONCLUSIONS

Colonisation, however it is defined, is an integral part of the biology of all species. The processes and qualities which permit an organism to invade a new environment are the same as those which give it the ability to expand its range in its home environment. As Barrett and Richardson (this volume) state, there is no single optimum genetic solution to the challenges facing the colonist, and, as the other chapters show, there is no optimum ecological solution either.

The brief examination I have presented in this overview of the introduction of vertebrates into Australia and the more penetrating observations of the contributions on specific vertebrate groups (see earlier chapters) lead to the following four general conclusions.

1. Amongst vertebrates, the possibility of colonising a new Australian environment is highly dependent on similarity between the climate of origin and climate of introduction (see Swincer, this volume). Unlike invertebrates, with their short generation times, vertebrates cannot however, in general, capitalise on genetic strategies for colonisation, but must already possess a genetic pool capable of supporting the physiological tolerances and ecological plasticity demanded of them. This conclusion is repeatedly supported by the contributions presented, and especially by the elegant demonstration for introduced birds of Nix and Wapshere (this volume).

It is equally important to note that evolutionary origins have effortlessly overridden the effects of domestication in the large herbivorous mammals. The camel, domesticated in 4000 BC in North Africa and Arabia and carried around the Mediterranean by Muslims as a beast of burden, is now extinct as a wild species. Eighty dromedaries introduced into southern Spain in 1829 died out within 20 years on the swampy lowlands of the Coto Donana. The British forces transferred 20,000 dromedaries from Sudan to the Ethiopian highlands in their war with Italy; all of them died in the alpine climate. Released by their Afghan masters in the Australian desert, the same species, which can lose 25 percent of body weight and live for as long as 3 weeks without water, prospered and increased to form the largest free-living herd in the world. The same kind of relationships held for the llama, donkey, various breeds of cattle, horse, sheep and goat, and some deer.

Evolutionary origins are also seen to be important in the smaller vertebrates, especially birds and fish. Even the smaller introduced mammals (lagomorphs and rodents) with their presumed greater genetic and ecological plasticity have found limits to distribution, based mainly on physiological tolerances or resource availability, which bar their further spread. The only species which has been able to colonise, with human help, most of the continent, viz. *Mus musculus*, has done so because of size.

2. A large number of introduced vertebrates in Australia owe their success and their continued existence to widespread human alterations to environment, either as invaders of human-made environments, or as colonisers of new environments from centres of high density created by human settlements.

The above statement is true for almost all introduced mammals, for most of the birds, and for many of the fish species. For Australia, where most of the full ecological equivalents have been removed, or had their status altered, it is thus rather questionable to try and discuss problems relating to the potential of communities for invasion (see Fox and Fox, this volume). It is likely to be far more profitable to compare the histories of establishment of the same species in different environments (where the data exist) or on different continents. Feral goats, for example, exist in large herds on offshore islands of northern Australia (Sir Edward Pellew, N.E. Island, St Helena) but not on the mainland nearby where the dingo is present. The European rabbit maintains large populations on offshore islands in North America but, despite more than 140 deliberate introductions, has never become established on the mainland inhabited by a full complement of closely related rabbit species and their predators and diseases.

3. Few ecological specialists have become established among the many vertebrates introduced into Australia, although many have failed. Those that succeeded did so due to strong human support (e.g. trout).

The veracity of this statement is clouded to a large extent by the lack of supporting information on numbers and frequency of releases of the different species. Mammals like the roe deer and mouse deer are so difficult to keep in captivity that the numbers released could not have been large. Species like the fallow, on the other hand which thrive in captivity, were released in large numbers.

Vertebrate species which have become established in Australia were almost without exception preadapted to the Australian environment and the resources it offered.

4. The Australian experience is a prime example of the supreme ability of humans themselves as a mammalian coloniser, extremely competent in predation, competition and environmental conditioning, including the use of fire. As human populations continue to rise, all species which compete with humans or serve as a resource, and all environments which are of human use, will change in status. But as far as the vertebrates are concerned, decisions on what species humans want to have live with them will, in the end, belong to the cultural rather than the biological sphere.

REFERENCES

Allen, D.L. (1974). Of fire, moose and wolves, *Audubon 76*, 38–49.

Bentley, A. (1978). *An Introduction to the Deer of Australia*, Koetong Trust and Forest Commission of Victoria, Melbourne.

Casperson, K. (1968). Influence of environment upon some physiological parameters of the rabbit, *Oryctolagus cuniculus* (L.) in natural populations. *Proceedings of the Ecological Society of Australia 3*, 113–119.

Caughley, G. (1977). *Analysis of Vertebrate Populations*, John Wiley and Sons, London.

Dunsmore, J.D. (1971). The rabbit in the south coastal region of New South Wales, an area in which parasites appear to exert a population-regulating effect. *Australian Journal of Zoology 19*, 355–370.

Frith, H.J. (1973). *Wildlife Conservation*, Angus and Robertson, Sydney.

Gibb, J.A., and Flux, J.E.C. (1973). Mammals. In *The Natural History of New Zealand* (ed. G.R. Williams) pp. 334–371, A.H. and A.W. Reed, Wellington.

Gill, A.M., Groves, R.H., and Noble, I.R. (eds) (1981). *Fire and the Australian Biota*, Australian Academy of Science, Canberra.

Hancock, W.K. (1972). *Discovering Monaro. A Study of Man's Impact on his Environment*, University Press, Cambridge.

Harrington, G.N., Wilson, A.D., and Young, M.D. (eds) (1984). *Management of Australia's Rangelands*, CSIRO, Melbourne.

Jarman, J.A., and Johnson, K.A. (1977). Exotic mammals, indigenous mammals and land-use. *Proceedings of the Ecological Society of Australia 10*, 146–166.

Long, J.L. (1972). Introduced birds and mammals in Western Australia. *Agricultural Protection Board of Western Australia Technical Series* No. 1.

Marshall, A.J. (1966). *The Great Extermination*, Heinemann, Melbourne.

Myers, K. (1971). The rabbit in Australia. *Proceedings of the Advanced Study Institute on Dynamics and Numbers in Populations (Oosterbeek, 1970)* pp. 478–506, Pudoc, Wageningen.

Myers, K., and Gilbert, N. (1968). Determination of age of wild rabbits in Australia. *Journal of Wildlife Management 32*, 841–849.

Myers, K., and Poole, W.E. (1963). A study of the biology of the wild rabbit, *Oryctolagus cuniculus* (L.) in confined populations. III. Reproduction. *Australian Journal of Zoology 10*, 225–267.

Newsome, A.E. (1975). An ecological comparison of two arid-zone kangaroos of Australia, and their anomalous prosperity since the introduction of ruminant stock to their environment. *Quarterly Review of Biology 50*, 389–424.

New South Wales Government (1901). *Royal Commission to Inquire into the Condition of Crown Tenants, Western Division of New South Wales. Summary of Evidence*. Government Printer, Sydney.

Olson, S.L., and James, H.F. (1982). Fossil birds from the Hawaiian Islands: evidence for wholesale extinction by man before western contact. *Science 217*, 633–635.

Parer, I. (1983). Dispersal of the wild rabbit, *Oryctolagus cuniculus*, at Urana in New South Wales. *Australian Wildlife Research 9*, 427–441.

Rolls, E.C. (1969). *They All Ran Wild*, Angus and Robertson, Sydney.

Sabath, M.D., Boughton, W.C., and Easteal, S. (1981). Expansion of the range of the introduced toad *Bufo marinus* in Australia from 1935 to 1974. *Copeia 3*, 676–680.

Seebeck, J.H. (1984). The eastern grey squirrel, *Sciurus carolinensis*, in Victoria. *Victorian Naturalist 101*, 60–65.

Stodart, E. (in prep.). Colonisation of the Australian mainland by the rabbit, *Oryctolagus cuniculus* (L.).

Strahan, R. (ed) (1983). *Complete Book of Australian Mammals*, Angus and Robertson, Sydney.

Strong, B.W. (1983). The invasion of the Northern Territory by the wild European rabbit *Oryctolagus cuniculus. Conservation Commission of the Northern Territory Technical Report* No. 3.

Taylor, M.J., and Horner, B.E. (1973). Results of the Archbold Expeditions No. 98. Systematics of Native Australian Rattus (Rodentia, Muridae), *American Museum of Natural History, New York Volume 150,* Article 1.

Veblen, T.T., and Stewart, G.H. (1982). The effects of introduced wild animals on New Zealand forests. *Annals of the Association of American Geographers 72,* 372–397.

Walker, J., Raison, R.J., and Khanna, P.K. (1985). The effects of fire on Australian soils. In *The Effects of Man on Australian Soils* (eds J. Russell and R. Isbell) in press, Australian Soil Science Society, Adelaide.

Wodzicki, K.A. (1950). Introduced mammals of New Zealand: an ecological and economic survey. *DSIR Bulletin* No. 98.

PLANT INVASIONS OF AUSTRALIA : AN OVERVIEW

R.H. Groves[1]

Approximately 10% of Australia's total of 15,000 to 20,000 species of vascular plants are introduced (Michael 1981). In some areas the proportion of introduced plants can be much higher than this average figure. For instance, for the Sydney region Fox and Adamson (1979) estimated there to be between 400 and 500 species of introduced plants and about 1,500 native species.

Kloot (1984) argued recently that several cosmopolitan species currently regarded as 'indigenous' may have arrived in Australia in prehistoric times by a process of long-distance dispersal. Such species seem to be associated particularly with aquatic environments. Following this reasoning, it is probable that up to about 100 of the so-called cosmopolitan species of the seashore or of wetlands may have established prior to settlement of the continent. These species may be regarded as 'introduced' when considering a longer time-scale for plant invasions. An example of this group is probably *Cakile edentula*. It is interesting to note that currently this species is being replaced along the southeast coast of Australia by the closely-related *C. maritima*, a pattern identical with that identified for the western coastline of North America (Barbour and Rodman 1970). *Cakile* and other strand plants have been shown to establish, disappear and re-establish on coral cays as a result of relatively short-distance dispersal over short-time spans (Heatwole 1984). The longer term implications of such natural 'invasion' sequences are more conjectural, however, especially as they relate to long-distance dispersal to Australia.

When Aborigines arrived in Australia more than 40,000 years ago they do not seem to have brought plant propagules with them. Although there is no evidence from this pre-European period for plant introduction, immigrants arriving subsequently certainly have introduced plants.

The first record of an introduction leading to a plant 'invasion' is that associated with the annual visits of Macassans who came to the northern shores of Australia from the South Celebes to collect the marine animal trepang or beche-de-mer (*Thelenota ananas* and other holothurians). They took dried trepang back to Macassar to trade with the Chinese (Macknight 1976). For up to 200 years from about 1700 the Macassans camped on the beaches of northern Australia. On their voyages they brought large quantities of tamarind fruit with them for their own diet. The first known plant to arrive and establish and become naturalised in Australia was thus the tamarind, *Tamarindus indica*. This species is now spreading naturally and its presence can no longer be used to indicate Macassan campsites (Macknight 1976).

Accurate historical records of plant introductions since European settlement in 1788 date from the first comprehensive botanical reconnaissance of the Australian coast conducted by Robert Brown in 1802, during Matthew Flinders' voyage of circumnavigation. Between 1802 and 1804, Brown noted 29 species of introduced plants collected at Sydney, including such well known species as *Plantago major, Erodium moschatum, Lythrum hyssopifolium* and *Poa annua* (Maiden 1916). Many of the species listed by Robert Brown were also present in South Australia prior to 1855 (Kloot 1985b). So began the invasion process for plants; it has continued even since. Plants have been introduced, sometimes accidentally (e.g. *Chondrilla juncea*), sometimes deliberately (e.g. *Echium plantagineum*), sometimes with Victorian English nostalgia for 'home' (e.g. *Ulex europaeus*) and sometimes with a blend of European nostalgia and arrogance (e.g. the continued spread of *Rubus fruticosus* by Von Mueller in the late nineteenth century). Since European settlement, the number of introduced species that have become naturalised in four Australian States (South Australia, Victoria, New South Wales and Queensland) has increased linearly with time (Specht 1981). This process is continuing at a rate of from four to six species a year (Figure 1); a rate of increase which is similar to that found for California (Frenkel 1970). These regions now have quarantine services of high competence.

[1] CSIRO, Division of Plant Industry, G.P.O. Box 1600, Canberra, A.C.T. 2601

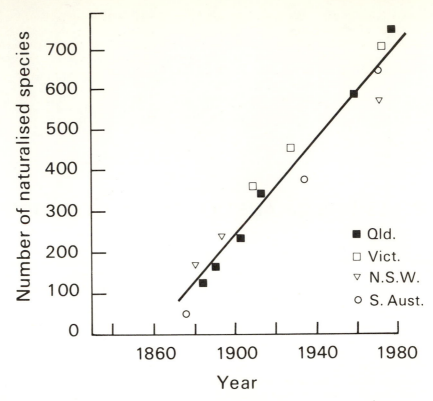

Fig. 1. Number of naturalised plant species in the four Australian States of Queensland, Victoria, New South Wales and South Australia 1870–1980 (Figure 14 of Specht 1981).

How long will it take to reduce the number of plants added to the naturalised flora of each of these regions each year as a result of the actions of contemporary quarantine services?

The authors of earlier chapters have tried to identify general features of these plant 'invaders'. Before attempting to draw together some of the threads from their contributions in this overview, however, I wish to comment briefly on invasions and biogeographic aspects of some of them.

INVASIONS

Recently (Groves 1985), I postulated three main stages in the invasion process: namely, introduction, colonisation and naturalisation. Many plants have been introduced to Australia, some deliberately and some accidentally. Some have failed to regenerate and establish; others have established successfully, formed self-perpetuating populations (the colonisation phase) and gone on to become permanent components of the naturalised flora. Quantitatively, there have been losses at each stage of the process. If we assign numbers to each stage the order of loss may be that for every 100 species introduced, perhaps only 10 successfully colonise new environments and only 5 of these eventually become naturalised. Of these 5 naturalised species, perhaps only 1 or 2 will become 'weeds' in that they will interfere with human activities in some way (Groves 1985).

Whilst we know very little about the quantitative aspects of invasions in any region, we do know that the introduction stage in the overall process can be complex. Let us consider *Echium plantagineum*, a colourful herb of Mediterranean origin, which is now widespread in southern Australia and considered to be a nuisance by most graziers. The species has also been introduced to South Africa, California and New Zealand. It was introduced deliberately to Australia a number of times in the nineteenth century as an ornamental (Piggin 1977). Kloot (1982) has claimed on the basis of both literature and herbarium records that it became naturalised (cf. introduced) in Australia in the late nineteenth century in two separate areas — one near Albury in southern New South Wales and the other near Gladstone in South Australia — and later at a third area in southwest Western Australia. The present almost continuous distribution of the plant in southern Australia comes from these separate and previously isolated sites from which it has spread subsequently.

Some of the major weeds of Australian agriculture have had similarly complex invasion histories, for example *Oxalis pes-caprae* (Michael 1964). But the most complex plant invasion known for Australia is that of *Trifolium subterraneum* (subterranean clover) (Morley and Katznelson 1965). The history of accidental invasions of southern Australia by three sub-species and numerous genotypes of this Mediterranean plant have been described for Victoria (Aitken and Drake 1941), South Australia (Cocks and Phillips 1979) and Western

Australia (Gladstones and Collins 1983), although even for these regions the story is far from complete. The apparent primary sites of naturalisation of subterranean clover genotypes recorded for part of southwest Western Australia by Gladstones and Collins (1983) are shown in Figure 2, which illustrates how complex the introduction stage of plant invasion can be. The naturalisation of this plant has been of great economic benefit to southern Australia, although some 'costs' are now being revealed, in terms of soil acidification (see later).

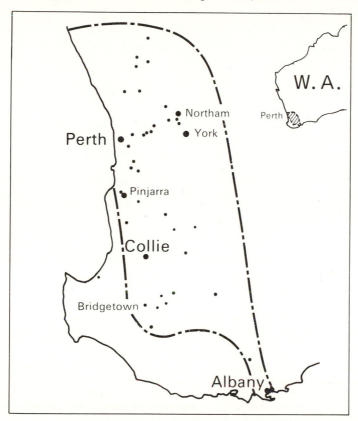

Fig. 2. Apparent primary sites of naturalisation of genotypes of *Trifolium subterraneum* (subterranean clover) recorded so far for part of southwest Western Australia (Figure 2 of Gladstones and Collins 1983).

The invasion process may also be complicated in terms of the genetics of the invading species (see Barrett and Richardson, this volume). Whilst the invasion process may be poorly understood quantitatively, it is often complex in space and time and involves, for some ornamental plants at least, multiple introductions of material which may already be genetically diverse in the country of origin, as seems to be the case for *Echium plantagineum*. In the case of the widespread form of *Oxalis pes-caprae* in southern Australia, it is a sterile pentaploid and thus genetically uniform, and reproduces only vegetatively (Michael 1964).

PLANT GEOGRAPHY OF INVASIONS

Australia's naturalised plants have come from many parts of the world — those in northern Australia coming predominantly from both temperate and other tropical regions and those in southern Australia from temperate and Mediterranean-climate regions of the world, especially Europe. Of 578 plants naturalised in Queensland, Everist (1960) found that 33% came from tropical regions and 40% came from Europe, Western Asia and North Africa. Furthermore, Everist found that there was little change in these proportions according to region of origin between an initial survey in 1883 and one made in 1959, although the absolute numbers of introduced species had increased (Michael 1981). Specht (1972) grouped the 654 species naturalised in South Australia according to their origins and showed that most (32%) came from the Mediterranean region and from Europe and Western Asia (Table 1), with a significant but smaller proportion (13%) coming from the Cape Province of South Africa. Generally, plants which have successfully invaded Australia seem to have come from areas of similar climate (see Swincer, this volume).

Currently, within Australia, there seems to be an increasing exchange of plant species between different regions. Previously, the Nullabor Plain was an effective biogeographic barrier to the natural movement of some species in the Australian flora. Now it seems that this and other barriers may be less effective, no doubt

TABLE 1. *The origin of species introduced to South Australia (Table 24 of Specht 1972).*

Region	Monocots	Dicots	Total
Mediterranean region	47	161	208
Europe and Western Asia	45	194	239
South Africa, especially Cape Province	34	50	84
Cosmopolitan plants	15	35	50
South America, especially Chile	6	29	35
North America, especially California	3	26	29
Southeast Asia	2	7	9
Total	152	502	654

because of human activities. *Acacia dealbata* is native to southeastern Australia but it now spreading naturally in southwestern Australia, following deliberate introduction for re-afforestation purposes after mining. An example of a reverse movement is provided by *Albizia lophantha*, endemic to Western Australia, which is now spreading naturally in southeastern Australia. Another species *Acacia baileyana* or Cootamundra wattle, has a very restricted natural distribution in southeastern New South Wales, but because of its horticultural value it has been widely planted in southeastern Australia and is now naturalised around Canberra, Melbourne and Adelaide. *Pittosporum undulatum*, a shrub of wet forests on the east coast, has also been planted widely for its horticultural value. As a result it has spread westwards about 200km through southwestern Victoria within the last few decades (Gleadow and Ashton 1981) and is now naturalised in the Adelaide Hills (Kloot 1985a). This regional level of invasion may become increasingly important as more and more natural barriers to invasion are removed by human activities, either accidentally or deliberately (see Robinson, Carr and Robin, this volume).

At the local level there are increasing chances for hybridisation between species indigenous to a locality and other species of the same genus grown for their horticultural value in that locality but native to other localities in Australia, as Robin and Carr (this volume) indicate. Such a situation has already occurred with natural hybrids between *Acacia baileyana* as one presumptive parent hybridising with several naturally occurring *Acacia* spp. in different areas of Victoria (Willis 1972, p. 244) and South Australia (Kloot 1985a). Robin and Carr point to five other common and widespread Australian genera, namely *Coprosma, Epilobium, Grevillea, Nicotiana* and *Pittosporum*, in which natural hybrids have been recorded. Thus, at the local level there is some evidence for increasing 'homogenisation' of the flora, as well as at the regional, national and international levels. Whether these natural hybrids are 'invasive' remains to be shown, however. More examples of such hybridisation will no doubt be recorded in future as Australian plants are utilised increasingly for horticultural purposes beyond their natural ranges.

My discussion of the plant geographic aspects of Australian plant invasions has concentrated so far on the origins of our invading plants. But an important aspect of the overall topic is the situation where Australian plants have themselves become invaders of natural vegetation of other countries. Species of many Australian plant genera are invasive in other countries, especially the woody genera of *Eucalyptus, Casuarina, Melaleuca, Acacia, Hakea* and *Albizia*. Such species have often been introduced deliberately to other countries for their ability to produce wood or to stabilise soil and they have and will continue to play a very significant economic role in this regard (see, e.g., Anonymous 1984a). Subsequent to their successful and planned introductions some of them have become invasive in natural communities, as for instance has occurred in the Cape region of South Africa (Stirton 1983).

Apart from indigenous woody plants several herbaceous Australian plants have also become invasive in other regions. *Vittadinia triloba*, a composite, is native to southeastern Australia and is now naturalised in the upper Waitaki valley and central Otago regions of the South Island of New Zealand (Williams 1980). The New Zealand native *Vittadinia* (viz. *V. australis*) never forms such extensive colonies as *V. triloba* but is more widespread throughout New Zealand. Kloot (1985a) mentions five examples of southern Australian herbs now naturalised in Europe — viz. *Cotula australis, Limosella australis, Acaena anserinifolia, Alternanthera nodiflora* and *Tetragonia tetragonoides*. All five species have been recorded as 'wool-adventives' although the latter three species were also introduced deliberately for horticultural purposes. With the increasing export trade in live sheep to Western Asia the chances for invasion of a number of Australian plants, especially herbs, to such semi-arid regions perhaps may increase in future.

A less obvious instance of an Australian plant becoming an invader internationally is given by Elton (1958). It is less obvious only in the sense that it concerns a small and inconspicuous red alga rather than a large shrub or tree. The alga *Asparagopsis armata*, known also as *Falkenbergia rufolanosa*, grows abundantly at low tidal levels along the south coast of mainland Australia, Tasmania and New Zealand. These two names represent alternate phases in the life history of the same species. *Asparagopsis* was first noticed on the extreme southern French Atlantic coast in 1923 and in the same year *Falkenbergia* was found at Cherbourg and *Asparagopsis* in

Algeria. This seaweed has since increased in density and spread along most of the coasts of western Europe and North Africa (Elton 1958, pp. 97-99). Discussion of invasions by Australian plants will be too limited in scope if it continues to overlook the marine in favour of the terrestrial or if it ignores the 'lower' plants in favour of angiosperms. An analogous oversight for animals may be the case of Australian barnacles invading northern European waters (Elton 1958).

CHARACTERISTICS OF INVADING PLANTS

Plant propagules arrive at a new site with certain inherent characteristics which previously enabled their successful survival and continued reproduction at their original site. This volume represents the collective ideas of a group of plant and animal ecologists about the nature of these plant characteristics, about how the genotype may be modified on arrival and during colonisation of different sites and about how plants interact in the longer term with their 'new' environment.

Is there an 'invasive syndrome' for plants? Some previous attempts have been made to answer this question (see, e.g., Baker 1965, 1974; Newsome and Noble, this volume); we may conclude that there is no one suite of characteristics which make a plant invasive. Rather, there are several predisposing factors which act either alone or together to increase the chance of a plant becoming invasive. I wish now to discuss some of these factors giving Australian examples.

Taxonomic position

Certain groups of plants have become more invasive in most regions than other taxonomic groupings. In temperate southern Australia, for instance, of the 88 plants identified as noxious in Victoria by Parsons (1973), 27 belong to the family Asteraceae, of which 15 are thistles. Of the 63 plants identified as noxious or secondary plants in Tasmania, 16 belong to the family Asteraceae, of which 8 are thistles (Hyde-Wyatt and Morris 1980). Despite problems associated with the legal definition of 'noxiousness', species from certain taxonomic groupings, such as the Asteraceae (for total numbers) and the Brassicaceae and Amaranthaceae (on a proportional basis), are more likely to be invasive, at least in regions of temperate climate.

Homoclimes

Swincer (this volume) makes the point for several insects that if an organism finds itself transported to a climate similar to that of its region of origin it may be better able to colonise and spread rapidly. This seems to be a factor in the success of certain plants too. For instance, *Chrysanthemoides monilifera* ssp. *rotundata* (bitou bush) is naturally distributed on dunes on the east coast of southern Africa, a region with markedly summer-incident rainfall. *C. monilifera* ssp. *monilifera* (boneseed) replaces ssp. *rotundata* the further west one goes along the southern coast of South Africa, as the rainfall becomes progressively more winter-incident. These two subspecies have been introduced to southeastern Australia (Weiss, this volume). Here, they are presently distributed in relation to rainfall incidence in a pattern similar to that in southern Africa. *C. monilifera* ssp. *rotundata* is confined to the east coast of New South Wales and southern Queensland, whilst ssp. *monilifera* occurs along the southern coastline of Victoria. Whether ssp. *rotundata* has reached its southern climatic limit in Australia is still uncertain, since it has been in Australia only since about 1908 (Weiss 1983). However, the similarity of climate (rainfall incidence) for its distribution in eastern South Africa and eastern Australia suggests that it may already have done so.

Ecological status

If a plant is a 'coloniser' in its country of origin, it seems more likely to become invasive in its new country. One of the habitats of *Chondrilla juncea* (skeleton weed) in southern Europe is on sandy beds and banks of river systems periodically disturbed by floods. It is thus a plant which on entering Australia was well adapted to a regime of regular disturbance in the form of cultivation of sandy soil for cereal growing. It rapidly became a major economic problem of the Australian cereal industry. *Emex australis* from South Africa is another early 'seral' species in its native region which has also become a major weed of regularly disturbed soils in southern Australia.

Dispersal characteristics

Allied to the early seral status of some invasive plants in their native region is the fact that invaders often have fruits which are morphologically adapted to disperse efficiently. Such plants are more likely to be moved around accidentally by wind or by birds or grazing animals on or in their products and thus arrive at a 'new' site. Two of the American *Xanthium* species (*occidentale* and *spinosum*), with their numerous hooked spines on fruits, are perhaps the most obvious examples of plants introduced accidentally to Australia having this characteristic. Both species are widespread in eastern Australia where they are weeds of grazing lands. Fruits of noogoora burr (*X. occidentale*) are also water-dispersed, thereby spreading the species along the inland river systems of central eastern Australia, where the species is common.

Seed dormancy

Many invasive plants show some level of seed dormancy, the effect of which usually is to spread the time for germination and establishment; the chances for effective colonisation are thereby increased. In fact, very few instances of the absence of seed dormancy are known for the group of Mediterranean plants which so successfully have invaded other regions of Mediterranean-type climate, including southern Australia (Groves 1985). The type of dormancy may be morphological (e.g. hard seeds in legumes) or physiological (e.g. after-ripening in grasses) or it may be a complex combination of the two types acting either synchronously or asynchronously.

Genetic systems

The number of reviews on the evolutionary significance of genetic systems in invasive or colonising plants has increased since the stimulus provided by the Asilomar conference in 1964 (Baker and Stebbins 1965). Barrett and Richardson (this volume) review this aspect well. In terms of factors predisposing plants to invasion it seems that polyploid inbreeding annuals or apomictic perennials are commmonly represented on lists of invasive plants. The conclusion of one recent review on this subject (Brown and Marshall 1981) bears repeating in the context of this overview, however; namely, ". . . colonising species are of interest not so much because they form a homogeneous group, but because they display a wide range of evolutionary pathways".

Mode of reproduction

Once a propagule has arrived at a new site it is advantageous to be able to reproduce rapidly and enter the colonisation stage of invasion. Plants having the ability to produce large numbers of seeds or those having both sexual and asexual (vegetative) modes of reproduction are advantaged. As an instance of the latter, *Chondrilla juncea* (see earlier) reproduces both from seed and asexually from buds on both the basal shoot and the root system. The plant is well placed thereby to become a dominant plant in frequently disturbed habitats as well as to invade new sites. An extreme but by no means uncommon case among invasive plants is provided by the water fern *Salvinia molesta* (see Arthington and Mitchell, this volume) and by *Oxalis pes-caprae* (see earlier and Michael 1964), both of which reproduce only vegetatively.

On the evidence presented in this volume I suggest that plants having at least some of these seven characteristics may more easily reach new sites and/or more readily compete with and eventually become dominant over plants which have evolved at this site. The invasion will be complete if the invading plant causes the extinction of the former occupant of the site. To prevent this extreme event happening is the task of the manager. The next section addresses some of the options available to management agencies, whether acting collectively as government instrumentalities or acting individually as a ranger of a conservation reserve or a farmer.

MANAGEMENT OF INVASIONS

Two of the most important options open to governments are to selectively prevent entry of new plant material and to regulate the entry of all such plant material. In Australia this is the task of the Plant Quarantine branch of the Australian Department of Primary Industry (see Navaratnam and Catley, this volume) which enforces the federal *Quarantine Act* 1908. Currently, 66 species and a further 20 genera of plants are prohibited entry (Table 2). In practice, as Navaratnam and Catley point out, the collective action of the quarantine services — both federally and in co-operation with the States — is to reduce the chances for entry of undesirable plants. As the data in Figure 1 show, new plants are still becoming naturalised in Australia. Navaratnam and Catley raise a number of important issues highly relevant to a consideration of plant invasions. I shall consider several of them briefly.

With an increasing knowledge of the characteristics of invading plants generally and increasing documentation of specific case histories, it should be possible to add to the list of plants not yet present in Australia but known to be invasive in other regions. For example, there are no species of *Hieracium* yet known to be naturalised in Australia. The genus *Hieracium* originated in Europe; several species have become naturalised in North America where they are major weeds of pasturelands. More recently, several species have been introduced to New Zealand. Two of these species, *H. pilosella* and *H. praealtum*, are known to have been at Timaru, a port of the South Island, about 60 years ago. On the lowland coastal plains around Timaru they had no economic effect. But when they arrived in the higher altitude tussock grasslands about 100km from Timaru they spread rapidly and in places now occupy not only all inter-tussock spaces but are causing the native perennial grass tussocks to break down (Makepeace 1985); consequently, the vulnerability of the montane region to erosion is increased. From a consideration of this scenario for a region similar to the Southern Tablelands of New South Wales and parts of montane Victoria and Tasmania, *Hieracium* species can be suggested as potentially 'successful' invaders of southeastern Australia. The genus possesses many of the characteristics already identified as those of invading plants — for example, they are apomictic members of the Asteraceae able to reproduce both by seed and vegetatively. And yet, on the basis of my understanding of existing quarantine procedures, *Hieracium* seed may not necessarily be prevented from entering Australia. Moreover, the chances of entry from New Zealand seem to be higher than, say, from Europe. There must be plants other than *Hieracium* and the 66 species listed in Table 2 for which sufficient is known of their biology, ecology and invasiveness to warrant absolute prohibition of entry to Australia.

TABLE 2. *List of species and genera of plants which are prohibited from entry to Australia under Quarantine Proclamation 80P of the* Quarantine Act *1908. Schedule 1 refers to species of plants and Schedule 2 to genera.*

SCHEDULE 1

Item	Botanical name	Common name
1	*Abrus precatorius*	Crab's eye
2	*Acroptilon repens*	Creeping knapweed
3	*Alhagi pseudalhagi*	Camelthorn
4	*Allium vineale*	Crow garlic
5	*Alternanthera philoxeroides*	Alligator weed
6	*Alternanthera pungens*	Khaki weed
7	*Baccharis halimifolia*	Groundsel bush
8	*Bromus commutatus*	Hairy chess
9	*Cabomba caroliniana*	
10	*Calatropis procera*	Calotrope, rubber tree or rubbish bush
11	*Cardaria draba*	Hoary cress or whiteweed
12	*Carduus nutans*	Nodding thistle
13	*Carthamus glaucous*	Glaucous star thistle
14	*Carthamus lanatus*	Saffron thistle
15	*Carthamus leucocaulos*	Glaucous star thistle
16	*Cenchrus gracillimus*	
17	*Centaurea solstitialis*	St Barnaby's thistle
18	*Cestrum parqui*	Green cestrum or green poisonberry
19	*Chondrilla juncea*	Skeleton weed
20	*Cirsium arvense*	Perennial thistle, Californian thistle or creeping thistle
21	*Convolvulus arvensis*	Field bindweed
22	*Cyperus aromaticus*	
23	*Echium plantagineum*	Paterson's curse or salvation Jane
24	*Eichhornia crassipes*	Water hyacinth
25	*Emex australis*	Three cornered Jack or doublegee
26	*Euphorbia lathyris*	Caper spurge
27	*Halogeton glomeratus*	Halogeton
28	*Helianthus ciliaris*	Texas blueweed
29	*Heliotropium amplexicaule*	Blue heliotrope
30	*Hydrilla verticillata*	Water thyme or hydrilla
31	*Hypericum perforatum*	St John's wort
32	*Ibicella latea*	Yellowflower devil's claw
33	*Iva axillaris*	Poverty weed
34	*Lactuca pulchella*	Blue lettuce
35	*Lagarosiphon major*	
36	*Lantana camara*	Common lantana
37	*Linaria dalmatica*	Dalmatian toadflax
38	*Malachra fasciata*	
39	*Mimosa invisa*	Giant sensitive plant
40	*Mimosa pigra*	
41	*Myriophyllum aquaticum*	Brazilian water milfoil or parrot's feather
42	*Myriophyllum spicatum*	
43	*Nassella trichotoma*	Serrated tussock
44	*Oryza rufipogon*	Red rice or wild rice
45	*Parthenium hysterophorus*	Parthenium weed or whitetop
46	*Pennisetum macrourum*	African feather grass
47	*Picnomon acarna*	Soldier thistle
48	*Pistia stratioides*	Water lettuce
49	*Proboscidea louisianica*	Purple flower devil's claw
50	*Rorippa austriaca*	Austrian field grass
51	*Sagittaria graminea*	Sagittaria
52	*Sagittaria montevidensis*	Arrowhead

TABLE 2
SCHEDULE 1 (continued)

53	*Senecio jacobaea*	Ragwort
54	*Senecio pterophorus*	African daisy
55	*Setaria faberi*	Giant foxtail
56	*Solanum carolinense*	Carolina horse nettle
57	*Solanum elaeagnifolium*	Silverleaf nightshade or white horse nettle
58	*Sonchus arvensis*	Corn sowthistle
59	*Sorghum almum*	Columbus grass
60	*Sorghum halepense*	Johnson grass
61	*Stipa brachychaeta*	Espartillo
62	*Stratiotes aloides*	
63	*Taeniatherum caput-medusae*	Medusa head
64	*Toxicodendron radicans*	Poison ivy
65	*Tribulus terrestris*	Caltrop
66	*Wedelia glauca*	Pascalia weed

SCHEDULE 2 +

Item	Botanical name	Common name
1	*Aegilops*	Goatgrass
2	*Ambrosia*	Ragweed
3	*Amsinckia*	Burrweed
4	*Berberis*	Barberry
5	*Conium*	
6	*Cuscuta*	Dodder
7	*Datura*	Thornapple
8	*Elodea*	
9	*Harrisia*	
10	*Helenium*	
11	*Homeria*	
12	*Mahonia*	
13	*Opuntia*	
14	*Orobanche*	Broomrape
15	*Prosopis*	Mesquite
16	*Salvinia*	Salvinia
17	*Striga*	
18	*Trapa*	
19	*Xanthium*	Burr

+ a plant, or any part of a plant, of a species of the genus *Cenchrus* that has burrs, is also prohibited entry.

Another aspect of plant quarantine which seems important in the context of the ecology of biological invasions is prediction of the regions from which invasive plants may most likely come to Australia. One of the taxonomic groupings most likely to become invasive is the family Asteraceae (see earlier) and especially, on the basis of their 'noxiousness', the thistles. Using a statistical method to assess natural distribution, Forcella and Wood (1985) showed there to be a subset of Mediterranean countries (France, Italy, Yugoslavia and Albania) from which *Carduus* species not yet present in Australia were most likely to come. This prediction, if valid, has potential to refine quarantine procedures. Both this thistle example and that of *Hieracium* apply prior to the introduction phase of invasion. They suggest that the chances to predict potential plant invaders could be increased even now.

Management options are more practicable after introduction, and usually after naturalisation. The early containment of an introduced plant and its effective eradication seems to have received little attention in Australia for plants, although this option has been considered for diseases and introduced animals. Why this difference should be so is not clear to me. In the complex Federal-State governmental system in Australia there exists a group called the Consultative Committee on Exotic Insect Pests, Weeds and Diseases. As a result of this committee's activity protocols already exist for the early containment and eradication of insects, vertebrates and plant diseases, but no such protocol seems to exist for newly introduced plants. A recent attempt by the Australian Weeds Committee to have the matter considered failed. I remain to be convinced that satisfactory mechanisms exist to combat the effects of a newly introduced plant known to be weedy outside Australia.

Auld and Tisdell (this volume) discussed the relationship between spread rate and pattern for several invasive plants, with pattern being summarised by the parameter 's' for two of them. A few plant scientists have tried to predict likely future spread once plants have arrived in eastern Australia. Medd and Smith (1978) studied the development of *Carduus nutans* (nodding thistle), which was first identified in New South Wales in 1950; they used their data to predict which other climatic regions would suit the plant's developmental pattern. Williams and Groves (1980) used a similar approach for the recently introduced *Parthenium hysterophorus* and confirmed the earlier prediction of Doley (1977), based on photosynthetic response curves, that *P. hysterophorus* had considerable potential to grow and flower in a wide range of environments in eastern Australia. Because the growth and developmental responses of a plant are wide does not mean necessarily that a plant will become invasive at all sites it could occupy. However, it does seem to me that this approach could be followed more often for plants introduced relatively recently. Prediction is always hazardous but results of the predictions cited have at least served to alert control authorities to adopt policies which may limit further spread. Modelling of the spread of invasive organisms generally is a much-needed activity, both nationally and internationally, and the overall SCOPE program has recognised this deficiency in the establishment of a working group to consider and develop such models.

Usually, however, control of invasive plants occurs after the plants are widely distributed. The aim of any control program is to minimise the number of propagules by manipulating the 'invaded' ecosystem in some way. Control programs for perennial plants and those annuals with dormant seeds are thus long-term and should involve careful monitoring of propagule numbers. Because of sampling problems for buried seeds or for buds on root systems, however, such monitoring is rarely long-term in practice. Nevertheless, some plants invasive to Australia have been controlled effectively by various methods — by cultivation in the case of agricultural weeds, by the application of chemicals or by biological means, including the methods of classical biological control using insects or other natural enemies. The use of desirable pasture plants to control the growth of some plants considered undesirable has been successful in agricultural areas of southern Australia, as has the planned use of fire to control weeds of land used less intensively. In this overview I wish to stress several ecological aspects of control.

It has been suggested elsewhere (Groves and Cullen 1981) that *Chondrilla juncea* in Australia has been controlled because of the interaction between a competing pasture plant of Mediterranean origin (*Trifolium subterraneum*) and the release of two natural enemies, also from the Mediterranean region (the fungus *Puccinia chondrillina* and the gall mite *Aceria chondrillae*). The ecosystem in southern Australia now more closely resembles the ecosystem in the Mediterranean. Integration of different control methods is usually more effective than those same methods used independently, but perhaps integrated control may itself be made even more effective if it seeks to match more closely the natural ecosystem in the way suggested for control of *Chondrilla juncea* in southern Australia.

Control of plants which have invaded natural vegetation may be more difficult than control of plants in agricultural systems because the range of methods available for control (see above) is more limited. For such plants the use of fire or biological control are more appropriate methods. The planned use of fire for weed control has been recently reviewed elsewhere (Johnson and Purdie 1981). Weiss (1983 and this volume) suggests the use of a certain regime of fire frequency and season of fire to favour the native species *Acacia longifolia* var. *sophorae* over the invasive shrub *Chrysanthemoides monilifera* which seems to be replacing it in eastern Australia.

Biological control programs have occasionally had a spectacular success in Australia, for example those for *Opuntia* spp. (Mann 1970), for one genotype of *Chondrilla juncea* (Groves and Cullen 1981) and for *Salvinia molesta* (Harley and Mitchell 1981). Two contributions to this volume (Barrett and Richardson; Murray, Tomasev and Hale) make the point that monitoring of biological control programs should not be confined to numbers of propagules but be extended to consider the genetic constitution of both the natural enemy and the host, as these too may change over time. Along with matching of sites between country of origin and the invaded region (Nix and Wapshere, this volume), the plea for genetic monitoring of populations seems relevant to developing a broader theoretical base for biological control activities.

Australian scientists are well placed to contribute to the wider study of the ecology of biological invasions not just because of their experience with biological control programs, however, but also because they have participated for many years in programs to deliberately foster plant invasions. Mott (this volume) describes one such program for northern Australia which is already showing signs of ecological instability within 10 to 15 years from initiation. Mott's example is interesting because it parallels a developing situation in southeastern Australia. In the latter region growth of the introduced legume *Trifolium subterraneum* has been promoted deliberately by applying superphosphate for as long as 50 years. Such applications have led to a drop in soil pH by as much as one unit and a consequent inability of some pasture and crop plants to be productive under these altered conditions. New plant genotypes have been introduced to Australia in large numbers (the Commonwealth Plant Introduction numbers for genotypes entering Australia through approved CSIRO channels now exceed 40 000) as part of planned invasions of both southern and northern Australia. A careful study of the failures and successes at each stage of the invasion process may add to present understanding of the ecology of biological invasions. It seems surprising from the large numbers of such introductions that so relatively few have been associated with complex and undesirable changes to otherwise agriculturally-productive ecosystems. But, as Auld and Tisdell (this volume) remind us, the status of invaders is changing; so too does the status of the invaded ecosystems change. Methods to control invading plants will also change.

FUTURE RESEARCH DIRECTIONS

One aim of the SCOPE program on the 'Ecology of Biological Invasions' is to assess the present status of research on the subject and to point to aspects to which a greater and a more co-ordinated research effort could be directed. Australia has been settled by Europeans for only 200 years and, as such, can provide many examples of accidental and deliberate invasions over a shorter time scale than for most other regions. Some of these invasions have formed the basis of present-day agriculture and forestry and are of considerable economic benefit. On the other hand, the losses to agricultural production caused by unwanted plants, or weeds, have been estimated conservatively to be about 500 million dollars per year. This level of loss is greater than the losses caused by either insect pests or diseases (Anonymous 1984b). To this estimate must be added a cost for the loss of natural values in areas of native vegetation on reserved land — a cost which is harder to quantify. If the economic losses resulting from plant invasions over the past 200 years are to be reduced, what are the aspects of plant invasions which may warrant increased scientific attention? I suggest there are at least five aspects especially worth pursuing.

1. The taxonomy of many introduced plants is imperfectly known. It was only recently, for instance, that a widespread *Senecio* species of coastal New South Wales was shown to be not the highly variable native *Senecio lautus* but the South African species *S. madagascariensis* (Michael 1981). As a result of this new knowledge, attitudes to its control have changed markedly. The recent elucidation of the taxonomy of *Salvinia* in the field in southeastern Brazil, its country of origin, appears to have greatly accelerated the successful biological control of *Salvinia molesta* in Australia (Harley and Mitchell 1981; Arthington and Mitchell, this volume). Currently, we do not know whether one of the most common thistles on the Southern Tablelands of New South Wales is a hybrid between *Onopordum illyricum* and *O. acanthium* or if it is a third taxon introduced separately from Europe (M. Gray, personal communication). Such lack of knowledge may delay initiation of a program for biological control of *Onopordum sens. lat.* There are many such taxonomic problems still to be unravelled by careful study of specimens collected in Australia and in their country of origin.

2. Scholarly research into the histories of introduction of plants of the calibre of Shaughnessy (1980) for Australian woody plants introduced to South Africa should be especially productive. More seems to be known for introduced animals (see, e.g., Rolls 1969) than for plants, particularly concerning the part played by the acclimatisation societies a century ago. Is this imbalance because of the lesser numbers of animals introduced? What types of plants were introduced deliberately but failed to become naturalised? If there is a 'successful' syndrome for invasive plants, are there any attributes shared by those plants which failed to become invasive? An answer will come only from increased attention to historic studies of plant invasions and from careful attention to taxonomy. A start has been made by Michael (1964) for *Oxalis pes-caprae* and by Kloot (1984a, 1985a) for South Australian plants generally, but many case histories remain to be researched. Auld (1977) has shown that *Eupatorium lindleyanum* was introduced over a century ago to two sites in northern New South Wales, but it has not persisted, unlike its close relative *E. riparium*, with which it has been confused in the past. Even the history of invasion by *Opuntia* spp. is imperfectly understood (but see Mann 1970), despite the success of their control by biological means.

3. Auld and Tisdell (this volume) present information on the economic effect of one plant introduced to Australia, namely *Nassella trichotoma*. Collection of data on economic aspects of other such plants, and especially for weeds of pastures and of natural vegetation, is needed urgently as the implementation of control programs becomes more contentious (as exemplified by the current controversy about the merits of controlling *Echium plantagineum* using introduced insects). Because such results are easier to obtain, data are more commonly available for crop weeds, but even for that group much remains to be done.

4. It should be especially rewarding to assess invasive attributes of plants by carefully comparing the life histories of 'successful' plants and their closely-related but 'unsuccessful' congeners, as Barrett and Richardson (this volume) suggest for *Eichhornia*. For instance, why has *Echium plantagineum* invaded Australia so successfully but *E. italicum* failed to do so? Why has *Parthenium hysterophorus*, introduced more recently, spread rapidly whilst its congener *P. argentatum* (guayule), deliberately planted at many sites in eastern Australia in the 1940s (Crocker and Trumble 1945), is still not even naturalised?

5. An underlying theme throughout this and other chapters has been the need for prediction — prediction as to which plants may be the most likely to enter Australia in the future, prediction as to which plants already introduced will become naturalised, prediction as to their likely rate of spread, and prediction as to their likely impact on Australian ecosystems. In this regard, the modelling of plant spread (Auld and Tisdell, this volume), the further development of a bioclimatic approach to invasions (Nix and Wapshere, this volume)

and the incorporation of a set of 'invasive attributes' into models of invasions (Newsome and Noble, this volume) have special relevance to the prediction of the success or failure of a plant to invade.

Exchanges of plants between regions have been occurring for millennia. The chapters in this volume have discussed the increased rate of invasions to Australia over the last 200 years, largely as a result of human activities. The plants which have become naturalised over that period often are very noticeable because they interfere with our earning of a livelihood or with our appreciation of natural landscapes. Whether the number of invasive plants per year increases further over the next 200 years depends very much on a better understanding of the invasion process and of the ecosystems being invaded. The purpose of this volume is to bring the present state of ecological understanding to a wider and more international audience in the hope that an increased understanding will lead to a decreased rate of invasion and the consequent maintenance of integrity of our natural, uninvaded plant and animal communities.

I conclude this overview on a note of mild surprise. A plant collector in the colony of New South Wales in the late eighteenth century, such as George Caley, was extremely busy. Joseph Banks' list of plants to be shipped by George Caley from Britain to the colony in 1798 (in addition to those already introduced in the first 10 years of settlement) included "hops, olives, carribs, lemon grass, spring grass, cactis, ginger, strawberries, camphor, vines, apples, pears, peaches, nectarines, mulberries, walnuts, chestnuts, filberts, quinces, pruient plums, oakes and willows, mint, lavender, tarragin, sage, savoury laurel, cammomile and wormwood" (Currey 1966). In addition to these living plants, the ship was to take six large bags of assorted seeds. All this plant "cabin" and its 18 earth-filled boxes were under the care of George Caley. So great was its weight (about 3 tons) that it even threatened to capsize the ship. Most living plants died on the voyage to Australia of about 5 months but among the plants which survived were "2 plaintains, mint, and . . ." (Suttor-Banks 1800, quoted in Currey 1966). There was an equally large trade in reverse — not just in dried plant specimens but, for instance, on April 28, 1803, Caley consigned "1 box of plant specimens; 1 box of living plants; 238 papers of seeds; 65 waratah pods; 149 duplicates; etc." (Currey 1966). On this basis it is perhaps not the number of exchanges which has increased so markedly but rather it is the increased chances for naturalisation of these species as a result of ecosystem modification over the last 197 years. In view of all the plant exchanges into and out of Australia from Caley's time and before to the present it surprises me that so few species have become naturalised and that even fewer have become weeds. Why should this be so?

ACKNOWLEDGMENTS

I appreciate the constructive comments of B.A. Auld, J.J. Burdon and P.M. Kloot on an earlier draft of this chapter. Tricia Kaye helped greatly at all stages of its preparation, for which I am also most grateful.

REFERENCES

Aitken, Y., and Drake, F.R. (1941). Studies of the varieties of subterranean clover. *Proceedings of the Royal Society of Victoria 53*, 342–393.

Anonymous (1984a). *Casuarinas : Nitrogen-fixing Trees for Adverse Sites*, National Academy Press, Washington.

Anonymous (1984b). Quarantine Measures to Exclude Weeds. Commonwealth Department of Health Plant Quarantine Leaflet No. 38.

Auld, B.A. (1977). The introduction of *Eupatorium* species to Australia. *Journal of the Australian Institute of Agricultural Science 42*, 146–147.

Baker, H.G. (1965). Characteristics and modes of origins of weeds. In *The Genetics of Colonizing Species* (eds H.G. Baker and G.L. Stebbins) pp. 141–172, Academic Press, London.

Baker, H.G. (1974). The evolution of weeds. *Annual Review of Ecology and Systematics 5*, 1–24.

Baker H.G., and Stebbins, G.L. (eds) (1965). *The Genetics of Colonizing Species*, Academic Press, London.

Barbour, M.G., and Rodman, J.E. (1970). Saga of the west coast sea-rockets : *Cakile edentula* ssp. *californica* and *C. maritima. Rhodora 72*, 370–386.

Brown, A.H.D., and Marshall, D.R. (1981). Evolutionary changes accompanying colonization in plants. In *Evolution Today. Proceedings of the Second International Congress of Systematic and Evolutionary Biology* (eds G.E.C. Scudder and J.L. Reveal) pp. 351–363, Hunt Institute for Botanical Documentation, Carnegie-Mellon University, Pittsburgh.

Cocks, P.S., and Phillips, J.R. (1979). Evolution of subterranean clover in South Australia. I. The strains and their distribution. *Australian Journal of Agricultural Research 30*, 1035–1052.

Crocker, R.L., and Trumble, H.C. (1945). Investigations of guayule (*Parthenium argentatum* Gray) in South Australia. Council of Scientific and Industrial Research, Australia, Bulletin No. 192.

Currey, J.E.B. (ed.) (1966). *Reflections on the Colony of New South Wales by G. Caley,* Landsdowne, Melbourne.

Doley, D. (1977). Parthenium weed (*Parthenium hysterophorus* L.) : gas exchange characteristics as a basis for prediction of its geographical distribution. *Australian Journal of Agricultural Research 28*, 449–460.

Elton, C.S. (1958). *The Ecology of Invasions by Animals and Plants*, Methuen, London.

Everist, S.L. (1960). Strangers within the gates. *Queensland Naturalist 16*, 49–60.

Forcella, F., and Wood, J.T. (1985). Colonization potential of alien weeds are related to their 'native' distribution. *Journal of the Australian Institute of Agricultural Science 50*, 35–41.

Fox, M.D., and Adamson, D. (1979). The ecology of invasions. In *A Natural Legacy* (eds H.F. Recher, D. Lunney and I. Dunn) pp. 135–152, Pergamon Press, Sydney.

Frenkel, R.E. (1970). Ruderal vegetation along some California roadsides. *University of California Publications in Geography 20*, 1–163.

Gladstones, J.S., and Collins, W.J. (1983). Subterranean clover as a naturalised plant in Australia. *Journal of the Australian Institute of Agricultural Science 49*, 191–202.

Gleadow, R.M., and Ashton, D.H. (1981). The invasion by *Pittosporum undulatum* of the forests of central Victoria. I. Invasion patterns and plant morphology. *Australian Journal of Botany 29*, 705–720.

Groves, R.H. (1985). Invasion of weeds in Mediterranean ecosystems. In *Resilience in Mediterranean Climate Ecosystems* (ed. B. Dell) in press, Dr W. Junk, The Hague.

Groves, R.H., and Cullen, J.M. (1981). *Chondrilla juncea*: the ecological control of a weed. In *The Ecology of Pests* (eds R.L. Kitching and R.E. Jones) pp. 6–17, CSIRO, Melbourne.

Harley, K.L.S., and Mitchell, D.S. (1981). The biology of Australian weeds. 6. *Salvinia molesta. Journal of the Australian Institute of Agricultural Science 47*, 67–76.

Heatwole, H. (1984). Terrestrial vegetation of the coral cays, Capricornia Section, Great Barrier Reef Marine Park. *Royal Society of Queensland Symposium, Capricornia Section, Great Barrier Reef*, pp. 87–139.

Hyde-Wyatt, B.H., and Morris, D.I. (1980). *The Noxious and Secondary Weeds of Tasmania*, Department of Agriculture, Hobart.

Johnson, R.W., and Purdie, R.W. (1981). The role of fire in the establishment and management of agricultural systems. In *Fire and the Australian Biota* (eds A.M. Gill, R.H. Groves and I.R. Noble) pp. 497–528, Australian Academy of Science, Canberra.

Kloot, P.M. (1982). The naturalisation of *Echium plantagineum* L. in Australia. *Australian Weeds 1*, 29–31.

Kloot, P.M. (1984). The introduced elements of the flora of southern Australia. *Journal of Biogeography 11*, 63–78.

Kloot, P.M. (1985a). The spread of native Australian plants as weeds in South Australia and in other Mediterranean regions. *Journal of the Adelaide Botanic Gardens 7*, 145–157.

Kloot, P.M. (1985b). Plant introductions to South Australia prior to 1840. *Journal of the Adelaide Botanic Gardens 7*, (in press).

Macknight, C.C. (1976). *The Voyage to Marege*, Melbourne University Press, Melbourne.

Maiden, J.H. (1916). Weeds at Sydney in 1802–4. *Agricultural Gazette of New South Wales 27*, 40.

Makepeace, W. (1985). Growth, reproduction and production biology of mouse-ear and king devil hawkweed in eastern South Island, New Zealand. *New Zealand Journal of Botany 23*, 65–78.

Mann, J. (1970). *Cacti Naturalised in Australia and Their Control*, Government Printer, Brisbane.

Medd, R.W. , and Smith, R.C.G. (1978). Prediction of potential distribution of *Carduus nutans* (nodding thistle) in Australia. *Journal of Applied Ecology 15*, 603–612.

Michael, P.W. (1964). The identity and origin of varieties of *Oxalis pes-caprae* L. naturalised in Australia. *Transactions of the Royal Society of South Australia 88*, 167–174.

Michael, P.W. (1981). Alien plants. In *Australian Vegetation* (ed. R.H. Groves) pp. 44–64, Cambridge University Press, Cambridge.

Morley, F.H.W., and Katznelson, J.S. (1965). Colonization in Australia by *Trifolium subterraneum* L. In *The Genetics of Colonizing Species* (eds H.G. Baker and G.L. Stebbins) pp. 269–282, Academic Press, London.

Parsons W.T. (1973). *Noxious Weeds of Victoria*, Inkata Press, Melbourne.

Piggin, C.M. (1977). The herbaceous species of *Echium* (Boraginaceae) naturalised in Australia. *Muelleria 3*, 215–244.

Shaughnessy, G.L. (1980). Historical ecology of alien woody plants in the vicinity of Cape Town, South Africa. Ph. D. thesis, University of Cape Town.

Rolls, E.C. (1969). *They All Ran Wild*, Angus and Robertson, Sydney.

Specht, R.L. (1972). *Vegetation of South Australia*, 2nd edn, South Australian Government Printer, Adelaide.

Specht, R.L. (1981). Major vegetation formations in Australia. In *Ecological Biogeography of Australia* (ed. A. Keast) pp. 165–297, Dr W. Junk, The Hague.

Stirton, C.H. (ed.) (1983). *Plant Invaders. Beautiful but Dangerous*, 3rd edn, Department of Nature and Environmental Conservation of the Cape Provincial Administration, Cape Town.

Weiss, P.W. (1983). Invasion of coastal *Acacia* communities by *Chrysanthemoides*. Ph.D. thesis, Australian National University.

Williams, P.A. (1980). *Vittadinia triloba* and *Rumex acetosella* communities in the semi-arid regions of the South Island. *New Zealand Journal of Ecology 3*, 13–22.

Williams, J.D., and Groves, R.H. (1980). The influence of temperature and photoperiod on growth and development of *Parthenium hysterophorus* L. *Weed Research 20*, 47–52.

Willis, J.H. (1972). *A Handbook to the Plants in Victoria. Vol. II. Dicotyledons*, Melbourne University Press, Melbourne.

ENVIRONMENTAL WEED INVASION OF NATURAL ECOSYSTEMS: AUSTRALIA'S GREATEST CONSERVATION PROBLEM

G.W. Carr[1], J.M. Robin[1] and R.W. Robinson[1]

The greatest conservation problem in Australia concerns environmental weed invasion of indigenous plant communities. In Victoria, thousands of taxa have been introduced accidentally or deliberately for agriculture and horticulture. The indigenous flora numbers approximately 2750 species whilst the naturalised flora numbers approximately 850 species (27.5%).

We estimate that of the introduced flora approximately 400 species pose serious threats to indigenous vegetation communities and that many more have this potential. Greater than 60% of all naturalised taxa have been introduced deliberately. Some of the declared noxious agricultural weeds also behave as environmental weeds.

Environmental weeds embrace all life forms and come from a very broad taxonomic spectrum. Most species were introduced from the Mediterranean basin or similar climatic zones in North and South America and South Africa. A significant proportion are species which occur naturally elsewhere in Victoria or Australia.

Invasion mechanisms are very poorly understood. Many species appear capable of invasion without apparent ecosystem disturbance but the full range of disturbance factors, whether natural or not, have yet to be identified. Superior competitive ability and faster inherent growth rates are clearly implicated in a large number of weed species whilst some (e.g. annuals) occupy structural niches previously unoccupied by native taxa, especially in open vegetation of woodlands.

Competitive superiority is apparently also possessed by introduced C_4 species over indigenous C_3 species, and allelopathy is also implicated in the success of many introduced species. Fire, or its absence, also plays a critical role by stimulating massive post-fire population recruitment or, because of unnaturally reduced frequency, by permitting the invasion of fire-sensitive species.

The problem of environmental weeds has received almost no attention in Australia despite the experience overseas, especially in South Africa. Over 100 species of these weeds are currently available in the nursery trade or are used by government agencies and others for ornamental or utility planting.

It is concluded that the long-term prospect for most Victorian vegetation is annihilation unless this problem is addressed as a matter of priority. Almost every plant community, from coastal saltmarsh to alpine herbfield, may be threatened.

[1]   Ecological Horticulture, P.O. Box 276, Heidelberg, Vict. 3084

THE GIANT TOAD (*BUFO MARINUS*): INTRODUCTION AND SPREAD IN AUSTRALIA

Robert B. Floyd[1] and Simon Easteal[2]

The giant toad occurs naturally in South America, north of 12°S and extends as far north as northern Mexico (27°N). Since the mid–1800s it has been introduced to many countries in the Caribbean and Pacific regions as a means of biological control of insect pests in crops, particularly sugar cane. The introduction of 101 toads to Australia in 1935 was to control coleopteran pests in sugar cane.

Toads were released in many of the cane-growing districts in Queensland during the years 1935 to 1937. From these locations the animal has dispersed to cover more than 40% of Queensland and a small portion of the Northern Territory and New South Wales. Detailed maps of the distribution of the giant toad in successive 5 year intervals are presented. These maps indicate that the spread of the animal has not been linear and continuous but has been discontinuous and possibly facilitated by human transportation. This conclusion is further supported by evidence from electrophoretic studies of *B. marinus* populations throughout Queensland.

Since the distribution of the species is still expanding, an attempt has been made to predict its ultimate range in Australia. Extensive experimentation on the thermal physiology of the embryos and larvae was carried out and the results synthesised into a bioclimatic model. The model predicted an extension of the present distribution to include northern Australia, as far west as the Kimberleys, and coastal New South Wales, south to the Hunter Valley.

Evidence suggests that the toad is posing an ecological threat to the native fauna. Control of the giant toad in Australia must be considered at two levels: firstly, the restriction of its future spread; and secondly, reducing its population size in areas already occupied. Since the spread does not appear to be natural, construction of fences to stop natural migration does not appear to be necessary or useful. It would be more beneficial to consider controls over transportation of produce and machinery from 'toad-inhabited' to 'toad-free' areas. Population control in 'toad-inhabited' areas has not been investigated in Australia.

[1]   CSIRO, Division of Entomology, PMB 3, Indooroopilly, Qld 4068
[2]   Department of Population Biology, Research School of Biological Sciences, ANU, Canberra, A.C.T. 2601

IMPACT OF INTRODUCED GRASSES ON FOREDUNES IN SOUTH-EASTERN AUSTRALIA

Petrus C. Heyligers[1]

Ammophila arenaria and *Elymus farctus* (syn. *Agropyron junceum*) are dune-forming grasses native to the coasts of western Europe and the Mediterranean. *E. farctus* is a pioneer of flotsam deposits and beach plains and grows best when groundwater is brackish. It forms long horizontal rhizomes and builds up low, broad foredunes. *A. arenaria* can establish only when the groundwater freshens. Owing to strong vertical rhizome development it is able to keep up with rapid sand deposition, forming dune hummocks and ridges 5 m or more high.

Both species are naturalised in Australia. *E. farctus* probably came with ballast as it was first collected on the shores of Port Phillip Bay in 1933. *A. arenaria* was introduced for reclamation of the sand-drifts near Port Fairy, Victoria in 1883 and has since been widely used for this purpose in the higher-rainfall areas along southern shores. *E. farctus* has been planted at a few sites in Victoria during the 1950s and '60s. Presently it appears to be spreading quickly; it has reached Kingston, South Australia, and Flinders Island, Bass Strait.

Festuca littoralis and *Spinifex hirsutus* are the native dune-forming grasses. The former is comparable to *E. farctus* in its tolerance to salinity and tidal inundation but lacks horizontal rhizomes and has only a moderate upward growth in accumulating sand. It forms low hummocky incipient foredunes. *S. hirsutus*, with its long stout stolons, is an excellent sand-binder in warm temperate or subtropical climates, but is a slow grower under cooler conditions and needs fresh soil water. It builds broad foredune ridges, up to about 3 m high.

Because of the differences in dune morphologies as a result of the properties of the species which dominated their formation, the following questions can be asked: What is the influence of the introduced grasses on local foredune formation? To what degree do foredunes stand to lose their original character? My observations, mainly along the south-eastern mainland coast, but also on some of the Dutch Wadden Sea barrier islands and along the Atlantic coast of England, have convinced me that in southern Australia, these introduced grasses are better colonisers of the backshore zone, especially under extreme conditions, than the native species; also, they are more efficient in trapping sand. Hence, because of their presence either foredunes are formed where none would have come into existence otherwise, or the formation of foredune terraces and ridges is enhanced and larger dunes are built up as a result.

Beside grasses, some introduced herbs, e.g. *Cakile* spp. and *Euphorbia paralias*, also leave an imprint on dune morphology.

---

[1]   CSIRO, Division of Water and Land Resources, G.P.O. Box 1666, Canberra, A.C.T. 2601

INVASIONS BY OSTRACODA (CRUSTACEA) INTO THE ITALIAN RICE FIELDS ECOSYSTEM

K.G. McKenzie[1] and A. Moroni[2]

The Italian rice fields ecosystem on the Lombardy-Padana plain was initiated in the late 14th-early 15th centuries during the period when powerful dukes, particularly the Estes (Ferrara) and the Sforzas (Milan), vied with each other in social conscience and prestige. Probably, rice was introduced into renaissance Italy from Persia and Macedonia where it has been cultivated for many centuries. The Statuto Ferrariae (1287) makes no mention of rice, so presumably it was first planted during the well-documented later bonifications — creation of new arable lands by draining swampland into the Po and Adige rivers — carried out by Ercole I of Ferrara and his immediate predecessor. By 1475, rice was sufficiently well established around Ferrara for Gian Galeazzo Sforza to request 12 sacks of seed rice in order to develop its cultivation around Milan. Today, rice is the region's major cereal crop and a distinctive staple of its cuisine.

Climatically, northern Italy is at the latitudinal limit for rice cultivation but, even so, summer temperatures regularly exceed 30°C. Regional soils are relatively poor and successful rice culture requires considerable nutrification via fertilisers. The crop cycle, of course, demands aperiodic flooding of the rice fields from irrigation channels.

Biogeographically, Italian rice fields can be regarded as aquatic islands. They are separated from the home of rice in Southeast Asia and other cultivation centres not only spatially but also, as indicated above, historically. They therefore make excellent laboratories for the study of biological invasions into Lombardy-Padana, our contribution confining itself to those by ostracode crustaceans.

Of the 50–60 Ostracoda which have been collected from Italian ricefields, about 15 have been introduced demonstrably from elsewhere, including Australia, Africa, South America, India, Southeast Asia and China. We call these species 'ospiti esteri' (foreign guests). Their occurrence in Italy can be attributed most probably to passive introduction of their desiccation-resistant eggs (about 50 μ diameter) with seed to trial rice strains in the ceaseless search to develop higher yielding, better quality Italian rice varieties. But a number of other plants may also have acted as vectors. The most important alternative possible plant vectors for Ostracoda into northern Italy are cannabis and mulberry. The excellent Italian historical records allow us to document many plant introductions in great detail, but others (e.g. wheat) arrived in pre-historical times.

Indeed, the list of useful plants introduced into Italy is so large that this dispersal mechanism for Ostracoda must be favoured over passive transport by birds or by high altitude air currents which have been emphasised previously. Similar studies seem warranted for Australian ricefields, especially since Ostracoda and other small crustaceans are also excellent indicators of water quality in rice fields.

[1]   Riverina College of Advanced Education, Wagga Wagga, N.S.W. 2650
[2]   Istituto de Ecologia, Parma, Italy 43100

ECOLOGICAL AND GENETIC DIFFERENTIATION BETWEEN AUSTRALIAN POPULATIONS OF INTRODUCED BIOLOGICAL CONTROL AGENTS

N.D. Murray[1], J.F. Tomasov[1] and C.B. Hale[1]

Introductions of successful biological control agents are examples of biological invasions where we often have detailed information on time, place, size, and source of the introduction. They therefore provide valuable opportunities to study genetic processes accompanying and following invasions. Described here are results of our work on the cactus moth *Cactoblastis cactorum*, the cactus cochineal *Dactylopius opuntiae*, St John's wort beetle *Chrysolina quadrigemina*, and the mosquito fish *Gambusia affinis holbrooki*. We have found morphological, electrophoretic and ecological differences between Australian populations, and between Australian and source populations. Genetic differentiation within Australia appears to be common in these organisms. The question of whether differentiation has accompanied or followed invasion can only be answered by improved documentation of the biological properties of the introduced and source material.

[1] Department of Genetics and Human Variation, La Trobe University, Bundoora, Vict. 3083

BIOGEOGRAPHIC ORIGINS OF INVADING SPECIES

H.A. Nix[1] and A.J. Wapshere[2]

Inevitably, through environmental modification and deliberate and accidental introduction of species, humans are moving biogeography towards a new global equilibrium. Vast areas are coming to be dominated by cosmopolitan assemblages of economically valuable species (livestock, crop, forage and forest), together with their associated weed, pest and pathogen species. But what factors and processes dictate the success or failure of an invading organism? How important is the provenance or biogeographic origin of the invading species? How important is the role of human environmental disturbance?

Review of an immense literature fails to yield any quantitative functional relationships between organismal attributes or organism/environment interactions and the probability of successful establishment in a new location. Obviously, the physical environment sets limits to the distribution of any organism. Thus, for example, homoclime analysis seeks to define these limits and to search for climatic analogues elsewhere. Whilst appropriate for analysis of single target species, results have been variable and homoclime analysis has proved incapable of yielding general functional relationships.

In this contribution a new methodology is applied to the analysis of comprehensive data sets relating to deliberate introductions of organisms by humans on a global basis. Essentially the method employs a non-hierarchical classification of some 4 000 global climate stations in terms of 18 climatic variables, selected for their biological significance. A lower triangle matrix of dissimilarity was computed for the derived 142 climatic classes. This provided a measure of bioclimatic distance between any two such classes. Given a sufficiently large number of cases that provide data for source and receival areas and success or failure of establishment, it then becomes possible to test for possible relationships between frequency of establishment and bioclimatic distance.

Results emphasise the importance of bioclimatic matching in achieving successful establishment. As expected, success is negatively correlated with increasing bioclimatic distance. Simple linear exponential or square root transformations of bioclimatic distance accounted for between 80 to 90 percent of the variance in frequency of successful establishment, on a global basis for (a) introduced birds, (b) invertebrate control agents of plants, and (c) parasites and predators introduced to control insects. More detailed analysis of the bird data reveals significant differences in response to bioclimatic distance between passerines and non-passerines and between selected families. Whilst there is evidence for differences in response for bird species from different biogeographic regions, it may be an artefact of differing sample size. Using the functional relationships developed, it becomes possible to generate maps of probability of successful introduction from any part of the world to a nominated target location or region. Of course these functions relate to groups of organisms introduced deliberately by humans into environments already modified by humans.

---

[1]   CSIRO, Division of Water and Land Resources, G.P.O. Box 1666, Canberra, A.C.T. 2601
[2]   CSIRO, Division of Entomology, G.P.O. Box 1700, Canberra, A.C.T. 2601

HYBRIDISATION BETWEEN INTRODUCED AND NATIVE PLANTS IN VICTORIA, AUSTRALIA

J.M. Robin[1] and G.W. Carr[1]

Thousands of indigenous Australian and non-indigenous plant taxa are cultivated outside their natural geographic range in Australia. This has brought about the elimination of intra-generic physical breeding barriers and many taxa have come into contact with wild inter-fertile populations of indigenous species. This has resulted in hybridisation and the establishment of hybrid populations, some of which are naturalised. Hybrid derivatives range from rare individuals to hybrid swarms numerically stronger than populations of the indigenous parent. In Victoria, by observation and reference to published sources, we have listed such hybrids in 6 genera involving 19 species. The genera involved are *Acacia, Coprosma, Epilobium, Grevillea, Nicotiana* and *Pittosporum*. Most introduced parent species are from elsewhere in Australia but one each comes from New Zealand, North America and Argentina.

The pollination ecology, breeding systems and seed dispersal in the taxa involved are considered. Pollination vectors include insects (bees, flies and moths), birds and wind. Parent species are mostly outcrossing. Active seed dispersal mechanisms may be absent or seed may be short- to long-distance dispersed (wind and birds). We also record naturalised hybrids between both parent taxa outside their natural geographic range (*Acacia* and *Grevillea*).

A further problem outlined concerns infra-specific hybridisation or 'genetic pollution' whereby non-indigenous provenances of cultivated species are brought into contact with *in situ* indigenous members of the same species. Unassisted regeneration or propagated nursery stock for revegetation schemes, it is suggested, may be of hybrid origin. This may have unknown but possibly detrimental consequences for the indigenous genome. Evidence for this however is so far lacking. Such hybrids, e.g. in *Eucalyptus*, would not be detectable according to morphological criteria.

Overseas examples of these genetic problems facing the Australian flora are cited. It is concluded that such gene exchange constitutes potentially major problems for the conservation of genetic resources and may result in hybridogenic speciation threatening native taxa or plant communities as environmental weeds.

The study of these phenomena is only in the preliminary stages but they do not appear to have been reported previously, except as isolated cases. We believe that hybrids between closely related morphologically similar species may also exist but would probably have been overlooked.

---

[1] Ecological Horticulture, P.O. Box 276, Heidelberg, Vict. 3084

PLANTS NATURALISED OUTSIDE THEIR NATURAL GEOGRAPHIC RANGE IN VICTORIA, AUSTRALIA: DIRE FOREBODINGS FOR THE FLORA

R.W. Robinson[1], G.W. Carr[1] and J.M. Robin[1]

The horticultural potential of the Australian flora is widely exploited in this country where thousands of taxa are cultivated outside their natural geographic range. At least 64 species and hybrids (25 genera, 13 families) have become naturalised in Victoria. Few are recognised as such in the botanical literature. Taxa are mostly woody — shrubs (31), trees (28), lianes (2) and herbs (3) — whilst genera involved include *Acacia* (13 species), *Eucalyptus* (13 species), *Melaleuca* (7 species), *Grevillea* (4 taxa) and *Hakea* (4 species).

Naturalisation has taken place in a range of situations from bushland to largely introduced communities on roadsides etc. Populations vary in size from a few individuals to the structural dominance or co-dominance of plant communities. The age structure of many populations, together with the ecological amplitude of species involved, suggests that most species will persist and reproduce. In many, exponential growth of populations is predicted. At least 22 species are serious environmental weeds capable of the destruction of native communities by invasion. Many more species will doubtless become naturalised.

Establishment of populations in indigenous or introduced communities depends upon a seed source and availability of sites for germination and establishment. Population establishment often follows human-caused disturbance but many species invade in the apparent absence of disturbance. In several species studied, the most effective establishment and recruitment episodes followed fire, after which germination sites became available and fire-stimulated germination of soil-stored seed occurred (*Acacia*) or seed stored in persistent woody fruits was released from parent plants (*Melaleuca, Hakea, Eucalyptus*).

The naturalisation of Australian species outside their natural geographic range gives cause for serious concern. The threat of these plants behaving as environmental weed invaders of indigenous communities is well established. Less obvious are genetic problems resulting from hybridisation with native and introduced taxa and the obscuring of the natural geographic distribution of species. These problems and their potential are illustrated by reference to the European flora so grossly modified by humans over millennia.

---

[1] Ecological Horticulture, P.O. Box 276, Heidelberg, Vict 3084

FERAL FRUIT TREES ON NEW ENGLAND ROADSIDES

J.M.B. Smith[1]

Introduced woody plants occurring in a wild state include several species of fruit tree growing particularly on roadsides. Surveys have shown that the variety and abundance of feral fruit trees on roadsides vary both with regional climate, and with traffic density on the adjacent road. Apple achieves the highest abundance, especially in cool climates. All species are commonest beside the busiest roads, reflecting their probable origin as seeds in fruit wastes discarded from vehicles. Only cherry-plum regularly displays 'mother and babies' clumping: other fruit tree species appear to seldom regenerate *in situ*, and are dependent upon the seed rain from vehicles for continual establishment. Numbers of individuals of different species on roadsides are roughly in the same proportion as numbers of seeds of those species 'exported' from a metropolitan wholesale produce market.

---

[1] Department of Geography, University of New England, Armidale, N.S.W. 2351

THE USE OF SPATIAL AND TEMPORAL SURVIVORSHIP CURVES IN PREDICTING INVASION BY *PINUS RADIATA*

F.J. van der Sommen[1]

The invasion by the introduced commercial conifer, *Pinus radiata* into adjacent fragmented 'islands' of indigenous vegetation appears to threaten the ecological integrity and long-term viability for such islands for nature conservation in South Australia.

The nature of this process has been evaluated from case studies on 23 well documented seed source/host community boundary zones. Within these zones, spatial density gradients were determined for 100m × 10m replicated transects. Growth ring analyses were used to determine age-frequency distribution of invaders within these transects. The dynamics of invasion were interpreted from: (1) the extent of deviation of the logarithmic decay density gradient of survivors from that predicted by seed dispersal models in the literature; (2) the gradient of the logistic cumulative survivorship curve predicted by seed production and niche availability.

The broad but comprehensive qualitative assessment of both biotic and abiotic properties of seed source and host ecosystems provided the basis for interpretation of results. These revealed that: (1) soil type, reflecting site quality for *Pinus radiata*, had a dominating effect on invasion irrespective of climax vegetation and type; (2) disturbance of both the seed source and host communities by fire or tree removal, although not a necessary prerequisite to invasion, increased its rate.

Invasion is constrained by dispersal efficiency. The movement of the invasion front, reflected in distortion of the dispersal curve and a break in gradient of the temporal survivorship curve is assisted by the relatively early age of reproduction of established invaders (estimated to be 10 years).

These results suggest that a management strategy should be based on: (1) selective treatment of vulnerable soil types; (2) the use of fire in a 100m boundary zone with a maximum 10 year burning frequency; (3) selective hand removal of related trees dispersed beyond the boundary zone to avoid initiation of a new invasion front.

---

[1] Roseworthy Agricultural College, Roseworthy, S.A. 5371

BIOGEOGRAPHIC ORIGINS OF INVADING SPECIES

N.M. Wace[1]

Human rearrangement of organisms may be intentional or unintentional. Intentional rearrangements at least on a continental scale, are usually documented, and the environments to which they are introduced are systematically altered for human economic gain. Unintentional rearrangements of plants and animals, which are in progress all the time, go largely undocumented. The volunteer organisms concerned often spread into little-disturbed environments which are not specifically designed or modified for their reception. These opportunist species comprise many of our weeds and pests.

Dispersal must precede establishment and naturalisation: it is therefore of interest to study the biogeographic origins of organisms which are involuntarily dispersed by people, in order to see how far they correspond to the origins of naturalised biotas. Motor cars and trousers both carry large numbers of viable plant propagules (usually seeds) from place to place. The following conclusions may be drawn from a biogeographical analysis of plants whose viable propagules are discovered in transit on the outside of cars and in trouser cuffs:

(a) Biogeographic regions whence most recent settlers in Australia came (northern Europe), and where early agriculture developed (Mediterranean) yield the majority of seedlings and species, and the highest seedling/species ratios. These are mostly tillage weeds, and all are herbs, with the notable exception of birch (*Betula*).

(b) Large numbers of Australian species are due to many composite herbs and sedges having small seedling numbers, but seedling numbers are high in some native pasture grasses (*Chloris, Eragrostis* and *Cynodon*). Many Australian native plants disperse easily and germinate readily, but are not primarily tillage-adapted.

(c) NE Asian species are mostly garden shrubs and trees with berries from China and Japan (*Pyracantha, Cotoneaster, Ligustrum, Buddleia, Sophora japonica*).

(d) South American species are largely summer-growing C_4 grasses (*Paspalum, Axonopus*) and wayside weeds (*Verbena bonariensis*).

This biogeographical mix of mostly northern temperate plants is ecologically an herbaceous flora of disturbed or managed ground with few shrubs and trees. Readily dispersed woody plants are mostly from local gardens.

Botanical yields from Canberra drycleaners' trouser-brushings are similar, but the yield of seedlings per species is lower than that of the largely mudborne carwash flora in Canberra.

These results suggest that the strategy of seed banking in the soil, linked with rapid germination in favourable conditions, is that most successfully deployed by species of Mediterranean or NW European origin. It is a strategy which takes advantage of tillage and the mobility of dirty mechanical tools and human clothing, and is well adapted to the chronic disturbance of the environment typical of a wide range of human activities outside the formal seasonal activities associated with agriculture.

Biogeographic origins of successful invaders of southern lands and remote islands undisturbed by human activities, also reveal a preponderance of northern temperate species. Comparisons between the naturalised floras of cool temperate to subantarctic islands show that a small group of short-lived (but not necessarily strictly annual) European grasses (*Poa annua, P. pratensis*) and herbs (*Stellaria media, Cerastium fontanum*) grow on almost all the islands. With very few exceptions, no native plants from the southern continents have become naturalised on southern cold temperate to subantarctic islands with wet isothermal climates. A few microtherm European species which are now widespread in the temperate zones of both hemispheres invade native vegetation on the southern islands, where they exploit situations disturbed by

---

[1] Department of Biogeography and Geomorphology, ANU, Canberra, A.C.T. 2601

natural processes, where they compete successfully with native species. These quick-growing and abundant-seeding herbs were established very early in this history of human contact with the islands, and are able to exploit natural, as well as human-made disturbance of the native vegetation. The 'aggressiveness' of the European floras in other temperate regions, first noted by Darwin and Hooker, is not exclusively due to the plants concerned being mere human camp-followers, adapted to situations created only by people. Invasiveness of southern temperate islands by introduced plants may be accentuated by their having recruited their native floras from distant continental lands which experience climates unlike those of the islands themselves.

INVASION OF COASTAL PLANT COMMUNITIES BY *CHRYSANTHEMOIDES MONILIFERA*

P.W. Weiss[1]

Several native plant communities in Australia have been invaded by the South African shrub, *Chrysanthemoides monilifera* (Asteraceae). The sub-species *rotundata* (bitou bush) has invaded extensive littoral areas in New South Wales. In some stands this has resulted in displacement of the structurally similar, and previously dominant *Acacia longifolia* var. *sophorae* (coastal wattle). This occurred particularly on the frontal dunes but less in the swale behind. The tussock-forming *Lomandra longifolia* has locally hindered the invasion, however.

The main factors in the success of bitou bush are flowering from autumn to spring, a yearly output of over 4000 seeds/m^2 under plants, efficient dispersal by birds and rabbits and low predation. This results in an overall soil bank of up to 800 seeds/m^2, with over 50 seedlings/m^2. Seedlings are able to avoid water stress to some extent by rapid root development and early closure of stomates as leaf water potential drops.

The effects of fire, slashing and herbicides were investigated as control measures. Fire resulted in 26% of adult plants resprouting, while over 20 seedlings/m^2 emerged. Growth was stimulated so that some new plants set seed within 12 months of burning. Double burning reduced resprouting to 5% but seedling emergence still occurred. More resprouting occurred after slashing than after fire.

Subsequent treatments of the herbicide, glyphosate, followed by either spring or autumn burning are promising so far. Autumn burning appears preferable in that a longer time is available between herbicide application and fire for seedling emergence. This treatment reduced subsequent seedling densities to 1/m^2 which may however still prove sufficient for invasion, since both seedling survival and seed production per plant are inversely proportional to density.

Despite selectivity to some native species by glyphosate, insufficient is known, particularly on rarer species, to recommend its widespread use. Further, burning kills some native species such as coastal wattle, so that subsequent reseeding is needed and some dunes may erode in the meantime. There are several potential organisms for use in a biological control program and if this was aimed initially at the reproductive stage, it would have the advantage of retaining plant cover, whilst limiting further spread of bitou bush.

[1] Woden College of Technical and Further Education, P.O. Box 666, Woden, A.C.T. 2606

INDEX